The White Rhino Saga

BY THE SAME AUTHOR

Men, Rivers and Canoes

Big Game, with TC Robertson

Wilderness and the Human Spirit. An Anthology, with Sir Laurens van der Post

Zululand Wilderness: Shadow and Soul

'*Voice from the Wilderness*' column in the *Daily News*, published as:

Voice from the Wilderness

More from the Wilderness

Man and the Wilderness

Reflections of a Wilderness Man

Along a Wilderness Path

People … and Wilderness

Ian Player

The White Rhino Saga

Jonathan Ball Publishers
JOHANNESBURG & CAPE TOWN

The publishers would like to thank Wildlife Protection Solutions for their generous donation towards the production costs of *The White Rhino Saga*.

www.WildlifeProtectionSolutions.org

Originally published in 1972 by William Collins Sons & Co Ltd
Revised 2nd edition published in 2013 by
JONATHAN BALL PUBLISHERS (PTY) LTD
A division of Media24 Limited
PO Box 33977
Jeppestown
2043

ISBN 978-1-86842-596-9
eBook ISBN 978-1-86842-597-6

Twitter: http://www.twitter.com/JonathanBallPub
Facebook: http://www.facebook.com/pages/Jonathan-Ball-Publishers/298034457992
Blog: http://jonathanball.bookslive.co.za/

Cover by MR Design, Cape Town
Design and typesetting by Triple M Design, Johannesburg
Printed and bound by CTP Printers, Cape
Set in 11/15pt Sabon MT Pro

To Magqubu Ntombela and all the other Game Guards who have taught us so much

Contents

Sponsor's Note

Few accounts of conservation efforts in the world today have what one would call a 'happy ending'. When *The White Rhino Saga* was originally published it was, indeed, one of those stories, due to the efforts of Dr Ian Player and his dedicated colleagues who worked from the 1950s onward to bring the white rhino back from the brink of extinction. Through their insight and actions the world has retained an incredible natural asset in the white rhino, and Dr Player's contributions cannot be overstated. Nowhere was this fact more evident to us than during two separate occasions occurring on a trip from South Africa to Southeast Asia.

The first time we came to understand the scope of what Dr Player had accomplished was when the Wildlife Protection Solutions team first had the good fortune to meet him in his home just outside Howick, South Africa. During our efforts to assess the current state of rhino conservation and secure land to start a rhino protection and breeding programme, we were eager to learn more about Dr Player's history and views on the status of rhinos today. As we made our way through Dr Player's kitchen and into his parlour, we were struck by the depth and breadth of his incredible library of literature, reflecting his passions not only for conservation, but for a great many other topics and philosophies as well. Under the watchful eye of a statue of Magqubu Ntombela (Ian's lifelong friend, mentor, and guide), he told us the White Rhino Saga in his own words. To describe such an experience is difficult at best; to describe its impact on us, less so. Not only were we incredibly moved by Ian's words and stories, but we also came to realise the broader implications of what he has accomplished. Through his efforts to save the white rhino, Dr Player has given the world a model that can be applied to many species currently under threat of extinction. By documenting the narrative behind the process, he has given us a manual vividly illustrating its execution. For both of these contributions, the world owes Dr Player an incredible debt of gratitude.

Fundamental to Dr Player's approach to recovering the white rhino was the idea that the species needed more land, more breeding pairs, and sufficient dispersion to protect the overall population from threats in any one area. Implementation of a plan to address these three issues would require intensive management actions on the part of conservationists, and Dr Player and his colleagues rose to the challenge by literally inventing the methods of rhino capture and transport (which are, fundamentally, the same ones still used today) needed to accomplish their mission.

The success of these efforts allowed the white rhino population to increase from the remaining 437 in one location to an estimated 20 000 animals worldwide within the span of 20 years. At that point, the white rhino was largely regarded as a key conservation success story. Sadly, the future of the rhinos is less certain today: the demand for rhino horn in the Far East is exploding as the middle class rises there and uses its newfound wealth to purchase products once only available to a fraction of the populace.

It was our investigation of this international rhino trade that led us to attend the 16th Conference of Parties held by CITES (the Convention on International Trade in Endangered Species) in Thailand. During this leg of our journey, the importance of Dr Player's work stood out to us again; this time on a global stage. The South African government, currently engaged in a literal war for the future of the rhinos, was soliciting suggestions from the international community on how to cope with the black market forces driving the rhinos toward extinction. As the debate became more and more heated, Dr Player was mentioned numerous times, and one speaker even elicited a round of applause through an impassioned plea to the delegates not to let the future of the white rhino and Dr Player's legacy slip into history as merely a fleeting success. The white rhino, its story, and Dr Player's lifetime of work, are simply too important to lose.

As it stands now, the future of the five extant rhino species remains uncertain. Though the rhinos are getting more attention than ever before, the numbers are simply not with the animals. For example, at the time of this writing, the Javan rhino population is estimated to be fewer than 50 individuals, surviving in only one park on the far western end of Java. The species (and the conservationists working to help them) must contend with issues of genetic homogeneity often found in small populations, loss of habitat, and pressures from invasive species which compete for the rhino's native food sources. The Sumatran Rhino is not faring much better, with fewer than 100 animals remaining in the wild, scattered amongst small, isolated populations with no possibility for migration to maintain genetic diversity.

In the end, if we are to ensure that rhinos live in the world our children's children inhabit, humanity must learn what works in species conservation and apply those lessons practically. *The White Rhino Saga* provides one such lesson. We at Wildlife Protection Solutions hope that its re-publication, which comes at a time so critical to rhino conservation, will catalyse not only conversation and awareness, but concrete actions that secure rhinos (and other endangered wildlife) the habitat, breeding populations, and genetic diversity each species needs for continued survival.

Eric Schmidt
Executive Director
Wildlife Protection Solutions
www.WildlifeProtectionSolutions.org
July 2013

Forty Years On – The Rhino's Plight

It is a sound you never forget. Perhaps because it is so unexpected in an animal of that size: a piercing, almost indescribable keening, like a child crying out in pain.

'The screams of agony from rhino that have had their horns chopped off while still alive should reach out into the hearts of all of us,' Ian Player wrote in 2011. I remembered his words when, months later, I heard those terrible cries myself for the first time. I can still hear them now.

It is June 2013. So far this year, more than 460 rhino have been killed by gangs of poachers in South Africa. The bulk of them – about 260 – have been slaughtered in the Kruger National Park.

The killing is relentless. Every year since 2008 a grim new poaching record has been set: 83 rhino that year, 122 in 2009, 333 in 2010, 448 in 2011 and 668 in 2012. Eight hundred will die this year. Perhaps as many as a thousand. It seems inevitable.

The first time Ian Player saw a white rhino was in 1952. He was a young relief ranger, out on patrol in the Umfolozi game reserve in KwaZulu-Natal.

'It was a misty morning,' he would later recall, 'and I was looking into a patch of bush when two white rhino came looming out of the mist, with steam rising from their flanks and their backs and hundreds of stable flies hovering above them. Something within me was deeply touched by this primeval scene, and I had an intuitive flash that somehow my life would be bound up with these great prehistoric animals. There was sacredness about their presence.'

'I still remember standing there and looking ... just looking,' he told me during an interview. 'Here was a living dinosaur. Somehow, inside of me, there was an intuitive flash that my life would be involved with them. And so it has proved to be.'

The White Rhino Saga is the beginning of that tale, but sadly not the end. It is a vivid record of South Africa's greatest conservation success story; the story of a small group of men who achieved what many believed was impossible and saved the white rhino from extinction. But today, 40 years later, that achievement is in real danger of coming undone.

'Until a couple of years ago I thought I'd done my bit as far as the rhino is concerned,' Player told me. Then he paused and looked away. 'Now we're in this terrible situation ...'

More than 2 000 rhino have been lost to poachers in South Africa in the past four-and-a-half years. That is more than seven times the number – 261 – that were poached for their horns in the 27 years between 1980 and 2007.

Official estimates suggest the 'tipping point' – the critical juncture when deaths exceed the number of births – will be reached in 2015. Some believe that it has already been passed. History is repeating itself.

In 1970, there were approximately 65 000 black rhino spread across much of southern, east and central Africa. By 1995, as result of rampant poaching, barely 2 400 of the animals remained.

Ironically, the bush wars in Angola and what was then South West Africa and Rhodesia, insulated South Africa's rhino populations from the worst of the slaughter in the 1970s and early 1980s. But through the latter half of the 1980s and the early 1990s, the killing moved inexorably south.

When copper prices plummeted in the 1970s and Zambia's economy collapsed, poaching in its national parks surged. Within six years its black rhino population had been reduced from 3 000 animals to fewer than 100. The country's capital, Lusaka, became a major entrepôt for illegal trade in rhino horn and ivory.

By 1983, gangs of Zambian poachers armed with AK-47 assault rifles and heavy machine guns had made their first forays across the Zambezi River into Zimbabwe. That year, after the rainy season, four rhino carcasses were discovered in the country's northernmost parks. Within three years the number of incursions by poachers from Zambia had risen to about 150 a year.

Zimbabwe implemented a controversial 'shoot-on-sight' policy. By the end of what became known as the 'Zambezi Valley War' at least 170 poachers had been killed, probably more. The violence of their deaths had little, if any, deterrent effect. Lusaka's black market dealers simply doubled their prices, from around $300 a kilogram at the time, to $800. The killing only stopped when there were no more rhinos left.

In Angola in the 1970s and 1980s, a similar slaughter of the animals played itself out, but for very different reasons.

Plunged into civil strife after the Portuguese colonisers abandoned the country in the mid-1970s, Angola became a proxy battleground for the Cold War superpowers. South Africa and the United States threw their weight behind Jonas Savimbi's rebel movement, UNITA. Cuba and the Soviet Union backed the MPLA. By the war's end, 600 000 people would be dead and a million more would be displaced.

In the 1970s, Colonel Jan Breytenbach, the founder of the notorious 32 Battalion and an ardent conservationist, described seeing teeming herds of animals that were so breathtaking they 'put the Kruger National Park completely in the shade'. A decade later, the landscape was eerily silent. The herds of elephant and the scattered rhino populations had all but vanished.

For years there had been mutterings in conservation circles about South African Defence Force involvement in elephant and rhino poaching in Angola and along the border of South West Africa, later Namibia. Savimbi boasted to his biographer that UNITA exported 'ivory, rhino horn and leopard and antelope skins to help pay for our war'.

There were whispered stories about stockpiles in military warehouses and secret factories churning out ivory carvings for export to Asia. There were the trucks trundling south that soldiers and police were prohibited from searching. And in one instance, a soldier looking for a new weapon in a military store came across packing cases stuffed with 'ivory and rhino horn and game skins, including sable, roan antelope, leopard skins and lion skins'. The cases were labelled 'dental equipment' and marked for dispatch to Waterkloof Airforce Base in Pretoria.

It would be another decade before the terrible truth was finally confirmed. The first cracks began appearing in 1988 when a US congressional oversight committee heard accusations that South Africa had become 'one of the largest wildlife outlaws in the world'. In 1989, Breytenbach broke ranks and wrote a letter to the *Sunday Times* revealing what he had discovered about SADF and UNITA involvement.

Six years later, a commission of inquiry chaired by Judge Mark Kumleben found that the SADF had 'aided and abetted the slaughter and destruction of elephant herds and rhino ... in Angola and Mozambique'. South Africa had become a 'clearing house' for the 'illicit and large-scale handling' of ivory and rhino horn.

Twenty-six rhino were killed in South Africa in 1994, double the number poached the previous year. Some like Ken Maggs, now head of environmental crime investigations at South African National Parks, warned that a storm was coming. 'Sufficient evidence exists,' he wrote that year, 'to indicate that an intensified onslaught on the elephant and rhino populations is imminent.' It was a warning that went largely unheeded.

Eight years later, in 2002, there was another spike in the numbers. Twenty-five rhino were killed, compared to six the previous year. Across the border in Zimbabwe 44 rhino were butchered in 2003, up from just four in 2002.

Then, in 2008, the onslaught that Maggs had predicted finally hit. The ferocity of it caught the South African authorities off-guard. In a single year, 83 rhino were killed, nearly half of them in the Kruger National Park.

But it was Zimbabwe that once again bore the brunt, with at least 126 rhino slaughtered there that year. More than 70 of them were killed in the Lowveld conservancies which had been established as safe havens for the rhino populations that had survived the 'rhino war' of the 1980s.

To some extent the poaching in Zimbabwe was fuelled by the country's economic collapse, widespread corruption, the land grabs orchestrated by 'war veterans' loyal to President Robert Mugabe and the widespread violence and instability that accompanied the 2008 presidential elections. There was also another element; the involvement of a number of ruthless South African safari operators, hunters and poachers who saw Zimbabwe's anarchy as an opportunity to plunder its resources.

Ian Player has often said that hunting is the reason for the enormous increase in South Africa's white rhino population after the 1960s.

'The great irony is that the rhino were nearly wiped out because of hunting in the nineteenth century,' he told me once. 'But it is through hunting in the twentieth century that rhino populations have exploded. When rhino were put back on the hunting list, it was the beginning of the game-ranching industry. The game ranching industry, at the time, were buying up rhino for a couple of thousand rand, selling them on to European or American hunters for $25 000, then putting that money back into conservation and buying more land and buying more rhino.

'I am very, very emotional about the rhino,' Player said, 'but, I'm not sentimental ... The fact remains that through death there is life.'

The refrain in hunting circles is that 'if it pays, it stays'. They call it 'sustainable use'. To exist in an unnatural world, animals must have a commercial value that can be exploited. Without it, their chances of survival are slim.

In 1968, when legal hunting of white rhino resumed, there were only about 1 800 of the animals in South Africa. Forty years later, South Africa was estimated to have a population of close to 19 000 with around 5 000 of that number on private land.

With money comes greed. In 2003, ten hunts took place on game farms in South Africa. They went largely unnoticed by nature conservation and environmental authorities. The Convention on International Trade in Endangered Species (CITES) trade database would later record that nine 'trophies' and two rhino 'horns' had been exported from South Africa. The destination: Vietnam.

No Vietnamese citizen had ever hunted a rhino in South Africa before then. In fact, Vietnam has no tradition of big game hunting and no recognised hunting associations. 'None of the Vietnamese can hunt,' Dawie Groenewald, the notorious game farm owner who faces hundreds of charges related to illicit rhino horn deals and illegal hunts, told me bluntly. 'They are not here to hunt. They are here to get the horn. That's it.'

Vietnam's emergence at the centre of a rapacious rhino horn black market took conservationists and law enforcement officials by surprise. For years the focus had been largely on China, Hong Kong, Taiwan and Yemen.

Chinese use of rhino horn dates back more than 2 000 years. Ancient Chinese medical texts, which heavily influenced the development of Vietnamese traditional medicine, prescribe rhino horn for a range of ills including the treatment of high fever, delirium, convulsions and headaches. A mixture of rhino horn, herbs and radish seeds can supposedly be used to cure cholera.

Eighth century records show that China obtained horn, first from other parts of Asia and later – when those animals were exterminated – from Africa. During the Tang Dynasty, which began in 618AD and lasted for 300 years, chroniclers recorded vast herds of rhinoceros along the Yangtze River. By the mid-nineteenth century, they had ceased to exist.

Hong Kong dominated the trade from the late 1940s until the mid-1970s. China also accounted for a significant percentage of legal shipments of horn prior to the international ban on trade agreed to by CITES in 1978. Other destinations at the time included Macao, Taiwan, Singapore, Japan, South Korea, Malaysia and Indonesia. For a brief period after the oil boom of the late 1970s, Yemen – where rhino horn was sought after in the manufacture of *jambiya* dagger handles – supplanted Hong Kong as the primary destination for shipments of horn. Between 1970 and 1977, Yemen received 22 tons of it, accounting for the deaths of at least 7 800 rhino. Taiwan was also a significant entrepôt and end-use market with direct ties with apartheid South Africa.

In 1993, after years of pressure and embarrassing revelations of its involvement in the black market trade in rhino horn, China imposed a blanket prohibition on sale, importation, exportation and possession. Traders were given six months to dispose of any remaining stock including medicines manufactured from rhino horn. References to it were deleted from the state-sanctioned pharmacopeia.

TRAFFIC, the wildlife trade monitoring agency established by the World Wildlife Fund and the International Union for the Conservation of Nature, conducted a number of consumer surveys in China in the mid-1990s. The last of them – published in 1996 – found that while a worrying residual black market continued to exist, China had 'been highly successful in implementing the domestic ban on rhinoceros horn'. Today, that 'success' is being questioned.

For a time, though, it seemed that the horrors of the 1970s and 1980s were a thing of the past. Rhino numbers in South Africa continued to increase and in places like Zimbabwe, there were slow signs of recovery.

Then, in 2008, the slaughter began again in earnest.

Why Vietnam? It is a complex question and the answers are, at best, speculative. Over the past 40 years, the new Asian markets for rhino horn have usually followed pockets of economic prosperity. Vietnam today is far removed from the apocalyptic cliché portrayed in Hollywood films. With a population of nearly 87-million, it is the world's thirteenth-largest nation and a 'communist capitalist playground' that is one of the fastest rising economic dragons of Southeast Asia.

New wealth has brought with it a demand for luxury products and the use of rhino horn, according to TRAFFIC, is 'another aspect of indulgent, status-conscious consumption'.

The 2003 hunts were a turning point. Hunting offered Vietnamese criminal syndicates a loophole that was all too easy to exploit. It gave them access to a steady, 'legal' supply of rhino horn which could be filtered into an illegal black market.

Between 2003 and April 2012, Vietnamese hunters accounted for at least 400 rhino hunts in South Africa, almost half the total number that took place. These became known as 'pseudo-hunts', little more than a sham to give a veneer of legitimacy to the acquisition of rhino horn for the black market. Between two and three tons of rhino horn are believed to have been 'legally' exported to Vietnam as trophies. In black market terms the shipments would have been worth anything between $200-million and $300-million. It was a sizeable profit, considering that the hunts had only cost the hunters about $22-million.

Tellingly, many of the trophies vanished once they arrived in Vietnam. Of the 607 rhino horns that South Africa recorded having exported to Vietnam between 2006 and 2010, only 154 were officially declared as imports on their arrival in Vietnam.

An urban myth which began circulating in about 2006 also seems to have added fuel to the fire. The story had it that a senior Vietnamese Communist Party official – sometimes described as a retired prime minister or an army general – had been diagnosed with terminal cancer. Regular doses of rhino horn, drunk with water or alcohol, were prescribed and within a matter of days or weeks, the patient had made a remarkable recovery. At least one popular newspaper reported the story as fact. The myth spread like a virus.

If you visit one of Vietnam's few specialist cancer hospitals, it is not hard to understand why the story gained the traction that it did. They are desperate places. Some days, as many as a thousand people will queue in the courtyard of the Vietnam National Cancer Institute in Hanoi. Many of them are from rural communities and have sought treatment when it is already far too late. It is not uncommon to find three or four people sharing a bed. They are the lucky ones who can afford it. Many other patients have to sleep on floors, in stairwells or on the streets. Many will spend their life savings on a piece of rhino horn. All too often, though, they fall victim to conmen and charlatans. In fact, much of the 'rhino horn' being hawked on the traditional medicine markets of Hanoi and Ho Chi Minh City is buffalo horn.

As a product, rhino horn is evolving. They call it the 'Ferrari factor'. Vietnam's nouveaux riches, it seems, are prepared to spend vast sums to acquire horns as investments or as status symbols to be flaunted and displayed, often in family shrines. In some circles rhino horn is used as a hangover cure: a 'party drug' that costs more than cocaine. Ground into rice wine, it has been described as the 'alcoholic drink of millionaires'. It is also a gift, shared among family members and given to the wealthy by those seeking to buy influence or as bribes to officials.

Take the case of Tram Be, a controversial Vietnamese businessman, who sits on the board of Sacombank, the second-largest bank in the country. In 2012, thieves reportedly broke into his home and sawed the horns off an 800 kg stuffed white rhinoceros that he kept there. The rhino had been given to him – illegally – as a housewarming gift. But, despite the fact that the banker did not have the necessary permits to allow him to legally own the rhino, he was not arrested. Vietnamese journalists looking at the case were warned by government officials to drop the story.

Attention is now also returning to China. At the 2013 CITES conference in Bangkok, I had a lengthy discussion with Do Quang Tung, the acting head of Vietnam's CITES management authority. He was clearly in denial and steadfastly refused to acknowledge Vietnam's role in the illicit trade. Unusually though, he pointed a finger of blame squarely at China and claimed that Vietnamese intelligence agencies had evidence that '99% of the horn that goes through Vietnam' ends up in China. There may be some truth to the claim. Recently I was shown undercover video footage of a factory near Hanoi where bangles and cups are being manufactured from blocks of rhino horn for Chinese clients. Among conservationists, there are growing fears that rhino horn is becoming a prized commodity for wealthy Chinese investors and collectors who are 'banking on extinction'.

The rot that has allowed the illegal trade in rhino horn to fester runs deep. It is aided by entrenched corruption in South Africa, Vietnam and transit countries like Thailand and Laos.

In South Africa game rangers, police, customs officials, soldiers, traffic cops and nature conservation officers have all been implicated in the trade. In Zimbabwe, gangs that once made a living smuggling zebra skins across the border to buyers in South Africa, now prey on the rhinos in the Lowveld conservancies. The 'zebra gangs' were supplied with hunting rifles fitted with silencers by a shadowy group of South African backers who have collectively become known as the 'Musina mafia'. There is also evidence that criminal syndicates previously linked to cash-in-transit heists, car hijackings and cigarette smuggling have also now turned their attention to rhinos.

Wildlife crime, they have discovered, is a low-risk, high-return enterprise.

Senior Vietnamese embassy officials in Pretoria have repeatedly been linked to the smuggling of rhino horn but their diplomatic status protects them from prosecution.

A Laotian rhino horn and wildlife trafficking kingpin I investigated, Vixay Keosavang, remains utterly untouchable and continues to ply his trade despite his growing notoriety – thanks in part to the *New York Times* – as the 'Pablo Escobar of wildlife trafficking'. His political connections extend to the highest levels of the Laotian government and military, he has reportedly accompanied the country's prime minister on official state visits to Vietnam and has ties to a key Vietnamese trafficking syndicate.

There are game farmers and hunters who knowingly aided and abetted the syndicates in their quest for rhino horn. Dawie Groenewald once told me that 'everyone who has rhinos has done hunts with the Vietnamese'. Groenewald, like many others, began by selling rhino hunts to wealthy American and European hunters. Then the Vietnamese came in and 'all of a sudden they started paying R50 000, R60 000 and R70 000 a kilogram,' he told me.

'Rhino prices shot through the roof,' Groenewald said. 'American hunters won't pay that. A guy who sells a rhino hunt to an American is f***ed up, because he's not going to make any money. What does it matter who shoots a rhino, an American or a Vietnamese? You go with whoever can pay the most money. That's the way it works. It's not my problem what they do with the horn over there.' There were many hunters and farmers who shared Groenewald's view. The money was everything. Damn the consequences.

John Hume, the largest private rhino owner in the world, argues that Groenewald is 'no different from ninety-nine out of a hundred farmers' in that he believes that 'I own the rhino, I bought it and if I want to kill it, I'll kill it'. Hume contends that legalising trade and farming rhinos for their horns is the only solution. No farmer, he says, would participate in the killing of rhino if trade was legal: 'If they give them an incentive to keep the animals alive, then they will keep them alive.'

Perhaps the most ruthlessly ingenious pseudo-hunting scheme exposed to date involved a Free State lion breeder and a group of Thai middlemen employed by Xaysavang Trading Export Import, a company registered in Laos by Vixay Keosavang. Initially dispatched to South Africa to acquire lion bones, they hatched a plan to ensure that their boss also received a steady supply of rhino horn.

South Africa's hunting regulations allowed a hunter to shoot only one rhino in a twelve-month period. In order for the scheme to work, Keosavang's men would need as many hunters as they could find. They secured the help of a pimp and trawled stripclubs and massage parlours in Pretoria, Johannesburg and Midrand. There they recruited young Thai women, many of whom had been trafficked to South Africa to work in the sex industry. The women would be offered a safari on a game farm and payment of about R5 000 to entertain 'Thai tourists'. In exchange they would have to surrender their passports. The passports were then used to obtain hunting permits in the women's names. Later, they would be driven to a farm, rhinos would be shot by a professional hunter and the women, in whose names the permits had been issued, would be made to stand next to the carcasses, rifle in hand. The trophies were sold to the syndicate by the farmer for R65 000 a kilogram. On the black markets of Laos and Vietnam, it would fetch ten times that.

When South African Revenue Service investigators detained one of Keosavang's key lieutenants, Chumlong Lemtongthai, they seized his laptop and found gigabytes of photographs, documents and video footage. A raid conducted by Thai police on Chumlong's Bangkok home uncovered a similar cache of incriminating data. Together, the seizures provided an astonishing record and a unique insight into the activities of an international wildlife trafficking syndicate. One of the documents seized gave a chilling insight into the syndicate's plans. It was an order placed with the farmer for 50 rhino: '1 month can shoot 15 rhino,' it read.

Chumlong was later sentenced to 40 years' imprisonment, the harshest sentence ever handed down in South Africa in connection with rhino horn smuggling. The game farmer, Marnus Steyl, is due to go on trial later in 2013. Charges had initially been withdrawn against him after Chumlong pleaded guilty, but public outcry over a shocking video of a botched pseudo-hunt in which he was involved, led to his re-arrest. But the nature conservation officials in North West province who signed off on the hunts and others who allegedly received gifts and money from the syndicate remain at large.

In 2012, nearly a decade after the first pseudo-hunts took place, South Africa's department of environmental affairs finally cracked down. Stringent new regulations required that hunters belong to recognised hunting associations and be able to show previous hunting experience before they would be issued a permit to hunt rhino. The flow of permits to Vietnamese and Thai nationals – along with Czech and Polish hunters who had been recruited as proxies by Vietnamese syndicates – ceased. The damage had been done, however. It is probably only a matter of time before the syndicates discover new loopholes to exploit.

'Elements of the game ranching-fraternity [who were involved in the pseudo-hunts] have done tremendous harm, not only to conservation, but to South Africa,' Player told me. 'The savagery and barbarism with which they treated those rhinos did our country no good at all ... The hunting and game-ranching fraternity should have moved quickly and taken these guys to task, but they didn't.'

Over the past decade, the criminal syndicates driving the rhino horn trade have grown increasingly sophisticated. They are better funded, better armed and able to evolve far more quickly than the forces marshalled against them.

Time has all but run out. The war – as it is currently fought – is being lost.

The investigators, prosecutors, game rangers and conservationists – as dedicated and determined as many of them are – simply don't have the money, the resources or the political and international support that they need. Diplomatic agreements between South Africa, Vietnam and Mozambique appear to be worth little more than the paper they are signed on.

At any time, a dozen gangs of poachers are active in the Kruger National Park. Firefights are growing in frequency and intensity. As I write this, Andrew Desmet – a seasoned Kruger National Park ranger – is fighting for his life in hospital after being wounded during an anti-poaching patrol. Dozens of poachers have been killed and hundreds arrested, but more keep coming. The impoverished villages that dot the Mozambican border with the Kruger offer few opportunities and are a ready recruiting ground for poachers who are prepared to risk everything for a few kilograms of rhino horn.

Many of the syndicates that once operated in South Africa have now shifted their activities to Mozambique where they are able to conduct their grim business with relative impunity.

Today South Africa is home to 73% of the world's last remaining rhinos; approximately 19 000 white rhino and about 2 000 black rhino. This is their last stand. If the war is lost here, then the world will have lost two iconic species that predate humankind by millions of years.

The plight of the rhino, says Ian Player, 'is symptomatic of what is happening environmentally all over the world. Wherever you go, you can see the destruction. There is not a single wildlife area in the world that isn't under some kind of threat. Where I grew up there used to be red *vinks* and yellow *vinks* and dams and waterbirds. Now it is as if a tide of concrete has swept over it.'

The White Rhino Saga is a book of its time but it remains as relevant today as it was when it was first published in 1972. Then, it was a celebration of a remarkable achievement. Today, it is reminder of the greatness that was once achieved and can be achieved again. All it took in the 1960s and 1970s for the white rhino to be brought back from the brink of extinction was an idea and the determination of a small group of people to succeed where others predicted failure. We should look to them for inspiration. Perhaps one day, as Player wrote at the end of the book in 1972, it will be possible to say, with some finality, that a species has been saved for posterity.

Julian Rademeyer, 2013

Foreword to the First Edition

This is a book for every lover of the wild. Its story is not only set in the beautiful country of Zululand, it not only describes its animals, trees, and grasses, it also tells of the salvation of a rare creature from extinction.

In earlier times the white rhino was found from the coast of Africa in the north to the coasts of the Cape, Natal and Zululand in the south. But it is a mild and inoffensive animal, and was easy prey for the hunter. It was much wanted for its hide and horn as well as for its flesh. During the last century it was reported as still being seen in considerable numbers in Mozambique, Botswana, South West Africa, Angola, Rhodesia, Swaziland, and Zululand. But Selous wrote in the 1890's that he doubted if there were twenty left alive. In 1894 a shooting party shot six at the junction of the Black and White Umfolozi rivers. This stirred the authorities to action. In 1897 the Umfolozi and other areas were declared game reserves. In 1953 Ian Player made an aerial count of 437 white rhino in the Umfolozi reserve.

The presence of so many white rhino in a relatively small reserve of 72,000 acres now presented new problems. The first was the deterioration in the conditions required to keep so many animals healthy and alive. The second problem was external, the pressure of the increasing Zulu population surrounding the reserve, leading to poaching and to squatting – that is, illegal occupation of reserve land – and the intrusion of thousands of cattle.

The challenge of these problems led to two tremendous projects. The first was to repopulate the game reserves of Africa where white rhino had once lived. The second was to supply white rhino to the zoos of the world. And how were these things to be done? How does one capture and transport the second largest animal in the world, so placid when at large, and so demonic when in captivity? It is the answer to these questions that forms the fascinating core of Mr Player's book.

Mr Player writes his story with a sure pen, simply and clearly, with now and then a joke, and now and then a touch of poetry. On to the stage comes Dr Toni Harthoorn, a British scientist of Dutch descent, working on the problem of the use of tranquillising drugs in the capture and transport of wild animals. An American, Red Palmer, had already invented the Capchur gun which fires a loaded dart into some part of the animal, the shoulder for preference in the case of the white rhino. The danger of the captures, the disappointments, the ultimate success, make a splendid tale. As Mr Player writes, 'It could be said that the species had been saved for posterity.'

Mr Player has the gift of imparting to his readers his intense love of the wild. He will no doubt infect some of them also. The Wilderness Leadership School is teaching people, especially young people, to value the natural treasures of our earth. Our schools are doing their part as well. My grandchildren, the eldest of whom is eleven, are all conservationists. They repeatedly assure me that they are anti-pollutionist and anti-erosionist, and they mean it. They were born and bred in the city of Johannesburg, but the intensity of their enjoyment of the space and beauty of a Drakensberg farm took me by surprise. I can only suppose that this is the work of our teachers, and that it brings hope that the young people of the earth are going to save it and us from destruction.

Mr Player is one of these teachers and I do not hesitate to commend *The White Rhino Saga* to the public. I commend it especially to the people of Kwa Zulu, whose duty and privilege it will probably be to administer and maintain the game reserves of Zululand.

Alan Paton, August 1972

Preface to the First Edition

In this book I have tried to tell the story of how the white rhino were caught and redistributed in their former habitat as well as being sent to zoos throughout the world. By 1965 the International Union for the Conservation of Nature was able to declare that the animal had been saved, and it was removed from the Class A Protection List.

Rhino capture was necessary for three main reasons. Firstly, it was unwise to have all our eggs in one basket. Secondly, there had been a steadily increasing invasion by squatters of the unoccupied state-owned land adjoining the Umfolozi Game Reserve.

Lastly, the Umfolozi Game Reserve has been maintained primarily as a sanctuary for the white rhino. But the increase of other game subsequent to the tsetse fly extermination campaigns meant that there was less *lebensraum* for the white rhino, and although the numbers of warthog, zebra, and wildebeest were drastically reduced, there was still a deterioration of soil and vegetation.

Until 1962 there was no fence of any kind around Umfolozi Game Reserve. Fencing was impossible because, except for the western boundary, the Reserve lay between the two Umfolozi rivers, their junction being the apex of the triangle. White rhino moved freely from the game reserve into the adjoining crown land buffer zones. Intensive agricultural developments, the increase of population, and the invasion of squatters put a stop to the rhino wanderings. The white rhino became compressed into a smaller area. The allocation of part of the crown or state-owned lands in 1962 meant that fencing could begin. As soon as restrictive measure becomes necessary in any wild life area, a management policy becomes imperative.

There were only two courses open to save the game reserve and the white rhino. Either a considerable number of rhino would have to be destroyed, which was unthinkable, or they would have to be captured. Fortunately for the white rhino and mankind, scientific advance made the latter possible.

Rhino capture has been written up in many scientific journals. Dr A. M. Harthoorn in particular has ably dealt with the subject in his wildlife monograph *Application of Pharmacological and Physiological Principles in Restraint of Wild Animals.*

Wherever possible I have avoided technical terms – even those elementary to the scientist – and have tried to write more about the small group of dedicated men who handled the early stages of this unique translocation of the white rhinoceros. I have also tried to describe the anguish felt by the men living in the Umfolozi Game Reserve during the struggle to have the boundaries altered to include ecological and administrative requirements.

If there is direct or implied criticism of other departments, the criticisms are included to convey the feeling of the times.

Preface to the Second Edition

The original edition of *The White Rhino Saga* was published in 1972 and then reprinted in 1973. At the time of writing I was still an officer in the Natal Parks Board and consequently I was unable to write anything about the politics of the day, all of which were rather unpleasant. It was difficult enough getting authority to have the book published, let alone then being mired in conservation's political problems.

To get the book published I had travelled to London to see Billy Collins, the great English publisher, who was very kind and accepted the book and then made arrangements for it to be co-published in the United States with Stein & Day. The book went into two printings, which was most encouraging, and two occasions, one in London and the other in New York, come to mind. The first was when I passed Hatchards Book Shop in St. James's Street. It was snowing and I looked in the window and there was my book and I was filled with pride and gave grateful thanks to my mother who had always encouraged me not only to read, but also to write. My very first book of canoeing journeys, *Men, Rivers & Canoes*, was only published in South Africa, and though it had given me a thrill to see it in the windows of local bookshops, the glamour of that snowy day in London was unsurpassed.

Then on a journey to New York I had the joy, again on a cold bitter winter's day, snowing heavily, with the roar of traffic about me, of seeing the book – with a very different cover showing a herd of white rhino surrounding a motor car, with one head right up against the door – amongst all the others in the shop. On both occasions I also remembered and thanked out loud the wonderful men with whom I had worked – Dr Tony Harthoorn, the veterinarian who brought the miracle drugs; Nick Steele and Owen Letley, horsemen of extraordinary skill; Magqubu Ntombela, John Clark, Norman Deane, Alpheus Ntuli and the magnificent gang of labourers who so tirelessly worked to load the rhino into the crates and then haul them by hand up gum-tree rollers onto the back of a three-ton truck. They were very hard days, but the camaraderie was unsurpassed and we knew that what we were doing was the best way of ensuring the survival of the rhino. Not only did we capture and translocate them to our own Parks, but also to other Parks in Southern Africa, including Mozambique, Zimbabwe and Botswana.

Operation Rhino, which we named in honour of the rhino, also owed its terminology to our respect for those men who fought in various actions in the Second World War. Our small group were like soldiers, tightly disciplined and dedicated to the task. We sought neither praise nor thanks; we were too busy with our task. All that was to come later and was received with much thanks by the whole team, but the greatest thanks of all came from the rhino in the sight of them trotting off into a new Park and a new destiny. There was also the great relief of knowing that we had succeeded, not only in re-establishing the white rhino – and the black rhino too – in its former habitats in South Africa, but that we had taken them overseas; first in pairs to zoos throughout the UK and the USA and then in the 1970s in groups of twenty to Whipsnade Zoo, San Diego Wild Animal Park, Orange County in California and Texas.

The politics of this particular translocation I have described in some detail to Graham Linscott who has captured it in the biography written about me, *Into the River of Life*. I do not wish to repeat it here.

When the first twenty white rhino were taken to Whipsnade Zoo, followed by another twenty to the Wild Animal Park, we really did celebrate, congratulating each other that we had now ensured the survival of the rhino if South Africa exploded, which could have happened all too easily. We all had a fierce emotional attachment to the rhino, the beginnings of which in every individual began at some point in their career in the iMfolozi Game Reserve. The reserve is a place of great historical importance in Zululand, if not in the world, because Zulus who were living there in the latter part of the 19th Century went off to war against the British army in great battles like Isandlwana, Rorke's Drift, Khambula, Ntombi Drift and Hlobane Mountain. Cetshwayo, the Zulu king, also took refuge there after the final battle against the British at Ulundi. Magqubu Ntombela, our very gallant and fearless sergeant game guard, constantly reminded me during Operation Rhino how his father had fought against the British and my grandfather had fought against the Zulus and now here we were fighting shoulder to shoulder to ensure the survival of the white rhino. Mkombe is the Zulu name for the white rhino, meaning 'to point' because it keeps its head down. 'Mkombe,' Magqubu said, 'is a peaceful animal and all of us now are working together for a peaceful cause.'

Our work went on day and night and no one ever asked for rest. As leader of the team I frequently had to order them to stop working because they were on the verge of exhaustion. It was always reluctantly obeyed.

We all owed much to our wives too who sustained us with encouragement and food and drink in desperate moments. They also had to deal with the fear of accidents that could happen only too easily and which inevitably did happen. Every member of the team was injured in some way or another, not the least a heavy rhino foot put on the hand that had recently been jammed in a crate or the boma.

Today, of the original team, only John Clark and I remain alive, but there were others after the first team who played equally important roles in continuing Operation Rhino and to this day it continues with wonderful telecasts by the BBC, Al Jazeera, SABC and others. It is important to honour and recall those who carried on after the first team, Dr Jacques Flammand, Dr Dave Cooper, Dr Mike Keep, John Tinley, John Daniels, Ken Rochat, Garth Carpenter, Gordon Bailey, John Forrest, Alan Herd, Graham Root, John Cauldwell, Hosias Mtetwa, Masuku Mzwantu, George Xulu, Moses Xulu, Nkomo Sefa; then later, Mark Cook and

Jeff Cook, two outstanding leaders flanked by their Zulu assistants, one of whom nicknamed 'Bomb' became famous in a BBC documentary on rhino capture.

By 2007 the fame and the success of Operation Rhino had spread around the world with innumerable documentaries, a major movie made in Hollywood, uncountable newspaper articles (including on the front page of the London *Times*) and magazine articles from *Sports Illustrated* to *Vanity Fair*, as well as continental magazines.

I continued to be peripherally involved with giving talks in South Africa, UK and the USA and I had reached a point where I felt I could say, 'My duty to this wonderful animal has now been done' and I could hang up my boots with some satisfaction. Then the latest and worst wave of poaching began.

Since 2007 more than 1,816 rhino have been killed for their horn, some of them under the most unbelievably cruel and barbaric circumstances; rhino with their faces half sawn off with a chain saw and left alive in indescribable pain and agony. How anyone can do this and call himself or herself a human being is totally beyond understanding. All the killing prompted television, magazine and newspaper reporters to come and see me to get historical background. There was hardly a day last year when I was not giving some sort of an interview and having to look at photographs of rhino in desperate agony. I thought I had had enough and could not continue, then one night I had a dream of a young white rhino calf climbing up onto my bed, lying next to me and putting its head on my shoulder. Here was a message coming from the unconscious – that deep autonomous side of ourselves – and it could only be ignored at my peril.

It is my hope that this book, a new edition, will go out into the world and remind people of the desperate straits that the rhino were once in, only to be rescued and now again to be threatened and how important it is for the sake of those as yet unborn, that we conserve this magnificent prehistoric non-aggressive, gentle and wonderful animal.

When I first wrote the original edition I sent it to Alan Paton who had kindly agreed to do the foreword. I had included a chapter on my journey to Uganda in 1961 to learn from professional game capturers how to make crates, build bomas and transport rhino. They were in the process of catching the last remaining northern white rhino, lassoing them from the back of a truck, and the experience I had with them was of critical importance in the job that I had to face when I returned to iMfolozi Game Reserve. In Alan Paton's opinion the chapter was not necessary, so it was left out. It has been included in this edition because the northern white rhino were eventually completely wiped out in both Uganda and what is now the Democratic Republic of the Congo. In the 1960s this was considered to be an impossible scenario, but such was the growing demand for rhino horn that all were eventually killed. With the growing rate of rhino poaching in South Africa it is a scenario that we constantly have to bear in mind.

Introduction

When I first visited Umfolozi Game Reserve in 1952 it was like entering a deserted world. Wherever I looked there was silent bush and mile upon mile of uncropped red grass. In a long walk through glades of scattered trees and waving grasslands, I saw nothing but a few solitary grey duiker. It seemed impossible that in seventy-two thousand acres of game reserve there were four hundred white rhino.

I camped out that night and no moths or other insects came to the lantern light. The aerial spraying with anti-tsetse fly insecticides had been too effective. In the morning only a few birds called. I was aware of a brooding sombreness, as though the land resented the intrusion of another human being.

It was not until the following morning, a dull overcast day, that I saw my first white rhino. Two bulls loomed out of the mist. I had a perfect view of their physical characteristics as they walked along a ridge. The mouth was square and the nuchal hump between the head and the withers bulged prominently. Flies clung to their flanks and steam rose from their backs. These were truly creatures from a bygone age. The two rhinos grazed as they moved, their heads swinging in a scythe-like motion as they fed on the grass. I watched them move through the grey nthombothi trees into a cluster of candelabra aloes, and disappear into the mist.

I had a sudden feeling that my life would in some way be bound up with these prehistoric animals. The mist lowered and it began to rain, heavy drops splattered on my khaki shirt and old felt hat. But I continued to stand staring towards the tall aloes hoping to catch another glimpse of the two white rhino. A soft wind blew towards me and I got a whiff of their body smell. This evoked another intuitive flash and I felt strongly that I had been here before. The mist lifted for a few seconds and I saw the white rhino again on the crest of a small hill, they had stopped grazing and were looking back towards me, their heads held high and tails curled in characteristic fashion. We stared at each other for a moment, then the mist slowly enveloped them and I was left with the memory.

It had been a dry year and only a few pans still retained water. That afternoon I pitched my camp near a secluded water-hole and as it grew dark the great grey forms of the white rhino suddenly appeared, ghost-like, from the nthombothi trees. Doves scattered and hadeda ibis squawked in alarm. More rhino padded out of the shadows and made their way slowly to the water. The bulls rumbled at each other and a cow laid back her ears when they came too close. When it was too dark to see properly I moved to my camp fire and sat alone.

I could think of nothing but the white rhino. Never had I been so impressed and at the same time so strangely involved with an animal. I was puzzled and faintly disturbed by my overwhelming reaction but just before I slept I had one of those lucid moments which occur between sleep and waking and I realised that these animals could become a cause to which I could give my life.

I was twenty-five, unmarried, and I had been sent as a junior ranger to the Umfolozi Game Reserve by Colonel Vincent, then Secretary to the Natal Parks Board. Although Colonel Vincent was senior in age and position, there was a bond of understanding between us from the day we first met.

For twenty years the Department of Veterinary Services had been in charge of the Reserve, concerned with the elimination of the tsetse fly. As the Veterinary officers relinquished control, poaching increased. Now the control was about to pass into the hands of the Province of Natal, and it would be my job to deal with this situation.

I carried out extended patrols through the Reserve and into the adjoining crown lands. These crown lands were known as the southern buffer zone, the western buffer zone, and the Corridor. The latter adjoined the Hluhluwe and Umfolozi Game Reserves. During the innumerable tsetse fly campaigns these open areas had been used as shooting-by-permit zones. In later years they became buffer areas between the stock farmers in the south and the Zulu Reserves on the west, part of them still later being incorporated into the Reserve.

After the 1914–18 War and the settlement of the land near the Umfolozi Game Reserve, various campaigns were conducted to eliminate the game. This culminated in an intensive drive from 1942 to 1950 when everything except the white rhino was shot in the buffer zones and in the game reserve. This was really blood lust and the story of it reveals the strange excuses that men will use to kill in the name of progress. It was one of the most disgraceful periods in South African history and the destruction of game did not eliminate the tsetse fly, as it was hoped it would. It took DDT and aeroplanes to do this.

On one of my patrols I went out into the western buffer zone, a beautiful piece of country stretching from the Mtunzini hills to the Hlungwana river. The red *Themeda* grass grew waist high and even during the driest times the two streams – the Hlinza and the Ngamazaneni – held water. White rhino wandered over their ancient footpaths as far as Nkonjane hill in the Zulu Reserve.

It was impossible to get a vehicle into the broken country so I tramped with a pack on my back, Lancer, my ridgeback dog by my side, and Alpheus Ntuli, my Zulu servant and companion, bringing up the rear. We camped each night near deep pools on the Hlinza or Ngamazaneni streams. Baboons screamed as the old dogs chastised the youngsters, nyala barked – a much deeper sound than the bushbuck – reedbuck whistled in alarm and white rhino snuffled and rumbled as they all came down to drink in the early mornings and evenings. Bird song came and went with the rhythm of the day. I lay rolled in my blanket listening to the orchestra of the bush while Lancer growled and whimpered at the nearness of the game.

White and black poachers hunted the area unmercifully. We came upon their signs, spent cartridges and snares which ranged from wire to unbelievably cruel spring traps. We had a brush with one group of Zulu poachers who had killed four lovely mountain reedbuck. I shot six dogs and Lancer killed another. When word of our presence got around all was quiet for a while. I knew there was little hope of getting the poaching under control without a big game guard force, so I concentrated on getting to know the country in preparation for the time when we would have more staff and would be able to smash the poaching gangs. So I walked hundreds of miles making notes and detailed plans of where every game guard camp would be established.

I returned from Ndumu Game Reserve to Umfolozi Reserve in 1955 with Ken Tinley who had joined me at Ndumu as a junior ranger. Our first task was to recruit Zulus from the Tribal Reserve to increase our game guard force. We drilled them intensively. One of the guards had a bugle which he used to summon them on to parade, until a Natal robin began imitating the sound and caused great confusion.

The tribal Zulu needed no training for bushwork and, of course, they excelled in tracking. Soon we were able to reinforce the outlying guard posts and begin to control the poaching gangs.

Jim Feely joined the Board's service later in the year and became an invaluable companion. He had an inexhaustible fund of technical knowledge and we soon nicknamed him 'The Brain'. In 1956, Hugh Dent, a tall lithely built man who had trained with the Rhodesian Police, joined the staff and took over the Game Reserve. Ken Tinley went to north-eastern Zululand to start his ecological reconnaissance, Jim Feely took charge of Richard's Bay, and I went to Lake St Lucia for a year to start the Research Centre at Charters Creek. In 1957 I married.

In 1958 Paul Dutton, an old canoeing friend, asked to join the Parks Board. I was delighted to recommend him, for he loved water and was able to take my place at the lake. A few months later Hugh Dent resigned to go teaching and I was transferred back to Umfolozi Game Reserve.

The results of the combined protective measures were now apparent. Poachers were more wary and the game much tamer. The white rhino, in particular, were seen far more frequently. They, too, were much calmer. In the past they would have fled at the sight or sound of man or vehicle, whereas now they carried on grazing peacefully. It became common to see baby rhino trotting across the veld in front of their dams.

A tremendous task lay ahead of me. From 1958 to 1964 there was no moment in which I was not concerned with the Umfolozi Game Reserve and the white rhino. But at the age of thirty and in the peak of physical fitness and moral resolve, I felt confident of overcoming any obstacle.

CHAPTER 1

White Rhino Territory

Since earliest times hunting, legal and illegal, had taken place in the Umfolozi valleys. Tshaka, the greatest of the Zulu kings, regarded the country in the lower regions of the two Umfolozi rivers as his private hunting ground, and he can therefore be considered the first game conservator. He conducted hunts with thousands of Zulus, extending from the Black to the White Umfolozi rivers. The warriors moved forward, chanting and beating their shields, driving the game to waiting game pits and concealed hunters. Hundreds of animals were slaughtered, some by Tshaka himself who rushed forward with the Zulu battle-axe and chopped at the tendons of fleeing giraffe. The Mhlopeni caves were sometimes his camping ground and in his despotic excesses he would have a man killed on the slightest pretext and had the body staked out on the bare ground across the river. He would then eat while the vultures circled overhead to land and feed on the corpse.

'The King's birds,' the attendant warriors would whisper as Tshaka watched the macabre antics of the vultures.

Tshaka was murdered by his brother Dingane, who in turn was murdered on the top of the Lebombo mountains overlooking the country of the amaTongas. Mpande, a pleasant, benign ruler, became king and the white man had an easier passage into Zululand.

Many men hunted in Zululand and you can read about their experiences. William Baldwin in his *African Hunting and Adventure* recalls that in 1852 he crossed the White Umfolozi river at Hlatikulu, then walked to the junction of the Gcoyi and the Black Umfolozi. He mentions passing King Mpande's Nondwengu kraal, and the presence of white rhino in this area. Today this is all part of the Umfolozi Game Reserve and is still a high density area for white rhino. Of all the men who hunted in Zululand during the benevolent reign of Mpande, it was Henry Drummond who left the most comprehensive record of what is now the Umfolozi Game Reserve. In his book *The Large Game and Natural History of South and South-East Africa*, he recalls how he hunted the rhinoceros in the country between the White and the Black Umfolozi rivers. To a modern generation the slaughter of the big game, particularly the rhino, makes sickening reading.

But in the 1860's when all Zululand was a wilderness, every wild animal was looked upon either as an enemy which had to be killed in defence of human life, or as an object of sport. Where some present-day 'sportsmen' in Africa have used jeeps, hunting brakes, lorries, and in some instances helicopters, to kill game, the early hunter went in on foot. The tsetse fly took care of any pack animals and malaria kept hunters to a minimum. Drummond must have been particularly tough, for he records trekking across the Umfolozi valley for thirty hours without even being able to 'moisten our tongues'.

Then, as now, in the early spring water-holes are few and far between and when Drummond and his companions found a mud wallow, they stripped and plunged into 'the beastly stuff, that though composed of every nastiness under heaven, we dignified with the name of water'.

Camp sites were primitive to an extreme. Each man had a Zulu mat and a few blankets which a Zulu retainer carried with the cooking pots and salt. For the rest, the hunters had to wait until they got back to waggons on the high ground. The Umfolozi area in Drummond's time was as wild a paradise as any naturalist could dream of. Eland, bushbuck, impala, elephant, buffalo, and hippo were common. By the turn of the century elephant and hippo had vanished, the former from shooting and human pressures and the latter because the rivers were silting up.

But it was the rhino that Drummond and his companions were after and the Umfolozi river valleys abounded with the prehistoric animals.

After one particularly trying day Drummond was grilling a bushbuck steak when a black rhino charged the fire. One warning snort and the animal was in the camp, scattering the fire in all directions and squealing with rage. Drummond surveyed the chaotic scene from a perch in a tree. Two great burning logs were smoking on the spread out bed and he could smell the smouldering blankets. The remains of a water calabash were strewn across the ground and the hard-earned bushbuck meat had disappeared, some of it trampled into the ground. Drummond's gun lay out of reach so he borrowed one from the nearest hunter. It was an elephant gun of six to a pound so he braced himself against the branches and fired at the shoulder of the trampling and squealing beast. Another hunter had a double-barrelled gun and he emptied both barrels into the struggling mass below him. He records: 'Its vicious temper was much sobered by the treatment it received. Ours were not, however, improved by the incident, and it was all I could do to prevent one of the hunters, who was almost speechless with rage at losing his supper, from giving chase on the spot.'

Drummond, like many other naturalists of his day, maintained that there were four species of rhino in Umfolozi, two of the so-called white variety and two of the black. He asserted that all rhino were the same colour, a peculiar shade of brown, except *Rhinoceros bicornis* which possessed a tinge of red. He admitted that to different observers and in different localities they did appear to be of different colours. William Baldwin even mentioned a blue kind.

Drummond classified the four species as follows:

Rhinoceros bicornis, or upetyane;
Rhinoceros keitloa, or unkombe tovote;
Rhinoceros simum, or umkombe wogobo;
Rhinoceros kulumane.

Drummond says the last one had not received a scientific name, or recognition, from the naturalists.

Scientists agree today that only the *Rhinoceros bicornis* or black rhino and *Ceratotherium simum simum* or white rhino, really occurred. There are, however, old timers and many Zulus who say that a sub-species of the black rhino – mpunyane – exists. It is supposed to be more bad tempered than the ordinary black rhino.

Drummond classified his rhino by the length of their horns and nature of the animals, hardly a scientific method, but in every other way he was a first class observer. He must have had a good memory, for in those early days, keeping notes could not have been easy.

His descriptions of the rhino are in many instances moving. He talks about the great white species being a noble animal when seen in undisturbed regions quietly grazing amid all the beauties of tropical vegetation with a flock of rhino birds (ox-peckers) lazily picking off an occasional tick, or a hornless little calf – a ludicrous miniature of its mother – running and gently being guided forward by the maternal snout. Scenes like this occurred towards evening on the edge of water-holes where the animal went to drink after the long heat of the day.

'Knowing no fear itself, and harmless towards all animals, it approaches the water in company with wild beasts of every description.'

He once saw a troop of lions walk past an old bull with its mouth buried in the pool, then they lay down and lapped the water a few yards away, each party ignoring the other.

Henry Drummond's favourite way of passing the nights was watching the game coming to the water-holes.

> There was the charm of solitude and silence, broken by the companionship of wild animals, the noises of a tropical night and the expectation of the unknown. The lion, the impala or duiker all came at different times to drink. Also many other animals that one rarely comes across in the daytime, such as wild dogs, hyenas, leopards, jackals, and wild cats of many kinds.
>
> There was one particular pool at which I spent many nights, sometimes when the moonlight was so bright that I could see the game approaching several hundred yards. At other times there was only the light of stars to assist my aim. When heavy thunderstorms covered the sky with black clouds I could only see when flashes of lightning

> lit up the scene. I found that buffalo and larger kinds of antelope avoided the water-holes during the bright moonlight, but it made no difference to rhinoceroses and to other kinds of antelope, while the worst of the storm was the time generally chosen by lions to make their appearance. I remember once during a lull in a thunderstorm hearing the cat-like lapping of one of these great beasts and when the next flash came, I saw three of them crouched flat on the bank still drinking. I levelled my gun at the spot and waiting for the next flash, fired a snap shot at the nearest and when the lightning enabled me to look again they had disappeared.

Drummond found one pool which by his description I would say was somewhere in what is now known as the Corridor, the land lying between the Hluhluwe and the Umfolozi Game Reserves.

> The pool was fed by a spring, never dried up and possessed such deep clear water, that game came long distances to it – preferring it to the river. It was about fifty yards long and surrounded by a fringe of thick evergreens, except at the upper end, where it was shallow and muddy. My hiding place was in the thick branches of a great cabbage tree. On one occasion I remained here without moving for two nights and a day, sleeping in the shade at the foot of the tree in the noonday heat and watching all night. A piece of sun-dried meat provided me with food. While watching from the hide, a little duiker antelope, its grey skin shining like silver in the rays of the setting sun, stole down and after gazing round for a few seconds, stooped to drink, the reflection of its head and tiny horns being quite plain on the surface of the dark still pool. A few minutes later another appeared on the opposite bank, followed by two more. Having all satisfied their thirst they returned to nibble the young shoots of grass in the glades. The next to arrive were a pair of reedbuck, mother and calf, which no doubt had been lying up in the long rank grass in the 'vlei' beyond.
>
> The bush partridge, a species of Francolin, had for some time been uttering their grating cry among the surrounding bushes, and now made their appearance to drink, while dozens of partridges of other

> kinds, mingled with turtle doves and paraqueets and the little long-tailed pigeon, alighted on all sides, attracted by the common want.

Henry Drummond was a hunter and he came to Zululand to kill. It was the vogue. Men came from all over the world to kill in the name of sport.

Roualeyn Gordon Cumming, a Scotsman who hunted in a kilt and shot a white rhino with the world record horn (still standing) of 62½ inches anterior and 52½ inches posterior, wrote a book about his adventures. This stimulated others like William Baldwin to copy his adventures in killing, and readers are almost assured of a killing a page.

Drummond killed too, and was just as ruthless, but at the same time he had finer feelings and found time to describe the beauties of the bush and the game living in it. Yet when he described a killing he did it in almost revolting detail. He writes about shooting a black rhino.

> Some hours had passed when I next awoke, half falling off the tree before I remembered where I was. The sullen gurgle of displaced mud warned me that there was something in the pool. Gently raising myself into a sitting position I saw, in the bright moonlight, a rhinoceros wallowing in the shallow water and mud, while its companion stood on the skyline on the bank above. Looking more closely, while my hand sought my gun, I saw by their small size and diminutive horns that they were both Upetyane (Black Rhino) – a species against which ever since I had been so roughly handled by one of them, I had always borne malice for their evil dispositions and vicious propensities and therefore though their horns were utterly worthless I was glad to get the opportunity to kill one. I could not at first decide which to fire at; for though the one in the pool was not ten yards off, it was lying in such a position that I doubted my being able to mortally wound it, while the other, unless it charged, would be out of sight the moment I fired and startled it. I fired at the latter. The bullet told loudly and the animal, puffing and snorting, disappeared while the one in the water, springing to its feet, sent mud spattering the surrounding leaves, trotted out and then wheeling half round listened for some indication of my whereabouts. I aimed as before at the shoulder and brought it to

> the ground, though it instantly recovered and charged for the place where it had seen the flash. Short as the delay had been, it enabled me to load one barrel and when it was within a yard of the tree I again fired down into its hump, making it swerve with pain. It lost its balance and fell bodily into the pond below. The water was deep and it floundered about for some seconds before it found its feet, enabling me to reload and again plant my balls right and left in its shoulder. It rushed off scattering the water as it did so and going over the rise, was lost to view.

Drummond described how the one rhino died, then buffalo came down to drink and he shot at one. Not satisfied he fired at a group of seven white rhino which arrived at the pool. For the next few days he had an orgy of killing at the water-hole.

At the end of his book Drummond realises that the game of Africa is not inexhaustible and when writing about elephants he says:

> I cannot leave this subject without adding my protest against the wanton and wasteful wholesale destruction of these animals that has now been going on for so many years. It is utterly impossible that it can last much longer, as any one who glances at the statistics of the export of ivory from the east coast must at once see, slowly but surely this most useful animal is being extirpated, merely for the purpose of supplying Europe with ivory ornaments and billiard balls.

Drummond had visions of the African elephant being used in the same way as the Indian, as a draught animal. He saw it as the only animal capable of becoming a beast of burden through the tsetse and fever infected regions of the African continent, the only animal that the traveller could rely upon and enable him to dispense with the costly and troublesome retinue of natives.

Drummond continued his hunting of the white rhino in Zululand, not knowing that by 1890 no more than forty to eighty of the species would be left in the whole of Southern Africa.

CHAPTER 2

Hunting the Rhino

The term 'white rhino' is a misnomer. The colour is grey rather than white. There are stories about the derivation of the name, ranging from the colour of the mud it wallowed in, to the theory that the old Boer hunters likened the white rhino to the white man because of its timid disposition as opposed to the black rhino which was wild and fierce, like the tribes of the interior.

The early distribution of the white rhino can be traced by the Bushman paintings. These little hunters and artists drew the rhino on rock faces from the arid regions of the Tsodillo hills of Botswana to the caves in Rhodesia, in the Cape and Naukluff in South West Africa.

In former times the white rhino was found over the greater part of Africa from the coast of Algeria to South Africa. Algerian petroglyphs showed that the animal was contemporary with early man. South African stone engravings twenty-five thousand years old indicate that palaeolithic man killed these huge beasts with primitive weapons.

The white rhino was known to early colonists long before it was scientifically described by Burchell who saw a dead animal in 1812 at Kuruman in the northern Cape. Burchell noticed the flat snout and long head, made drawings of it and gave it the specific name of *simum* (flat nosed) in scientific literature in 1817. Other popular names were square-lipped, square-mouthed, square-nosed, but the term 'white rhino' has stuck.

By 1839 explorers noted that the animal had almost ceased to exist in the Kuruman district where it had been discovered. It was one of the easiest wild animals to shoot because of its inoffensive nature. A growing demand from oriental countries for the horn, where it was valued as an aphrodisiac, made hunting the rhino an economic proposition. This hastened its end. It seemed unbelievable that such a widely distributed animal could disappear. Hunters and explorers had reported them from all over Southern Africa, in Portuguese East, Botswana, parts of South West Africa, Angola, Rhodesia, Swaziland, and Zululand.

Captain William Cornwallis Harris, in his book *The Wild Sports of Southern Africa*, mentions that in 1836 while travelling through what is now known as the Magaliesberg district in the Transvaal 'eighty were seen during the day's march, of which we were obliged in self defence to slaughter four'. About himself he was later to say, 'I have been taxed by the facetious with "shooting madness" and a truly most delightful mania I have ever found it.'

Sir Andrew Smith is also reported to have seen between a hundred and a hundred and fifty rhino, half of them white, in the same country.

But it was the French explorer and naturalist, A. Delegorgue, who first mentions seeing the white rhino in Zululand during an expedition in 1847. He reported their occurrence from slightly south of the White Umfolozi river northwards to the Mkuze and Pongolo rivers. C. J. Andersson, who between 1850 and 1854 travelled in the country near Lake Ngami, mentions killing nearly sixty rhino of both species during one season. Other hunters in the 1850's in former Bechuanaland shot scores of white rhino from blinds erected near a water-hole. In this arid region, animals had to trek for miles to water and could then be shot at a few yards' range.

F. C. Selous, one of Africa's most famous hunters, says, 'In 1847 or 1848 Messrs Oswell and Vardon are credited with having killed eighty-nine rhino, the majority probably white rhino.' The unfortunate defenceless beast, being unaggressive and living in more open country, was an easy target. The black rhino habitat, on the other hand, was in dense bush and the animal would charge anything at the drop of a hat, consequently it was not hunted too assiduously. The once big numbers of white rhino from the Cape to the Zambezi were seriously reduced. This increased the value of the rhino horn and the hides became greatly sought after as waggon whips.

In 1873, Selous hunted near the river Gwaai in Southern Rhodesia and found the white rhino plentiful. The following year he hunted along the Chobe river and still found white rhino common. Three years later he saw only the tracks of two animals. By 1879, during eight months spent in hunting in Bechuanaland, he did not see the spoor of a single white rhinoceros. It is not surprising. One European trader on the Bechuanaland border employed four hundred native hunters and rhino were exterminated in a big area through his agency alone. Selous wrote: 'His store always had huge piles of rhino horn, the spoils of a hundred animals at one time. They were sold to other traders and eventually made their way to England.'

The demand for all sizes of rhino horns was probably caused by the fashion in knife handles and combs. Whatever it was, it meant the end of the white rhino in most of Southern Africa. A host of Boer hunters, deadly shots and completely at home in the bush, shot the rhino left and right for sjamboks (hide whips). Many hunters would shoot a white rhino simply to eat the nuchal hump which was baked in clay and said to be most palatable. The natives and Bushmen also obtained rifles and ammunition more freely and they lost no time in putting the finishing touches to the death of the rhino.

In 1892 Selous completed his term of service with the British South Africa Company and went after some remaining white rhino on behalf of a museum. He fell from his horse while chasing an ostrich and was unable to complete his mission. He said, 'Therefore the two white rhinoceros which I shot in 1882 are the last of their species that I have ever seen alive, or am ever likely to see and when I left Africa towards the end of 1892 I fully expected that these animals would become extinct within a short time and remain forever unrepresented in the collection of any European museum.'

But a few months later R. T. Coryndon and Arthur Eyre, members of Rhodes's pioneer column, came across a family of white rhino. They wounded the cow and the bull and killed the calf by mistake. The next day while following the wounded animals, they came upon another cow and very young calf. They shot the cow and captured the calf, but it soon died. In 1895 Eyre tracked down and shot the last bull in Southern Rhodesia. It was presented by Cecil Rhodes to the Cape Town museum.

At the end of 1893 a few white rhino were said to inhabit the low, inaccessible, tsetse fly haunted country between the lower courses of the Black and White Umfolozi rivers in Zululand. Over the rest of Southern Africa they were extinct. The long and terrible slaughter was surpassed only by the extermination of the bison in North America.

So the dismal story went on, and Selous wrote in his memoirs:

> Thus it will be seen that the great square-mouthed rhinoceros, the largest of the terrestrial mammals after the elephant, which sixty years ago, was excessively common over an enormous area of country in Southern Africa to the south of 17° South latitude, and which even so lately as thirty years ago, was still very plentiful throughout many large districts of that vast country, is now on the verge of extinction. A few, a very few, still survive in one small district of Zululand, whilst perhaps a dozen others yet wander over the Mahobohobo forests between Angwa and Manyani rivers in N. East Mashonaland. But that twenty of these strange old-world creatures are alive today, I very much doubt, and in spite of game laws, which may be more or less efficient in Zululand, but in the nature of things must be entirely inoperative in an outlying district of Northern Mashonaland, I cannot think that the species will survive very far into the coming century.

Then in 1894 a shooting party in Zululand, of whom C. R. Varndell was one, shot some six white rhino at the junction of the Black and White Umfolozi rivers. The news had tremendous impact on responsible people in the colony of Natal. Sir Walter Francis Hely-Hutchinson became Governor of Natal in 1893. He had much sympathy with the preservation of wild life. In February 1895 C. D. Guise wrote a letter to the Resident Commissioner of Zululand, M. Clark, referring to the near extinction of the white rhino. He suggested that white rhino be put on the royal game list and that no permits be issued by the governor, and that an area of Zululand containing their habitat be beaconed off as a game reserve, and no shooting nor destruction of game be allowed therein. The extent and limits of the area could be ascertained from parties who had hunted there.

Mr Guise's letter was minuted by the Secretary to the Resident Commissioner, who forwarded it to Sir Hely-Hutchinson, saying that he had instructed all magistrates on no account to grant applications to shoot rhino, that a proclamation was being framed to make rhino royal game, and that, 'I have before me all the papers connected with the proposed establishment of game preserves, and the question is receiving my consideration.'

On the 22 April 1897 a proclamation was issued declaring Hluhluwe, Lake St Lucia, and Umfolozi as game reserves. The area of Umfolozi Game Reserve was some 72,000 acres, situated between the White and Black Umfolozi rivers. The western boundary was the Manghlagazi footpath named after the Zulu tribesmen who used it.

By this time Sir Charles Saunders was the Resident Commissioner of Zululand. He knew Zululand intimately and had for many years, when he was still a junior official, advocated the creation of reserves. For fourteen years Saunders was the champion of the game reserves and the white rhino. He was a most active man and made long trips by horseback and waggon to all parts of the territory. The Zulu people of today still speak of him with admiration – a sure sign that he was a man in all respects.

The Lands Delimitation Commission of 1902-4 made provision for land to be opened up in Zululand to European settlers. This was notwithstanding many pledges from His Majesty's Government that the country would not be taken from the Zulus. The Zulus would in one way or another be able to take care of themselves, but the same was not true of the game. Serious trouble lay ahead. Just prior to his retirement before Natal became part of the Union of South Africa, Sir Charles Saunders wrote a letter to the Colonial Secretary recommending the appointment of a Game Conservator for Zululand. It was virtually his last official act and indicative of his concern for the wild life of Zululand.

CHAPTER 3

The Umfolozi Reserve

By October 1953, after eighteen months' service, I had been to almost all the Zululand game reserves, relieving other rangers who were on leave or who were ill. But it was to Umfolozi that my thoughts kept returning. So I was overjoyed when Peter Potter, then Chief Conservator of Zululand, sent for me and instructed me to go to Umfolozi Reserve where I was to help old Willie Foster who had arranged for an aerial count of the white rhino.

My forefathers had been associated with Natal and Zululand since 1850. My great-grandfather had been a founder member of the Natal Carbineers in 1855, and my grandfather had fought at Inyezane in the Zulu War of 1879. Anything to do with the history of Natal and Zululand fascinated me.

I took the old track leading out at the Nqabatheki gate of the Hluhluwe Game Reserve down to the main road and through the Corridor, a strip of unallocated State land between the Hluhluwe and the Umfolozi Game Reserves. In 1905 Government Notice No. 93 had proclaimed this area a game reserve, and it stretched from the source of the Hluhluwe River to where the Mzineni stream entered Lake St Lucia. Foolishly, it had been deproclaimed a few years later. My old jeep clattered up the road towards Masundweni hill (Place of the Earthworm). I could see common reedbuck grazing on newly burnt grass and a few blue wildebeest and zebra on the hills. A population build-up in the Hluhluwe Reserve was forcing some of the game out.

As I crossed the Skovana stream (Place of the Owl), three light aircraft in exact formation flew low overhead. These were the tsetse sprayers, piloted by wild but most competent young fliers. Day after day they flew at tree-top height spreading clouds of DDT in the valleys. I did not know it but it was the end of an era. The tsetse fly was nearly wiped out and with it was going years of terrible strife between cattle ranchers and game conservationists.

When I reached the Nagana (tsetse fly) Research Station at the bottom of Masimba hill, Will Foster was sitting in his rondavel, staring out of the door of his hut. Two Zulu game guards squatting in the shade of a marula tree greeted me. One was Magqubu Ntombela, a man who had been in the service of Umfolozi Game Reserve since 1918. Five years later he was to be my Induna (head) game guard, a close companion and the greatest teacher I ever had in the bush.

Will Foster greeted me ponderously. He was then in his seventies, a man who had given a lifetime of service to the Department of Veterinary Services, and who knew more about the Umfolozi Game Reserve and its history than any white man. We became great friends.

While we drank tea he told me he had arranged for one of the young pilots to do the first aerial census of the white rhino.

'This man is an excellent pilot and knows the game reserve,' Will Foster said. 'Hendrik van Schoor, the ranger at Gome, is coming in this evening, he'll accompany you in the aircraft.'

While it was still dark the following morning, Hendrik van Schoor and I waited at the airstrip while the pilot checked the small Piper Cub. Hendrik said it was his first flight and he was apprehensive. A tall man with huge arms and very strong calves, Hendrik could lift a forty-four gallon drum of petrol from the ground to the back of a truck. It seemed impossible that anything should worry him. We both laughed when I confessed that one tight turn in an aircraft was enough to make me sick for the rest of the day.

The pilot called us over, gave us maps and we climbed into the aircraft.

The pilot explained that he would do the spotting and we would record the number of rhino and their distribution on the maps.

The hot October winds blew early in the morning so we took off soon after dawn. By 10 a.m. the light plane was being buffeted by the wind, and the stench from the DDT spraying tanks and high octane fuel made me dizzy and bilious.

The pilot saw me looking pale and shouted above the roar of the engine, 'If you spew down my neck I'll give you a ride you're never likely to forget,' and I immediately felt better.

We flew at 500 feet, counting every rhino we saw. Hendrik van Schoor looked from one window, I from the other. The pilot kept the map on his lap and recorded the numbers. There were moments when I felt so ill I did not dare speak and merely held up the appropriate number of fingers. The pilot watched me carefully and made gestures which left me in no doubt what would happen if I were ill.

When we could not determine the number in a group, the pilot would circle and dive until the rhino were flushed out like partridges.

There was no mistaking the difference between the white and the black rhino. The white moved slowly, keeping their heads close to the ground, hence the Zulu name *umkhombe*, meaning to point. The black rhino moved fast, its head held high.

After three days' flying we counted four hundred and thirty-seven white rhino, the most accurate figure it was possible to get. For the next few days I camped in the reserve, writing reports and drawing maps.

One evening I drove to Will Foster's hut and encouraged him to talk about the early history of Umfolozi and Zululand.

'Try to imagine Zululand in its virgin state, before the advent of civilisation,' he murmured.

I did, as you might do.

A beautiful country rising from the Indian ocean in terraces. First the dense coastal dune forest with its array of bird, insect, animal, and reptile life; then the coastal plains – a wonderland of flora; gigantic fig trees fringing the river banks, forests of acacia and fever trees and the wild hyphaene palm with its fan-shaped fronds, dotted across the plains as far as the eye could see. Then the fields of wild gladioli ablaze with salmon-coloured blooms, and the ground orchids which spring up after the veld fires. Game in countless number grazed or browsed. Long lines of elephant moved from pan to pan, feeding in summer-time on fallen marulas. Tremendous herds of buffalo accompanied by flocks of *ama-Hlalanyati*, the Zulu name for ox-peckers, and meaning 'the birds that sit on the buffalo'. Groups of white rhino grazing, or making their way to water, there to drink or wallow. Lions and cheetah lying on the hillocks watching impala, wildebeest, zebra, or tsessebe. There were hyena and wild dog, serval and leopard too, all part of the pattern of nature.

A few Zulu huts – the old ones, the real beehive shape – were dotted about. These people were outcasts from the upper class Zulu who lived in the highlands. Generally speaking they were degenerate, and riddled with malarial parasites.

Then there were the highlands, lovely country with clusters of huts on the windswept hills; forested kloofs with clear water running into the main rivers; bushbuck in the forests, eland on the hills, and oribi lying in the waving fields of red *Themeda triandra* grass; crowned eagles soaring above, their plaintive whistles rising and falling in a sad melody. It was in the high country that the Zulu kings concentrated their selected armies. Men walked the length and breadth of Zululand to build the great kraals and do their military service.

The old man sat silent for a while. Then he shook his head.

'Now compare this with the Zululand of' today,' he said. 'Imagine seeing it from above, like a bird. As far as you can see the bush has been cleared and replaced by stretches of cane and cotton fields, a network of motor tracks and a snake-like railway line winding its way from the south. Masses of farm-houses dotted all over the land. Fenced off paddocks, grazed to the ground. Native reserves congested with people, their stock causing soil erosion. Streams and rivers running red with mud and the remaining wild animals confined to small game reserves.

'My life is ending,' Will Foster said. 'You young people have a long hard task before you. The increasing tide of people, both black and white, will soon be knocking on the door of the game reserves. They will demand that the land be made available for farming or native reserves. It is going to be a long and bitter fight for you. I know what lies ahead because we lost many battles and the game was wiped out in the Umfolozi Game Reserve. But the reserve is still there. Now you must see to it that the crown lands are included, otherwise the rhino will not survive. Even if you save the reserves, people in their tens of thousands will be coming, and if you are not careful they will turn it into a zoo. You will have to fight hard to prevent this.'

It was dark now, and I could only just make out the shape of the old man.

'Tell me, what does the word "Umfolozi" really mean ?' I asked.

'I have discussed this with many Zulus,' Will Foster said. 'The word "Umfolozi" is a corruption of *mfulawozi*, which means "rivers of fibre". The rivers get their name from *Urera tenax*, a fibrous bush of the nettle family which grows along the banks and is used by the Zulus in mat making.'

Will Foster spoke about an old Zulu of the Mbonambi regiment who told a little story about the two rivers.

'In the early days of the Zulu people,' he said, 'the Black Umfolozi was a narrow but deep and dangerous river. It was known as Mfulawozi Nketabewesi – the river of fibre which picks off the ferrymen. The old warrior coupled the two rivers by saying that the Black Umfolozi would only be crossed by the brave people, while the White Umfolozi was only of great strength in flood.'

I was camped on the Black Umfolozi opposite the Masimba krantzes and I went back to my tent to eat the meal Alpheus had prepared. Lancer greeted me wildly and we ran to the river to wash.

After I had eaten I took Alpheus back with me to old man Foster. We sat on the steps of the rondavel in the darkness and listened to the early history of Umfolozi.

'I have been writing up the history of Umfolozi. You can have a copy if you wish,' the old man said.

He had written it in longhand. I accepted gratefully, but asked that he tell us the history too. For a while he spoke in Zulu, telling the story like a tribal elder. Alpheus sat, entranced by the faultless Zulu, and muttered to himself, 'Umuntu' (this man is an African). He shivered at the intonation and depths of expression as the old man told the story.

'The Mtetwa clan lived in the country between the two Umfolozi rivers, from the junction to the Mpila range of hills. This was at the beginning of the nineteenth century.'

'Their king was Dingiswayo, son of Jobe and grandson of Khayi after whom it is said that the word assegai originated, for it was Khayi who introduced the long-handled throwing spear.

'Dingiswayo, whose real name was Ngodongwana, fell foul of his father who tried to have him killed. He escaped into the Emawunzi bush and hid there. He was looked after by his sister while he made plans for an escape. The new name he gave himself – Dingiswayo – meant "he who is caused to want and is at a loss as to what to do". When he was well, he made his way to the Hlubi in the mountains and became famous for killing single-handed a lioness that had caused havoc amongst the cattle.'

Alpheus moved slightly and in the faint light I could see the intent expression on his face. He was entranced by the old man's knowledge of Zulu history.

'After many years absence,' Foster went on, 'Dingiswayo returned to lead the Mtetwa tribe. It was said that he had met Europeans and seen their soldiers drilling, because he introduced new strategy and tactics unknown to Zulus of the day.

'He built many kraals. One of them was on a ridge not far from the water pan Dadethu (sister). The king named the pan when one of his sisters was taken by a crocodile. After the tragedy Dingiswayo did not drink from the pan and his people followed his example. To this day the Mtetwas refuse to drink the water.'

We sat silent again while a lone hyena called from the side of Masimba hill.

'In the latter part of his rule, before he vacated the area between the two rivers, the king only kept his herd of white cattle. These white cattle were known as Inyonikayipumuli, after the cattle egret, because there were so many that the birds never had time to rest. The white cattle were said to be less susceptible to the disease carried by the tsetse fly, which, at that time, the Zulus called *umunca*.'

As if anticipating my question, Will Foster gave a brief description of the possible derivation of the word which is now used throughout most of the African continent.

It is in all probability related to the Zulu verb, 'ku-naga', which means to care, or to be anxious concerning anything or anybody. Some animals infected with nagana appear to walk in the most deliberate manner. The actual cause of this apparent caution is sheer weakness.

'It is an interesting thing,' Will Foster said, reverting to the royal white cattle, 'that when we were carrying out experiments with the Harris fly traps in the 1930's it was soon obvious that the tsetse was not attracted to a trap covered in white material. In Dingiswayo's time, when the nagana outbreaks were bad, the cattle were driven to the Mpila range of hills.

The Mpila range of hills is where the present rest camp is situated.

'Do you know what "mpila" means ?' Will Foster asked Alpheus.

'Health,' Alpheus answered triumphantly.

'Yes, that is so,' Will Foster said ponderously. 'But it is also the name of a little white daisy and this is what the range of hills gets their name from, because at certain times of the year, there is a carpet of white flowers over the slopes. The range forms a natural division between the eastern and western sections of the game reserve.

'But the Mtetwa left the area and moved south towards the Enseleni River because of the increase in malaria and the high mortality amongst the cattle. The king moved his kraal to a site at the source of the Mpapoza stream near what is now the Ntambanana farms. The stream got its name from one of his daughters who drew water from a pool. To this day when the stream dries up the people gather and pray and make offerings in the form of a goat to placate the long departed Mpapoza.'

I asked about the western section of the reserve.

Speaking in English and Zulu alternately, Will Foster went on with his story.

'The western part was at one time densely populated, probably by the Ndwandwe people. There are many old kraal sites and grinding stones. I have also seen exposed graves with skeletons showing. The old men of the Telapakati regiment state that they were born in the western area, so the reserve was probably occupied up to 1870-5. The men say that their forefathers were harassed and finally driven away by raiding parties of the Mandhlagazi tribe. This is the origin of the Mandhlagazi footpath which became the western boundary of the game reserve when it was proclaimed in 1897.'

'The fighting must have been bad,' Alpheus muttered.

'Yes,' Will Foster said. 'On the plains below Ntaba-amanina (The Hill of our Mothers) men of the Mtetwa and Mandhlagazi fought pitched battles. When they stopped fighting they went to the women-fold on the hill – hence its name – and demanded beer.'

The old man laughed quietly.

'Even though they fought they were still gentlemen,' he said.

'Nondwengu, the original kraal of King Mpande, was also in the western area before Mpande moved to the Ulundi site. There are also many smelting sites where the old Zulu blacksmiths melted down iron ore for the manufacture of assegais, hoes, and axes. They were fine craftsmen.'

It was late when old man Foster had finished talking. The night sky was full of stars and a hyena moaned from the river. We drove back to my tent while reedbuck whistled shrilly from the conical-shaped Masimba hill.

Alpheus sat in the vehicle shaking his head.

'Hau! Mashiya' – Will Foster's Zulu name, which referred to his particularly bushy eyebrows – 'Mashiya speaks Zulu better than the Zulu people. He knows the old, old language,' Alpheus said.

Will Foster died in 1956. He had been a loyal employee of the Natal and the Union Governments, and a fighter for the survival of game in Zululand.

I returned to Umfolozi Game Reserve in 1958. While I had been stationed at the lake, a ranger's house and a rest camp had been completed on Mpila hill.

The view from the house had no equal in Zululand. To the south lay the White Umfolozi river with golden sandbanks and dark green sycamore fig trees. I could see waterbuck standing in the water and among tall phragmites reeds. Troops of baboons played on the sand or fed in the fig trees while grey duiker, bushbuck and warthog followed below, eating what the baboons dropped. To the south-east Dengezi hill ('the Place of Broken Pots', so named from Tshaka's depredations) towered above the river, its wooded slopes a favourite nesting place of the bateleur eagle.

Further to the south lay Mpanjane, Tjokolwane, Butulezi, and Gome hills. And beyond lay the Ntambanana farms and the Omendo hills.

To the east was the whole spread of the game reserve; rocky ridges, tree savannah and dense patches of purple nthombothi trees which grew so well in the clay soil. Siyembene hill which marked the junction of the two Umfolozi rivers stood out like the tip of a rifle foresight in the inverted V of the rivers. Beyond Siyembene was Ncebe ('banana palms') hill with the flat plains of Magayisa to the northeast. This was the favourite haunt of wildebeest and zebra.

Black rhino liked the dense bush along the Black Umfolozi river. White rhino colonised the open areas and used the thick bush to lie up in during the day. Beyond Ncebe hill and Mcacaso stream were the bare hills of the tribal reserve.

To the north-east was the Corridor, the land between the Hluhluwe and Umfolozi Reserves. To the west lay Little Mpila and Nqabaneni hill ('the fortress') and the wooded White Umfolozi valley ringed by Nqoloti, Lubisana, and the Mantianna hills. This valley had been the home of the Ndwandwe people led by the great Chief Zwide who had been defeated by Tshaka. Bits of old pottery, beads, forges, and smashed grinding stones could still be found if you knew where to look.

Beyond all this were the Mtunzini hills and the open plains where the white rhino concentrated. Ukuku and Unoma hills dominated the landscape beyond Mtunzini but on a clear day I could see the mountain, Dingane's Seat, like a nipple pointing to the sky forty miles away.

Umfolozi Game Reserve cast a spell over every man who worked there, though some could describe it only in geological or geographical terms. It became a place with a distinct soul.

There was a tremendous difference between the two seasons; the roar and tumult of summer, thunderstorms, lightning and howling winds. Thick green foliage everywhere, choking dust storms, heat waves and mirages. Floods. Many times I saw the White Umfolozi come down in a raging torrent, brown waters hissing and roaring as they swept past the towering krantzes. Sandbanks vanished and reeds bent before the rush of the water. Logs, animals, pumpkins, and rubble were borne by the flood. Each year there was a toll on the white rhino, too, because unlike the black rhino, they could not swim. They would be lying on the warm sands, unaware of danger, and the flood would sweep them along. Some were washed as far as the sugar lands at Mtubatuba.

Then summer faded and the fire lilies of May bloomed. Winter came. Streams ran quietly or dried up, the sun was mild, the grass shortened and the insects disappeared. The White Umfolozi bared its broad white and gold sandbanks. Dry debris caught in the top branches of a sycamore fig was the only reminder of the summer violence.

In the past, many other men had crossed its rivers, drunk from its pans of grey water, made fires with its wood and heard the calls of birds and animals in the day and in the night. Primitive men using stone-age tools roamed the hills and deep bushy valleys. Their artefacts – hand axes, arrow heads, bark and skin scrapers – were still there. The brown, wrinkle-faced Bushmen lived there too. They had left their traces of occupation in rock paintings of eland in overhangs on the Nqutu ridge and Nqabaneni hill.

In the fourteenth or fifteenth century the Bantu migrations came down from the north, naming everything they saw with appropriate and poetic names.

Every hour in the game reserve had its charm and every section its attractions. The narrow Black Umfolozi river and the broad White Umfolozi river; the cool, misty Mpila hills; the stony kopjes and the barren, desert-like portions of the Thobothi country; the dense, closed bush of the Meva area, the wonderful outlooks from the top of Nqoloti hill and the humid, low-lying country at the junction of the two rivers where the fish eagle called with such haunting beauty.

CHAPTER 4

Magqubu Ntombela and the Wilderness Trails

Magqubu Ntombela was born in a kraal on the Ongeni hills which are situated midway between Hluhluwe and Umfolozi Game Reserves. As a small boy he had walked this wild stretch of country and he knew Umfolozi intimately. The reserve and everything in it was part of his life. He remembered seeing some of the last elephants in the game reserve, when he was a tiny herdboy looking after his father's goats. At twelve he was a guide to the white hunters who came shooting in the buffer zones near the Hluhluwe and Umfolozi Reserves. He joined the game reserve service in 1918 under Vaughan-Kirby.

Magqubu Ntombela was now appointed Head Game Guard. We walked and rode through the reserve together as I renewed my acquaintance after my absence at Lake St Lucia.

Magqubu stood about five feet seven inches tall, with strong chest and arms. He was a little bandy but his thighs were the most powerful I have seen on a man. His face seldom showed anger, but when it did the other guards were frightened. Rage made him stutter, and then become more angry. He was a Shembe (a Zulu religious sect) and would not drink liquor or eat pork or butter, nor would he accept any European medicines. He never told a lie, and would stand up to any man and speak out if he knew he was right. He was one of the hardest working men I had ever known.

On our long patrols he was the teacher and I was the pupil. He was a historian as well as a naturalist, and knew the origin of every place name in the Umfolozi Game Reserve, as well as the history of the Zulu people from the time of the early Mtetwa migrations. He was an excellent mimic and I often watched him call up the honey-guide bird by imitating the grunting call of the honey-badger, then prove the legend by getting the bird to lead us to the honey.

Sounds of white rhino fighting and baboon calling were his specialities. Everyone would be in fits of laughter at his baboon mimicry, but he never lost his dignity or played the clown. He loved to sit round a glowing camp fire at night and tell of the warriors of old. He would stand up and demonstrate, with swinging arms and stamping feet, the frenzied charges of the Zulu impis as they swept down with their short, stabbing assegais.

'Usutu! Usutu!' he would cry, lunging with an imaginary assegai, making the sounds of rifle shots and cannon, and the dying gasps of Zulu and British as they fell below the sphinx-shaped hill called Isandlwana.

He was a superb tracker, an artist in the field. He was a deadly shot with a rifle and could stalk so close to an animal that he never missed.

Magqubu hated poaching dogs. On one of our first patrols we bumped into a gang of poachers with a horde of thin, mangy dogs. He dropped ten with ten shots before I had my second. During his service he had to fight for his life when attacked by poachers, but he was afraid of nothing. After knowing him I no longer wondered why so large a British army was needed to conquer Zululand in 1879.

Magqubu and I were together until 1964 when I was promoted to Chief Conservator, and he decided it was time to retire. But in 1969 when I was transferred to our Head Office in Pietermaritzburg and came to live on a farm in the beautiful Karkloof valley of Natal, I asked Magqubu to come with me and look after my family while I was away on long trips. He agreed and once again we are together.

I will always be in his debt, for in every conversation we have, he teaches me something. He is a unique human being.

One of my first jobs was to recommend setting aside 36,000 acres of Umfolozi Game Reserve as a wilderness area. It embraced the country from the junction of the two rivers to Nqoloti hill in the west. It was an area where no motor vehicles were to be permitted, only people on foot or on horseback. In the interests of a good report I explored the proposed wilderness country. I told Magqubu to show me all the caves because I saw them as points at which future wilderness trailers – tourists on foot and not more than six in a group – would camp at night.

Magqubu first took me to the Mhlopeni krantzes.

From Nkonjane (Swallow) hill and the Hlungwana river junction, the White Umfolozi flows due east until it reaches the southernmost ridge of the Mtunzini. From here it abruptly sweeps and turns to flow west then east once more. Over thousands of years the continual flow has worn cliffs and caves on the south bank. It was in these caves, the Mhlopeni, that the Mandhlagazi tribe slept before their final assaults on the Mtetwa tribe during their periodic internecine wars. The cliffs are red, dotted with rich green strangler fig trees. In some places the vegetation is so thick that the mouths of the caves are closed, and give shelter to hyena and warthog. Birds abound – mocking chats, black saw-wing swallows, pied and black crows, hammerheads, mousebirds, kestrels, and owls.

We camped the night after a long walk through the dense thorn scrub of black rhino country. Later, after Magqubu had made a fire and I had washed in a pool of brown water, Magqubu told me tales of different tribes who had used the caves, of white and black poachers who had hidden there, thinking they were safe from the pursuing rangers. We talked until late into the night.

As we sat near the fire I wondered how long it would be before the idea of wilderness trails caught on. It was new in South Africa. Jim Feely had first drawn my attention to literature about the wilderness concept in America. The more I read the more I was sure that without wilderness areas no game reserve or National Park in Africa would survive. I was convinced that by getting visitors out on foot into the reserve we would make far more friends for conservation. Tourists in cars never properly understood or appreciated a game reserve. The thoughtless actions of the many who threw refuse from their cars was evidence of this lack of appreciation. People who travelled along the trails were different. With few exceptions they appreciated how privileged they were to experience true wilderness.

A few months later, when the story of our proposed trails first appeared in a Sunday paper, we had over three hundred letters asking for details. No more proof of interest in the trails was needed. Nick Steele and I bought donkey pack saddles, billy cans, sleeping bags, air mattresses (which were soon punctured by thorns), bivouac tents, tin plates, knives, forks, spoons. Before a month was over I had taken out the first trail.

Magqubu was the guide. He walked in front, his rifle slung across his shoulders. Some trailers were foolish enough to try to make him walk fast. They did not know that Magqubu could walk as fast uphill as he could on the flats. I remember two women plunging into a rhino wallow, chasing out some warthog, and lying down to suck up the brown water with relish. They had tried to race Magqubu up Nqoloti hill.

Each wilderness trail was an experience for me. I never knew what people were going to be like. It was the first time some of them had ever slept out of doors, and one woman confessed that it was the first time she had really seen the stars.

Everyone looked a little disdainfully at the White Umfolozi water when we walked across in the first half hour of the trail. 'Is it safe to drink?' they asked.

But after a few hours in the dehydrating heat of Umfolozi they would flop on to the sand and gulp the water as though it were nectar. Some of the streams were crystal clear but so salty it took a strong stomach to contain the water. Trailers would run eagerly forward to a clear pool and splash the water into their mouths, only to spit it out. Magqubu would stand nearby, a polite smile on his face, and say in Zulu, 'You would not have believed me if I had said it was salt.'

Once a lion passed a few yards from the camp and roared loudly. The donkeys bolted and wilderness trailers stood upright in their sleeping bags and jumped like children in a sack race towards the fire. They babbled about the experience, a reaction I saw many times; the rush of adrenalin to the system had to be dissipated somehow.

On one particular trail we left early and made our way over

Amatshenyama ('Black Rocks') towards the isivivane. I explained how the Zulus never passed an isivivane without picking up a stone, spitting on it, and throwing it on to the pile. It was a tradition. Magqubu maintained that during the times of the early Zulu kings men came from all over Zululand to do their military service. Many of the old ones died on the way, usually after climbing a steep hill. They were buried in a shallow grave with stones piled on top. From then on no Zulu would pass without adding to the cairn.

As we rested in the shade of a marula tree I told the trailers a story about an isivivane on Dengezi hill. Magqubu and I had been out on a long patrol and reached this isivivane late in the afternoon. I was tired and anxious to get home to my family, and I strode past the cairn. Magqubu called out to me.

'You have forgotten to pick up a stone, spit on it, and throw it on to the isivivane,' he said.

I said, 'Look, Magqubu, I am two hundred yards from the cairn. I am tired, thirsty, and soaked in sweat. We have walked a long way today. Home is still another five miles. Also it is your superstition. I do not believe evil will befall me if I pass it by.'

Magqubu stood firm and spoke loudly.

'I have taught you many things and you have always listened. It is important not to ignore the isivivane. It is the law.'

We stared at each other for a few moments. His eyes did not waver.

'It is the law,' he repeated.

'All right,' I said. 'I'll come back and do as you say, but do not think that I believe in your laws.'

Magqubu smiled.

I shambled back, found a small stone, picked it up, spat on it, and irritably flung it on to the heap.

'*Asihamba* – now let us go,' Magqubu said and he loped off along the winding mountain reedbuck footpath.

Lancer, my ridgeback dog, trotted nearby, his long pink tongue covered in white froth. It had been a long walk for him, too.

We had walked about a mile further and I was too tired to do more than concentrate a few feet in front. Suddenly between Magqubu and myself I saw the end of a black tail slithering through the grass. I was too late to stop myself and put my foot on the tip. In a flash a black mamba raised itself above the grass. It seemed to tower above me, but was probably shoulder height. It made a peculiar 'tsi tsi tsi' call and I saw the scales at the back of its head. This was an ndlondlo, the almost legendary crested mamba.

The snake and I stared at each other for what seemed an age to me. Then it dropped and slid off gracefully, practically on top of the grass. It was then that Lancer saw it, and rushed forward barking. Again in a flash the mamba turned, and came for the dog, who at once retreated to my side. I froze, unable to move. The snake stopped a few yards away, still making its 'tsi tsi tsi' call. It swayed slightly from side to side and I clearly saw the scales raised like hackles. It dropped slowly and moved over the grass to a patch of bush. This time I grabbed Lancer's collar and held on to him until the snake had disappeared. The whole incident had probably taken no more than two minutes.

Magqubu turned to me, a faint smile on his face.

'You see,' he said. 'The isivivane is important. If you had not returned to throw the stone, the mamba would have bitten you. But you showed respect and the spirits guarded you.'

It might have been coincidence but I never walked past a cairn again without completing the ritual.

I knew that in the wilderness areas we had resources that were vital to the well-being of the people of the world. These were like a fountain that they could return to for nourishment; a spiritual recreation, something desperately needed in the twentieth century.

In 1957 I had taken boys in their matric year into what were going to be the wilderness areas of Zululand. Some of them wrote to say that the experience had changed their lives. For the first time they had realised that a wild area was just as important to man as to animals. Each of them had gained something different from the wilderness.

This gave me the idea of starting a wilderness leadership school. I wanted to take out boys who had already proved themselves to be leaders and subject them to a wilderness experience, show them the effects of over-population in game reserves and what it did to the land, then show them the same thing where human beings lived; show them soil erosion, muddy seas, pollution, and overcrowded beaches, contrasting all this with a wild environment, clear rivers, and lonely beaches.

I wanted them to appreciate the tremendous importance of every wildlife sanctuary and how wrong it was that so few were now being proclaimed.

I hoped that from the young leaders who went out into the wilderness there would one day be some who would hold influential positions, that they would take the initiative and make their communities realise we had to live with nature and not exploit her.

In 1957 this was still a dream. Today the Wilderness Leadership School exists and is well on its way to becoming an international movement.

CHAPTER 5

Toni Harthoorn and Rhino Capture

In September 1957 Nick Steele was transferred from Hluhluwe to Umfolozi Game Reserve, and stationed at Gome outpost across the river. He had a fanatical love for horses and was responsible for the important part they came to play in rhino immobilisation and in Zululand ranging work.

Communications were primitive until 1960 when we got radio. If I wanted Nick I sent a runner with a note, or a man on horseback. Nick would reply and the man would return. But I knew the southern areas were safe, for Nick did not spare himself or his guards. While he watched the south I looked after the west, the game reserve, and the Corridor. We met every month end for three days to pay the game guards and labourers. If there was trouble we joined forces and patrolled together. We did not know it at the time, but we were really happy.

One afternoon we rode for miles, discussing a series of problems, each one so vital to us at the time; poaching, the settlement of the crown lands issue, and the stream of squatters. The solution of these problems meant so much to us.

We were quiet, each busy with his own thoughts. As we rode I said to Nick that the white rhino population was increasing to a point where we would have to capture and translocate them to former habitats. Nick was horrified.

'Is the reserve safe?' he asked. 'Won't it be deproclaimed if the white rhino are moved? Without the white rhino everyone will say there is no need for the game reserve.'

I said it was a risk we had to take, our first duty was to ensure the survival of the white rhino.

'But how would we catch them?' Nick lamented.

I told Nick that I had recently met Dr Hans Nel, a geologist, on one of the wilderness trails. While we drank coffee round the fire we had discussed the problem of moving rhino. I mentioned that while we were trying to chase hippo away from farms near Lake St Lucia, I had thought of drugging them. When I spoke to a local doctor and asked him how much morphine we would have to give a hippo, he replied irritably, 'A bucketful man, a bucketful.'

Dr Nel was interested and wrote to friends in the Mineralogy Department of Harvard University. A professor replied. He said although he had made many telephone enquiries, he could not get an answer to 'the rhinoceros problem'. He suggested I wrote to the Director of the Whipsnade Zoo.

I wrote immediately and had a letter by return of post. People were working on tranquillising drugs, but the outcome of using them on wild animals was uncertain, particularly if a dart gun was used. But it was encouraging to know that experiments were being made. The next time I saw Colonel Vincent he told me that a Dr Harthoorn and a Dr Hal Buechner were working on the problem in Kenya. Later I read a magazine article about a man named Red Palmer. He and a group of professors at the University of Georgia had developed an anaesthetic gun. The gun was powered by compressed carbon dioxide gas and fired a hypodermic needle designed to inject controlled quantities of drug.

I enthusiastically told Jim Feely. He calmly said that he, like Colonel Vincent, had read in scientific journals of work being carried out in this field.

Colonel Vincent went to a conference of the International Union for the Conservation of Nature in Warsaw in 1960. Here he met Dr Harthoorn and discussed our problem; too many white rhino in the Umfolozi Game Reserve. He invited Dr Harthoorn to South Africa to experiment with drugs suitable for white rhino capture. This meeting changed the course of wild life conservation in South Africa.

On the 6 December 1960 I drove to Mbuzane ('the place of the gnats') to tell Jim Feely that Dr Harthoorn was coming.

Jim was leaving soon for Zambia. After five years with the Natal Parks Board he wanted wider experience, and had always longed to work in the Luangwa valley amongst big game. I was going to miss him very much. Jim was an intellectual. When he was asked for his opinion he gave it unequivocally, which was not always appreciated, but to me he was a very valuable friend because he could view problems objectively. We had grown very close over the years, and I always consulted him on any important issue; he could weigh up the pros and cons like a judge and come straight to the point. He had the rare ability of being able to talk, smoke, drink tea, and simultaneously work out the answer to a problem I had given him half an hour before.

I drove to Mpila after receiving a message that Dr Harthoorn and Mr de Burgh Whyte, the Parks Board Public Relations Officer, had arrived. At my office de Burgh Whyte handed me a letter from Colonel Vincent.

After explaining that 'The following are the points I wished to mention to you – quite haphazardly put down and typed by myself', the Colonel had produced a lucid and detailed list of instructions which became a blueprint for rhino capture.

He said, *inter alia*: 'It is extremely important that you, Deane, Carpenter, and Clark learn as much as possible in the short time available. Much of Dr Harthoorn's information is technical and extremely important. I must implore you all not only to listen carefully but also to write copious notes.'

The Colonel said that we would have to do the bulk of the rhino work once Dr Harthoorn had left, and 'It has to be remembered that some losses may be incurred. The Board has asked Dr Harthoorn here because we accept that we are prepared to lose two or three rhinos – if in the outcome we can know in the future how to deal with the species.' He stressed that the visiting public must not overhear our conversations or see the experiments, 'because at this stage I do not want publicity or interviews. That can wait until we know what we are doing.'

I got a small clue to Dr Harthoorn's nature from the Colonel's penultimate paragraph when he wrote: 'D.H. is a man who quite obviously likes often to be quiet – I hope you will ensure he has enough leisure in his rondhavel to write up his notes,' and he repeated the point about our writing notes of what we could glean from Dr Harthoorn.

In a postscript the Colonel said that Dr Harthoorn had a lot of information about the winching of rhinos on to lorries, and about tranquillising the beasts in transit.

I read it twice then drove with de Burgh Whyte up the hill to Mpila camp and hut number four. It was an important meeting, but all I could think of as I knocked on the door was Jim Feely's remark, 'I understand he's tall.'

Dr Harthoorn was a most impressive man; he was over six foot tall, with light brown, greying hair, deep-set blue eyes and a mouth that suggested a ruthless streak. This was an energetic person, one who would keep working until he or we dropped. We introduced ourselves, he speaking with a slight accent, a trace of his Dutch upbringing.

After the inevitable tea and talk about game, I suggested we go to the western area of the reserve, the area of high rhino population. He agreed eagerly, and we drove to Magqubu's kraal. Magqubu ran towards us, buckling his belt. He stopped to slap the butt of his .303 rifle in a smart salute.

I told him that Dr Harthoorn had come from Kenya to show us how to capture white rhino.

As we drove out to survey the ground I pointed out the rhino grazing patches, the effect of shade on *Themeda*, and pans that had been deepened by years of rhino wallowing. We passed the artificial rhino pans and saw a herd of waterbuck and impala. These two species seemed to thrive in a deteriorating habitat.

Near the Thobothi stream we saw a fully grown rhino. Dr Harthoorn asked me how much one would weigh. I glibly said three tons, having been told this by many of the old-timers. Dr Harthoorn looked dubious, and with reason, as we found later. In the area near the Mtunzini range, which had been bush cleared during a tsetse fly campaign, we saw rhino in groups of two, three, and five.

We stopped below Sokwezela hill, got out of the Land-Rover and followed a pair of young bulls as they grazed along the hill slope. Dr Harthoorn made aiming movements.

'Would we have to get any closer?' I asked.

'No – this would be all right,' he replied.

His voice disturbed the rhino and they turned and blundered towards us.

'Run!' I shouted and we legged it to the Land-Rover. 'Harmless animals,' I said, 'but they can get confused and run over you.'

'Which would be unpleasant,' Dr Harthoorn added cheerfully.

It was getting dark, and fires from the squatter huts were blinking in the fading light. I pointed them out and told Dr Harthoorn how glad we all were that he had come, because only by moving some of the rhino out would the species be safe.

On the way back to Mpila I questioned him about the Capchur gun. He was not communicative that evening, so our conversation was on a question and answer basis.

'What powers the Capchur gun?' I asked.

'Two soda syphon type CO_2 powerlets which build up to a pressure of two thousand pounds per square inch.'

'What's the range?'

'Depends upon the size of the dart,' Dr Harthoorn said.

There was silence.

'The Colonel mentioned in his letter that the gun was erratic.'

'Well, it shoots better in the heat of the day,' Dr Harthoorn grunted.

'How do you unload a dart?'

'Use a long piece of grass – or medical forceps. Blowing down the barrel is not advised,' he said with a sideways glance.

'What drugs do you use?'

'Gallamine triethiodide has been successfully used by myself and John Lock on the black rhino. Succinylcholine chloride works on some of the antelope, like Uganda cob.'

The names were incomprehensible to me and I had to ask him to spell them so many times he became irritable. Eventually I memorised the names and looked forward to mentioning them casually to rangers the next day.

I returned to my questioning.

'Why do you have a telescopic sight?'

'Easier to shoot in fading light,' said the doctor. 'Possible to watch the flight of the dart – less losses this way. Once you are used to the size of different animals you are able to estimate the range with more accuracy.'

It was too dark to stop and write but I made mental notes and couldn't wait to reach home so I could write it all down. The Colonel's instructions were not to be taken lightly, and he had stressed the need to take notes.

That evening Dr Harthoorn came to dinner. After a meal he relaxed and we talked until the lights went out at ten o'clock.

Conversation turned again to the Capchur gun and darts. He said he had developed a great deal of affection for this weapon and although there were many who derided its uses, no one had yet perfected anything superior. Some people swore by the cross-bow, but in his opinion it was not as reliable. Difficulties had been experienced with the darts. The acid-loaded darts were difficult to carry in the field without accidental triggering of the activating mechanism, or creep of the plunger from acid leaking past the brass seal. They could only safely be carried needle up, which made stalking difficult.

John Page, then Secretary to the Parks Board, arrived late that evening. He had come to see the capture of the first rhino so that he could give a first-hand report to Colonel Vincent.

The following morning, on the Colonel's instructions, Norman Deane and Garth Carpenter arrived from the Hluhluwe Game Reserve. Norman, wiry and very fair, was an ex-insurance clerk and air gunner. He had spent some months in the Mkuze Game Reserve before being transferred to the Hluhluwe Game Reserve, where he had done an outstanding job. Garth was a recent employee, doing game control work at Hluhluwe.

Nick Steele rode over from Gome outpost and as usual arrived well before he needed to. During the years he had worked with me he had never been late.

Everyone was introduced to Dr Harthoorn and I was delighted at their looks of astonishment as the doctor expounded on drugs, the intricacies of the Capchur gun, and his modifications of the dart.

'Phew, this is a complicated business,' Norman said despairingly, as we walked to retrieve a dart Dr Harthoorn had fired into a grass-filled sack while testing the gun.

'Oh, not really,' I said. 'Gallamine triethiodide and succinylcholine chloride have a common effect in that they check the transmission of the nerve impulse at the neuro-muscular junction.'

Norman looked at me blankly and I had to walk away fast to stop myself laughing. It had taken me minutes of repetition to learn that sentence.

Dr Harthoorn gave us a lecture in the afternoon.

'I never understood one word from the moment I walked in until the end,' Nick said afterwards.

Dr Harthoorn explained the Capchur gun again.

'Because of its many defects and idiosyncracies it is doubtful whether it could be effectively used for all the game animals we hoped to capture,' he said. 'However, it has proved to be quite adequate for shooting darts into rhino, and it could also be adapted for marking rhino – but remember it is a dangerous weapon, and don't travel with it loaded. This is most important for it is all too easy for the weapon to be accidentally fired.'

Norman leant across and whispered, 'At least I can understand him when he talks about the gun.'

'Wait, he hasn't really started yet,' I said.

'The small darts have a maximum range of forty-five yards and the large ones, twenty-five yards. Experience has shown that they are easily deflected by wind,' Dr Harthoorn said, putting the gun on the table.

'As far as the darts are concerned, I have made some modifications to the original, but it's a simple mechanism.' He pulled out a dart and stripped it down.

'There is the dart body which is made from aluminium; the needle, and the tufted nylon flight. Now for the drug to be injected into the rhino, we have a rubber plunger which we grease with silicone then move it up and down the dart barrel to lubricate the whole thing. Into the recessed flight we drop a small ball bearing and a carbonate tablet, and seal it off with a piece of *Uganda Argus* – it has to be *Uganda Argus*.'

He paused, and continued. 'Then between this and the plunger we put in citric acid. Now on impact the split shot forces the carbonate tablet through the paper into the acid, a gas is formed, the rubber plunger is forced down the barrel, and the drug is injected. Simple, isn't it?'

We all sat quiet for a moment then John Page asked, 'Does that piece of paper have to be *Uganda Argus* – will nothing else do?'

Dr Harthoorn turned away as the rest of us laughed. John Page had grasped the intricacies of the gun and the dart while *we* had only appreciated that one piece of newspaper was the same as another.

Dr Harthoorn then gave a dissertation on the merits and demerits of the drugs he had experimented with in Rhodesia, Kenya, and Tanzania.

'Flaxedil – or gallamine triethiodide to give it its technical name – is the only drug we have used successfully on rhino so far. John Lock, my colleague in Uganda, and I have caught black rhino in the hunting areas of Tanzania and also at Kariba in Rhodesia.'

He digressed to tell us how he and Rupert Fothergill, the Rhodesian game ranger in charge of Operation Noah on Lake Kariba, had lashed a drugged black rhino to a raft of drums and towed it across the lake to release it on the other side.

He returned to the drugs and said the other drug that had been used on antelope was scoline, or succinylcholine chloride.

'How do these drugs work, Doc?' John Clark asked. He was leaning forward with pencil raised ready to take notes.

'Well!' Dr Harthoorn said. 'As I was telling Ian Player this morning, the two drugs have a common effect in that they check the transmission of the nerve impulse at the neuromuscular junction. Gallamine triethiodide does this by blocking the transmission across the myoneural junction or voluntary muscle. It paralyses the muscles of locomotion, causing the animal to lie down. It also changes the pattern of breathing. Scoline does it by persistent depolarisation of the muscle and plates. Now the gallamine can be partially reverted by physostigmine or neostigmine. In other words this is an antidote to the gallamine.'

He quickly drew a diagram to show what he had just explained.

'There you are John,' he said. 'Simple, isn't it? Q.E.D.' Someone behind me whispered, 'What the hell is Q.E.D. – another bloody drug?'

'What dose do you have to give a rhino?' John Page asked.

'Approximately point five eight milligrammes per pound body weight.'

'Can you tell me what this is in c.c.'s?' Norman Deane asked desperately.

We were walking out of the door when Dr Harthoorn said, 'I forgot the tranquilliser Largactil, or chlorpromazine hydrochloride.'

Everybody groaned.

'This is too much for me,' Nick cried.

'You will be using this one a lot,' Dr Harthoorn continued calmly. 'This tranquilliser, because that's all it is, has a soporific effect and also counteracts the action of adrenalin. But don't give it intravenously because it may cause a fall in blood pressure.'

'How long before it takes effect?' John Page said without looking up and writing quickly.

'About twenty minutes, but be careful not to give it when the weather is cold, because it destroys the animal's ability to regulate temperature – this could be fatal.'

We trooped out like a bunch of schoolboys released from class.

'Thank God that's over,' Norman Deane said drily. 'Another five minutes and I'd be drinking the stuff to calm my nerves.'

By 8.30 a.m. the next day we were all on our way to the western area. It was a beautiful December day, hot with scattered white cloud. Herds of reedbuck were on the open patches of green grass at the Madhlosi headwaters ('place of ancestral spirits'). The only jarring note was the sight of distant squatter huts and the goats and cattle on the ridges of Mtunzini hill.

We decided that only fully mature males would be darted until a dosage was perfected. Everything was a little hazy; none of us knew what to expect. As we entered the bush-covered zone Magqubu spotted two bulls slowly making their way towards the pans and shade. Dr Harthoorn asked us the weight of the biggest one. We all guessed. He filled a dart with drug mixture, transferred into Norman's open Land-Rover and drove towards the rhino.

The two rhino grew agitated. One trotted off rapidly to the reserve. The other ran towards Sokwezela hill then stopped. Tension mounted as we saw Dr Harthoorn raise his rifle only to lower it and point towards the rhino. Norman drove a little closer. The rhino swung round, uncertain. Dr Harthoorn aimed and fired. There was a 'clunk' from the dart as it struck the shoulder.

The rhino galloped forward a hundred paces, then stopped to turn towards the Land-Rover. I saw Dr Harthoorn put up his hand, and Norman stopped. For a full minute the rhino stared at the Land-Rover then it moved towards the reserve. Norman swung the vehicle round and raced after the rhino to turn it from the thick bush.

The rhino, by now panic stricken, ran northwards towards the Thobothi stream. Norman's Land-Rover jolted across the veld. Through binoculars I saw Dr Harthoorn gripping the door and bracing his feet against the shock of the rough riding.

The rhino was now running fast towards us. It crossed a donga and Norman could no longer follow close behind. We drove forward, hooting and shouting at the unfortunate animal until it was running parallel to the bush. By now seven minutes had passed and we expected the rhino to succumb, but it was going stronger than ever.

'That muthi isn't working,' Magqubu said matter of factly as he clung to the spare wheel.

We hit a hidden stump. The steering wheel jerked in my hands, but we kept going and turned the rhino. It now ran southwards towards the Icibiletank pans. Norman had crossed at the lower end of the donga, driven over the veld and caught the rhino up again, but it turned into the bush, disappearing in the long grass and trees. Everyone jumped out of the Land-Rovers and ran after the rhino, but it was a futile chase.

Magqubu, calm and collected as ever, took over and painstakingly began to track the animal. After half a mile he told us that it was still running fast.

'It's no use following it any further,' Dr Harthoorn said. 'We will have to step up the dose with the next one.'

As we walked back to the Land Rover I discussed the darting with Nick, and he agreed we could work out a more efficient way of following darted animals.

'We'll use horses and postmen with radio-telephones on high points,' I said.

Nick agreed. He said it would be hard following the rhino on horseback, but it could be done.

'Owen and I should be able to keep after them,' Nick said.

Owen Letley was a young ranger who had been recently transferred to Umfolozi from the Drakensberg mountain resorts where he had been in charge of jackal hunting. He was an excellent horseman.

The horses, the tracker, and the gunner were three essentials of capture.

I spoke to Dr Harthoorn about our plans.

'That's your side of the show,' he said, looking up suddenly from wiping a dart. His blue eyes were piercing.

This became the pattern. He respected our judgment on the practical side while we depended completely on his knowledge of the drugs. It was a good working partnership, based on mutual respect.

By the end of the first capture Dr Harthoorn was our hero and any passing scientist who dared to criticise him felt our wrath.

Dr Harthoorn sensed our affection for the rhino and soon felt the same way himself. 'Those splendid beasts,' he called them. He appreciated how urgent it was to move rhino in numbers to other areas to ensure their survival, and he supported my plea to have the animals sold to overseas zoos as an extra precaution. This view was not currently very popular. There were few conservationists who could bear the thought of seeing one of the 'splendid beasts' caged. But in 1960 the political future of all Africa seemed uncertain. If we had been forced to fight for our existence on the African continent against outside invaders, as well as keep down possible insurrections in our own country, wild life would have received little sympathy. The poor-sighted, gentle white rhino would soon have been exterminated.

Magqubu strode off to get the tea mugs and billy from the Land-Rover. We collected wood and soon had a fire going. The smell of woodsmoke and the sound of water boiling in a blackened old billy seemed to relax people, and soon everyone lay sprawled on the grass, sipping the hot liquid.

Someone asked Dr Harthoorn to demonstrate the gun again, and he was questioned about the drugs. Slowly we were beginning to get a grasp of what it was all about, and 'gallamine triethiodide' and 'succinylcholine' were bandied about by everyone.

Dr Harthoorn showed no emotion but there must have been times when he felt like laughing or screaming. To have five sunburnt, rugged game rangers muttering drug names like a litany and asking one another how many grammes in an ounce must have been too much for him, particularly when everyone, obeying the Colonel's orders, followed him with notebooks open and pencils drawn.

As we drove home that afternoon I saw some squatters against the skyline at Reedbuck Rocks on Mtunzini. They must have had a perfect view of us all day. Next day the game guards told us the rumour amongst the squatters was that we were going to catch all the white rhino so that they could move on to the land. It was a sad but dangerous situation.

It was late before we got back to Mpila but Nick immediately set about organising everything for the following day. Saddles and bridles were examined then loaded into the Land-Rover. A groom received careful instructions to take the horses out early and have them in position by eight o'clock.

By nine o'clock the next morning we were all up again. The horses were saddled at Madhlozi guard camp, then Owen Letley and Nick followed the Land-Rovers on to the plain where Magqubu spotted a rhino. I studied the animal through my binoculars and recognised it by its missing posterior horn. It was an animal we all knew as Onehorn.

Dr Harthoorn greased a dart and poured acetic acid into the space above the rubber plunger. He drew four and a half c.c. of drug mixture from a rubber-capped bottle and carefully squirted it into the dart with the syringe. These preliminaries took a good ten minutes. The rhino grazed peacefully.

When everything was ready the rhino was stalked from the Land-Rover. It took no notice of the vehicle. This was to be expected because since

October 1958 more and more tourists had driven round the loop road and watched the rhino at close quarters. Nevertheless we tensed as Dr Harthoorn motioned the Rover to stop. He aimed, fired, and the dart hit the shoulder. Instinctively the rhino swung round, bellowed, then began running north below the Sokwezela ridge, disappearing now and then in patches of invading *Tarchonanthus* bush. Nick and Owen sped off on their horses, cantering fast after the rhino which had taken fright and gone towards thick bush along the Thobothi stream. I drove my Land-Rover down the boundary road then over the veld to get between the rhino and the bush, keeping parallel with it for more than a quarter of a mile, until it crashed into my left mudguard. I braked hard and it got ahead. Norman and Dr Harthoorn took over and were able to turn it away from the bush. The rhino ran in a circle, and stopped close to where it was darted.

There were no visible signs of the drug taking effect. The rhino slowed down to a walk and was grazing again. We kept it under observation for a quarter of an hour, then Dr Harthoorn decided to dart it a second time.

The drug was mixed, a dart was prepared and the now skittish rhino was approached. This was not easy. It now associated vehicles with danger. Dr Harthoorn took a long shot. The dart went in and the chase was on. We managed to keep it away from the thick bush for five minutes then it crossed the Thobothi stream and vanished among the trees. Nick and Owen galloped after it, bending low in their saddles, and were soon out of sight. Half an hour later Owen appeared, leading his horse. We leapt expectantly to our feet.

'What's happened?' we asked.

'It kept going until it reached a wallow and now it's lying in the water,' Owen said casually.

We followed him on foot through the bush along narrow rhino paths. A grey duiker got up under our feet, frightening us; more than one pair of black rhino lived in this section of bush. We perspired freely from heat as we walked with bent backs. Magqubu was leading, talking to himself as he pointed out rhino spoor, hoof marks, and branches that had been broken by the fleeing rhino. The bush thickened and the trail was lost. We looked at Owen.

'I think it's over there – not far,' he said, and he whistled. There was a low whistle from Nick in reply. He came quietly through the bush and led us to the rhino.

It was still lying in the wallow. It raised its head as we approached. The hump and the back were covered in sweat, and flies were still present. We spoke in whispers. Did Dr Harthoorn want to dart it again?

He shook his head, staring at the rhino.

It was breathing fast, its heaving flanks making ripples that crashed in miniature waves on the edge of the pan. It shifted its position. Involuntarily we moved towards some trees, but the animal only wanted to drink. It lumbered to its feet, swaying a bit, then drank the dark brown wallow water in long draughts. We could see the neck muscles moving and hear the water being sucked into the mouth. The rhino flopped down again, still breathing hard. A cloud of flies buzzed above it, looking for a dry spot to land. There was a strong smell of mud from the wallow and the dank scent of wet rhino.

'It does not care about us here,' Magqubu said loudly.

We all turned to hush him, expecting the rhino to get to its feet. But Magqubu was right. The rhino was indifferent to us and to our voices.

I moved to fifty feet away and took photographs. Everyone began talking in normal tones, laughing and discussing the darting and the chase. The rhino was ignored, and it was only when we heard water sloshing that we looked, and saw it move out of the wallow, have one last drink, then trot away into the bush.

Dr Harthoorn had been making notes on his leg with a ball point pen. This was a habit of his, though he sometimes favoured his arm. He transferred the notes to a small red notebook then looked at me and said, 'Well, what now? Not much point in doing another one; it's getting late.'

I was feeling the strain and the excitement and was glad to call it a day.

CHAPTER 6

Early Experience

The next night John Page and Dr Harthoorn came to dinner and the doctor gave a resume of events to date. He gave technical details of the imperfections of the dart needles, and the need for a further supply. John Page asked questions which showed he had soon grasped the mechanics of dart and gun. He said there was a chance of getting a Pietermaritzburg firm to make the needles and eventually the darts too. John Page's interest in the operation, and his technical ability, made him a useful ally when we needed equipment. Even if money was tight – and in the early days there was no special allocation for rhino capture – he would always find some vote which could be milked to supply us.

The lights went out before everything had been discussed, but I had a feeling of relief. I knew John Page would take care of the organising of supplies and equipment, and this left me free to work out the best areas for darting rhino – more efficient retrieval techniques – and other practical problems associated with the operation.

Next morning Dr Harthoorn dismantled the Capchur gun and showed us the component parts. The whole thing was far too complicated for me but John Page grasped its intricacies immediately. An hour later they had everything they needed for another try at the rhino.

We did not reach the Mtunzini area until after two o'clock. The rhino were lying up in bush near the cleared zone and were hard to find. We stalked what looked like a big bull, but it turned out to be a cow with a tiny calf which could not have been more than a week old. I pointed out to Dr Harthoorn that for about the first week of its life a white rhino calf follows the cow, like a black rhino calf. When it is a week to a fortnight old it runs in front of the cow. Many observers have missed this.

'What prompts it to do this?' John Page asked.

I didn't know, but Magqubu said it was because the cow knew the area in which it lived. When the youngster became familiar with its home range, then it preceded the mother. This seemed a reasonable explanation.

I had noticed many times how much keener the senses of the calves were. Whenever I stalked a group of rhinos to photograph them it was always the youngsters who gave the warning, if the ox-peckers were not there. The only way I could overcome their suspicions was to bounce along on my backside. It was surprising how close I could get to them in this fashion before they took fright. If I stood up or got to my knees they were off, trotting away with tails curled.

Sitting on top of the Land-Rover, Nick Steele sighted a bull.

Dr Harthoorn asked if it was as big as the one yesterday. Nick translated and Magqubu said '*Gefana*' – it was the same size.

The doctor poured out six c.c. of gallamine triethiodide.

'This is more than we used before,' he said. 'If this doesn't bring him down I'll be very surprised.'

He unscrewed the dart flight and poured acid above the plunger, put the flight back and loaded the gun.

Norman Deane drove him towards the rhino. We kept behind the two horsemen until the rhino stood up. I looked at my watch; half past three. We still had four hours of daylight left.

Dr Harthoorn aimed and hit the rhino in the shoulder – a perfect shot. The rhino galloped forward until Norman cut it off. It headed towards Sokwezela and stopped. Nick reined his horse in and held up his hand. Owen joined him and they spoke together. The rhino turned. We leapt into the Land-Rover and the horsemen were off at a canter, the light mane of Nick's horse waving in the wind. We bounced over the veld, hitting antbear holes and trying to avoid hidden rocks.

1. Colonel J. Vincent, MBE – 'A Great Leader'.

2. Magqubu Ntombela – 'philosopher, naturalist, and historian'.

3. Norman Deane.

4. Toni Harthoorn, with Capchur gun.

'It's going to cross the Thobothi,' Magqubu said. 'Turn here, nkosaan, and get across.'

Exactly as Magqubu had foreseen, the rhino went down a path and crossed the Thobothi. I accelerated and got alongside it. Sweat was already showing in beads on the nuchal hump and along the back. I managed to keep up with it but could not turn it. Then the Land-Rover hit a small boulder, I lost control for an instant and the rhino crashed into the mudguard. Instinctively I jammed on brakes. The rhino shot past and ran down a game path leading into thick bush.

We jumped out to run after it, but the horsemen passed us at full gallop. Minutes later we heard them crashing through the bush. We ran until we were out of breath. As we stopped, we heard the squealing of a rhino in distress. It is an unmistakable sound, a low moaning rising to pig-like squeals, pathetic in their intensity.

Owen came cantering up the game path, leaning low on the saddle to avoid branches.

'We've found it,' he said breathlessly. 'Come quickly, it's in a bad way.'

We all ran after him. The rhino lay almost on its back in a small glade of nthombothi trees.

'Quick, get it on its brisket,' Dr Harthoorn ordered.

We moved forward cautiously. This was an enormous rhino which to us was very much alive.

Dr Harthoorn rapidly filled a syringe with the antidote Prostigmin, moved in behind the rhino and injected it in two places. The rhino's movements had grown slower and we tried to roll it over. The scent of man revived it; it rolled over almost unaided, then lay quiet, just breathing.

'It's dying,' John Clark announced sadly.

'Artificial respiration,' Dr Harthoorn said crisply.

I looked at him incredulously. How did one give a fully mature white rhino artificial respiration ?

Dr Harthoorn sprang on to the rhino and began to jump rhythmically up and down.

'Don't watch – get on with it,' he snapped.

Norman's face was a picture of amazement and horror. 'Get up!' Dr Harthoorn said loudly.

We sprang on to the belly. While Norman steadied me I leapt up and down. I glanced at Magqubu; for once he was at a loss for words. As soon as I tired Norman took over, jumping up and down in his big combat boots.

'Raise a vein someone – quick!' Dr Harthoorn said urgently.

Raise a vein? Everybody rushed about as though they knew exactly what the doctor meant, but their movements were aimless, except that each man carefully watched Dr Harthoorn. As soon as he moved towards the rhino's head we all followed him, almost jostling him out of the way.

He grabbed an ear; someone grabbed the other ear.

'Hold here,' he said.

A hand shot forward and held the rhino's ear in a vice-like grip.

Dr Harthoorn filled his antidote syringe, put a finger on a vein and as it swelled he stuck the needle in and injected the antidote.

'So that's what raising a vein is,' I thought.

John Clark and Garth Carpenter climbed on to the rhino, slipping on the sweat, to take their turn at jumping.

Dr Harthoorn knelt dejectedly near the rhino's head, his hand just covering the animal's nostrils. The rhino had become an inert mass, quivering only as the boots of Carpenter thumped on its side. I could see by Dr Harthoorn's expression that there was no hope. The intravenous injection had failed to revive it.

He stood up and said, 'We're wasting our time.'

John Clark and Carpenter kept on jumping, their boots thudding on the hide. Their faces had a fixed look, as though they believed that their continued movement would bring the animal back to life. Now that the heat of the chase was over and we were actually touching the animal it became personal, and we desperately wanted it to live.

'It's no use, John,' I said. 'Come down now.'

The rhino lay still, a thin trickle of blood running down its ear. A few *Stomoxys* flies settled on the flank but the slightest movement made them disperse. A bloated tick the size of a ten cent piece crawled down a back leg away from the anus.

I heard a white-browed scrub robin whistling, and realised it was getting dark. The sun had already sunk behind the Okuku range. I became aware of other sounds; an isikwehle partridge calling, the high-pitched whistle of the mountain reedbuck on Sokwezela hill. It was strange to have been separated from it all in my concern for the rhino when, however subconsciously, I was used to having within me the rhythm of the bush.

'It won't be a wasted death,' I heard Dr Harthoorn say. 'We will have to come here tomorrow and weigh every part of this beast. It obviously got an overdose.'

As we walked back to the Land-Rover I thought how optimistic I had been. A little drug in a dart, injected into a rhino, and that was how it was captured. How foolish of me to believe that science was so easy. This was going to be a long hard task with many disappointments.

I looked at Dr Harthoorn walking ahead with his long stride, his head jerking backwards and forwards, his hands behind his back. We learnt that this was his pose when he was deep in thought. Someone was speaking to him but he was not really listening.

'Thank God he has come to help us,' I thought.

This was the kind of man who would not give up until he had found the answer.

We returned the following morning; rigor mortis had set in and the grey belly of the animal was distended. I ran my hand over the rhino's back and was surprised to feel hair. I looked carefully and saw tiny single hairs all over the body, which made me think of the woolly rhinoceros of prehistoric times. Nick Steele examined the horns and found maggots under the posterior horn which we later discovered were from the *Gyrostygma* fly.

'No wonder the poor blighters scratch their horns at every opportunity,' Nick remarked.

Dr Harthoorn was looking at its teeth and called us over. 'Look at this ridge on the lower lip.'

It was very prominent, running the whole way along the tip.

'This is because it grazes so close to the ground,' Dr Harthoorn explained. 'It can crop shorter grass than a horse.'

We started to cut up and weigh the rhino, and after half an hour in the overpowering heat we were all stripped to the waist.

Dr Harthoorn gave the rhino another careful examination and helped us to take measurements.

Point of horn to occiput	34½″
Half breast girth behind right shoulder	57¾″
Shoulder height	69″
Circumference left hind foot	34½″
Anterior horn	27″
Posterior horn	9″
Occiput along back contour to tail	111″
Tail, base to tip	25½″
Half greatest girth	71½″
Right front foot length	12½″
Right front foot width	12″
Ridge along lower lip	9½″
Width of ridge	¼″
Width of lower jaw	10½″
Ear	10½″
Overall length from mouth to base of tail	130″

This set the pattern for every animal captured. After the first inspection to see that the rhino was safe, it was always measured.

Magqubu, who had stripped to a sleeveless grey pullover and shorts, led the guards who were expertly cutting up the rhino.

The guards chanted quietly as they worked. Garth Carpenter and Norman Deane twisted a length of wire and tied the scale to an acacia tree red with blobs of resin. Dr Harthoorn spread out a canvas sail to catch every drop of liquid and blood. This was poured into a galvanised iron bucket and weighed.

A leg was dragged to the scale and weighed, then the head. There was a gasp of amazement when Norman said, 'Four hundred and ten pounds.'

All four legs and the head were now off. The body lay oozing blood with a horde of blue flies hovering over the exposed sections. Everything stank of rhino. Three hopeful pied crows flapped and squawked in the sky, and far away I saw the soaring speck of a vulture. They knew there was a feast coming. The blood spattered guards dragged the legs through the bush and threw them into the dry bed of the Thobothi stream. A few minutes later the crows swooped down and strutted round the bloodied meat.

The heat and the flies grew worse.

'All right Magqubu,' I nodded to the swollen belly.

Magqubu picked up a hand axe, spat on his palms and walked, chanting, to the rhino. Talking and singing to himself he twisted the axe then struck with quick hard blows at the chest. The meat and hide parted before the steel and he was into bone. Everyone waited expectantly for the stomach to burst.

Faster and faster Magqubu chopped, from chest to belly. Then he called for a cane knife and carefully slit the skin at the navel. White fat and body tissue showed. He cut deeper through the meat right to the stomach lining. Everyone moved a few paces back. A cicada began screeching in a tree behind and I turned to look when the cane knife went into the belly. With a sickening hiss the gas forced its way out, tainting the air horribly. Fluid and bits of muck splattered over Magqubu but he laughed and flicked them off.

Dr Harthoorn stalked forward to peer into the rib cage.

'Tell them to be careful when they pull the intestines out,' he ordered.

Magqubu nodded when I explained. He took hold of a piece of intestine and began pulling. Dr Harthoorn helped him and they dragged the intestines out of the rib cage. If a piece stuck, Magqubu used his penknife to slit the connecting tissue. When it was laid out Dr Harthoorn explained all the related functions while we took hasty notes.

Two guards cut the penis out and carried it to the scale. 'Good God, look at this,' Norman exclaimed. 'Sixty-two pounds! Strewth, what a weapon.'

We crowded round the scale and stared at the dangling penis.

'*Hau ndoda*, what a man,' a game guard called out, his hand across his mouth in the pose of astonishment.

By one o'clock the weighing was finished. The stench was intolerable and we had to be careful not to open our mouths too wide or a blue fly would be trapped inside.

Magqubu swilled out the bucket that had been used to weigh the blood and liquid. He poured fresh water into it from a drum and we took it in turn to wash. Congealed blood stuck to our fingernails and had to be scraped off with Magqubu's knife.

Dr Harthoorn washed, then stood in the shade of the acacia tree and studied his notebook.

Norman walked across to us.

'That bloke is always so deep in thought,' he said.

Dr Harthoorn looked up, serious for a moment, then he smiled.

'The total weight is four thousand, four hundred and thirteen pounds,' he said. 'It is made up like this,' and he read out the weights.

Head	410 lbs
Pelvis	256 lbs
Penis	62 lbs
Nuchal hump and neck	425 lbs
Stomach	107 lbs
Intestine, small	64 lbs
Intestine, large	708 lbs
Lungs and heart	90 lbs
Liver	64 lbs
Kidneys	20 lbs
Spleen	11 lbs
Body	818 lbs
Left foreleg and shoulder	332 lbs
Right foreleg and shoulder	310 lbs
Left hind leg	265 lbs
Right hind leg	283 lbs
Liquid (including estimated loss in evaporation)	188 lbs

We were scribbling hard.

'Don't worry chaps, you can copy it from here,' Dr Harthoorn said, holding up his notebook.

CHAPTER 7

A Long Day

John Clark and Magqubu left early on the morning of the 10 December to find a bull rhino of suitable size. Nick Steele, Hugh Dent and Owen Letley left just before dawn on the horses for the Ncebe area. Nick alternated between two horses, Ben Gunn and Zoom, while Owen Letley used Boy or Bomber. The horses had become a vital part of operation rhino.

'The horses are our contribution to the saving of the rhino,' Nick said. 'But remember they can only take so much; the doc seems to think horses can go on for ever,' Nick groused. 'And you are catching on to his way of thought.' He nodded at me.

When they had left I worked in the office until John Clark's voice came over the radio.

'We have found a bull, about four thousand pounds, on Ncebe,' he reported.

I collected Dr Harthoorn and John Page and we headed or Ncebe in the Land-Rover.

I counted over forty warthog before we reached the Black Umfolozi bridge. Their population was exploding, and although we were shooting daily we were making very little headway. The warthog were dangerous in that they could overgraze parts of the rhino range.

A white rhino cow with calf at heel trotted across the road. We slowed down and a bull quickly crossed too. Dr Harthoorn studied it critically. He leant forward, chin on hands, his brow furrowed and his deep-set eyes watching every move it made.

'Really splendid beasts,' he said.

The female was coming on heat and she laid her ears flat when the bull approached too close. All three ignored us. The bull tried to get between the calf and the cow but every time he came too close the female would bellow and, with ears laid flat, charge a few paces. The bull retreated, pretended it was very interested in eating grass, then tried to get near again.

I explained to Dr Harthoorn that once the bull got between the cow and the calf it would immediately chase the calf away. I had seen them chase one for over a mile. This happened only with calves three years old or more.

We drove into the Corridor. As we crossed the Black Umfolozi bridge a herd of waterbuck came out of the reeds.

This was another animal which was increasing too quickly. When the habitat at Hluhluwe Game Reserve began to deteriorate seriously in 1954, the waterbuck started to move out into the Corridor and the Umfolozi Game Reserve. In the Mbuzane section they could be found at any time of the day.

We found the horsemen resting in the shade of a grove of nthombothi trees on the Tjevu stream crossing. The horses munched grass, their bridles jingling when they swiped at the flies with their tails.

John Clark came down the hill in the Land-Rover.

Dr Harthoorn mixed the drugs. I checked the Capchur gun, my heart beating a little faster at the thought of creeping on hands and knees towards a big rhino.

Owen Letley saddled his horse quickly then stood watching Dr Harthoorn.

'What are you giving it, Doc?' he asked.

'Gallamine at nought point five milligrammes per pound; about five c.c.'

'Means nothing to me. I'll just follow the rhino,' Owen said, pulling himself into the saddle. There was a faint whiff of saddle soap.

When everyone was ready we drove along Ncebe hill to within eight hundred yards of the rhino. I stalked it on foot for five hundred yards then began crawling towards it. Magqubu followed close behind me, a reassuring presence. When we were seventy yards away I lay for a few moments to get my breath and take the thorns out of my knees.

Magqubu laughed quietly, his teeth still white and perfect although he was over sixty. There was not a trace of fear in his face. He had lived so long among wild animals that he knew instinctively how they would behave.

Moving along in an unaccustomed position soon made me pant. I looked back for the horsemen. They waited about three hundred yards behind, both men leaning forward on the saddles, staring at me. It was good to know that they were there. If there was trouble these men would not hesitate to gallop in and lure the rhino away. Behind the horsemen I saw the Land-Rover with the small group of men looking in our direction, some with binoculars.

I checked the gun again, wiped away some dust, then closed the bolt. The faint click was enough to stir the rhino and it stopped eating to look in our direction. I looked at Magqubu. He placed his finger over his lips and whispered in Zulu, 'Wait.'

I looked at the time: nine twenty-eight. At half past nine Magqubu touched my leg and we started creeping forward again. The rhino had partly turned its back and was grazing, unaware of the danger. A minute later we were forty paces away – still too far to shoot. I motioned to Magqubu to stay where he was and began to slide on my belly as fast as I could towards the rhino. From my prone position it looked enormous, and the chomping sound of its eating was deafening. A zebra yodelled on the side of Ncebe. I froze, but the rhino took no notice. The sun was beating down on my neck, sweat ran into my eyes and tiny pepper ticks crawled busily along my arms.

The rhino now had its back to me and I wanted to shoot it in the shoulder. I wiped the sweat from my eyes, quickly checked the Capchur gun again, loaded it and hissed softly. The rhino swung round. I fired and the dart hit the shoulder. The rhino hesitated, then tore off in the opposite direction. The time was nine thirty-three.

5. 'Daisy' – the first success with new drugs.

6. Mpila Rest Camp, Umfolozi Game Reserve.

'*Ushayile kahle* – you hit it well,' Magqubu said smiling and he shaded his eyes to watch the horsemen chasing the rhino.

Two minutes later a Land-Rover bumped across the veld to pick us up.

'Good shot,' Dr Harthoorn said as he busily wrote, first on his bare leg then on his bushjacket sleeve.

The relief from tension was wonderful; a surge of joy swept over me. These were important days and it was good to be here with a fine group of men.

'There they go,' John Clark shouted, pointing to the rhino being closely followed by the two galloping horsemen.

I looked up as they disappeared into a patch of yellow-flowering *Acacia karroo* scrub on the upper reaches of Tjevu stream. We followed immediately in the Land-Rover. Owen Letley rode across the open flats on Bomber.

'It's going down,' he called when within shouting distance, then turned and we followed in the vehicle. We reached the rhino a few minutes later.

'What time did it go down?' Dr Harthoorn asked.

'O-nine-forty,' Nick said, glancing at his palm where he had written the time.

'I gave it five c.c. of Prostigmin in the hump,' Owen said, handing over a syringe and a small bottle of antidote.

Dr Harthoorn quickly injected more antidote into the hams. Norman tagged both ears. The rhino did not appear to feel anything.

After we had been there for five minutes the rhino began to sweat, first in the folds of the skin on the nuchal hump, then under the neck and along the back. Soon it was sweating so profusely we could gather drops of the amber-coloured liquid in plastic bottles.

At ten-thirteen the rhino was on its feet. We stood in a semicircle at a safe distance while it moved slowly away. Dr Harthoorn watched it very carefully.

'It seems that the animals that go down quickest have the best chance of survival,' he said. 'The large one that died was more inclined to fight the drug than this one was. I also have a feeling that the younger the animal, the greater the range of tolerance.'

'How does all this compare with the black rhino at Kariba?' John Page asked.

'We caught seven without loss, one of the reasons being that it was easy to follow them on the islands. In Tanzania we experienced considerable difficulty in following the black rhino in hunting areas.'

For the rest of the morning we searched for another rhino of a suitable size. In the late afternoon we found one which I stalked and darted, but the dart did not penetrate the skin. Nick and Owen were after it before we could call them back, and they followed it for half an hour.

It was getting dark when we returned to Mpila.

CHAPTER 8

The Charge of Two Rhinos

The following day Nick and Owen left at dawn with the horses for Maqayisa in the Corridor. John Clark followed later and reported by radio that Torn Ear, a rhino known to many of us, had been located not far from the boundary of the tribal reserve. A cow and an immature calf accompanied him.

We got there an hour later. Cattle were lowing in the distance, and dogs barked, reminders of threats to our wilderness. A pair of crowned plover came hurtling overhead, screeching their call. This flat open stretch was a favourite place of theirs.

Dr Harthoorn quickly mixed the drugs as we watched his every movement.

'Is it the same drug?' Owen asked vaguely.

Dr Harthoorn had an intimidating habit of looking one straight in the eye, but not answering, when one asked a silly question. He did this now.

Nick kicked Owen softly and laughed. 'Of course it's the same drug.'

'How did I know? All these damned drugs look and sound the same to me,' Owen said despondently.

The rhino grew restless and the cow and calf trotted off. Torn Ear followed for a hundred yards then stopped. We followed in a Land-Rover and drew up close. Dr Harthoorn aimed and fired, and the dart went home. The rhino took off at a canter, running east towards the tribal reserve. The horsemen followed at an easy pace and we jolted along behind in the Land-Rover.

The rhino only went three hundred yards then collapsed. We roared past the horsemen, leapt out of the Rover, and Dr Harthoorn injected Prostigmin into a proffered ear vein. I was about to pull out the precious red tipped dart when the rhino got to its feet. It looked dubiously at us. Dr Harthoorn pulled his syringe needle out of the rhino's vein and a spurt of dark red blood covered the ear. The rhino shook its head and stirred.

'Run!' John Page yelled.

We vaulted on to the Land-Rover. The rhino trotted straight towards us. We jumped off just as it put its horn under the vehicle and through the tool box. It battered the Rover again and then stood up as though puzzled. I could see the unhappy beast was bewildered. In its partly drugged state it probably thought the Rover was another bull trying to take away its cow.

Norman Deane shouted and clapped his hands. Everyone joined in and the rhino turned and lumbered off. It ran a hundred yards, then collapsed. We ran after it and tugged fearfully at the dart. Every time the rhino moved an inch we leapt back hurriedly.

'This rhino is well and truly down,' Norman said after we had run away a few times.

He took a pair of pliers and tugged at the dart. Dr Harthoorn watched him and said, 'Treat it carefully, Norman, those things are precious.'

Norman withdrew it and wiped it on his khaki trousers before he handed it to Dr Harthoorn.

Antidote was injected at ten-minute intervals and after the fifth injection Dr Harthoorn remarked, 'This is most unusual – a much smaller dose of Prostigmin can kill an animal.'

He shook his head and murmured, 'This is something of a record.'

Large doses of penicillin were also injected. I winced each time the thick needle was pushed into the flesh. Dr Harthoorn held it between two fingers like a dart, then rammed it in with one quick movement.

Eventually, using some logs, we propped up the rhino on its brisket.

'It can damage the lungs and head if we leave it for too long on one side,' the doctor explained.

The rhino sweated profusely and Dr Harthoorn looked anxiously at the sky.

'We need water to cool this beast down,' he said.

We gathered water from a nearby spring in every container we had and poured it over the rhino. The south wind had been blowing softly all morning, bringing with it a smell of rain. As the sky grew overcast there was a great contrast in the colour of the rhino, its grey skin wet with sweat, and the bright green grass of the Maqayisa plain.

Later, squalls of rain swept across the veld and we sheltered under trees and in the lee of the Land-Rover. The ox-peckers arrived and settled on the rhino's back and ran up and down the flanks, picking ticks out of the folds of the skin.

There was a symbiosis between the bird and the rhino. The birds provided a warning system while they fed on the ticks. They had a great variety of notes but when they gave their chattering alarm call both white and black rhino reacted at once.

The drugged rhino lay flicking its ears as one bird got right inside. I stood up to get a better look and the birds flew off with their alarm cries. The rhino reacted and tried hard to rise to its feet, its whole body shaking.

We waited another half hour then returned to Mpila. We got back late in the afternoon. The rhino had moved a short distance and was lying down again.

'I'd better give it another shot of penicillin to stop it getting pneumonia,' Dr Harthoorn said, walking with his long strides towards the rhino.

He was only twenty feet away when the rhino lifted its head and rose to its feet in seconds. Dr Harthoorn dashed back to the Land-Rover and leapt into the back as we jerked away in low gear, the rhino snorting behind us.

As I saw Dr Harthoorn running and the rhino coming, I had visions of writing reports to Colonel Vincent to explain how our visitor had got horned. It was a close shave.

We saw the rhino again as it was getting dark. It was trying to copulate with a cow.

Norman looked at me and laughed. 'Maybe there's more to that drug than you think,' he said.

The seventh rhino was the biggest bull I had ever seen. It ignored the Land-Rover when we drove up to it and only trotted away when I got out with the gas gun. I followed it into a gully and darted it in the shoulder as it climbed out on to the bank. The dart hit with a thud, knocking bits of dry red mud into the air. I signalled to the horsemen and they cantered slowly behind as it ran down towards the White Umfolozi river.

We sat waiting for one of the horsemen to return. Dr Harthoorn leant against the Land-Rover wheel writing in another red notebook.

We heard a shout and saw Nick waving to us.

'Action stations,' I said and we climbed into the Land-Rovers.

Nick trotted his horse up to us.

'You won't get the long wheel-base Land-Rover to the rhino. It's lying in the donga' (gully) – he pointed to the west.

Dr Harthoorn got into Norman's short wheel-base Land-Rover and Garth followed him.

Driving in bottom gear low ratio, I reached the top of the donga where we had a grandstand view of the rhino lying on the sand below. We watched Norman drive ten yards away from the rhino, then the three of them got out. Dr Harthoorn held up a bottle and drew some antidote with a steel syringe. Norman gripped the ear tagger which flashed brightly in the sunlight. Garth followed with a notebook and pencil.

They approached the rhino cautiously because it was moving its legs. Dr Harthoorn injected some antidote and Norman strained to clip in an ear tag. The rhino moved and they jumped back.

'They had better be careful, that damn thing is going to get up,' John Page muttered as he filmed the scene with his camera.

Dr Harthoorn moved forward again and was giving more antidote when the rhino stood up. The reaction was instantaneous. The three men dashed towards the Land-Rover. The rhino was bewildered for a moment then chased after them.

'Run, run!' John Page shouted, forgetting to film.

They all reached the Land-Rover together and I saw Dr Harthoorn's green shirt separate from the two khaki-clad figures and leap into the front seat. Norman was with him in a moment and Garth scrambled into the back. Norman looked round quickly to see if Garth was aboard, by now the rhino was alongside the vehicle. Norman let the clutch out and the vehicle shot forward like a rocket. At this critical moment Garth stood up to get a better seat and as the Rover jerked forwards he sailed over backwards and fell off, but somehow managed to grab the back flap.

Garth hung on for dear life but his legs were drawn under the mudguard and brushed against the moving wheels. The rhino was still following the Land-Rover. Garth said later he was afraid to draw Norman's attention to his plight because if the vehicle stopped he would have been gored by the rhino.

We banged our Land-Rover doors, blew the hooter and shouted ourselves hoarse trying to draw Norman's attention to Garth.

Norman told us later that after he had gone a hundred yards with his foot flat down on the accelerator he heard a mild voice above the screaming of the engine: 'I've fallen off Mr Deane, I've fallen off Mr Deane – but I've got my notebook.'

Fortunately the rhino turned off and disappeared into the veld.

We ran down to the Land-Rover to find Dr Harthoorn, Norman and Garth in fits of laughter.

'Why is it that game rangers always laugh when someone nearly gets killed?' Dr Harthoorn asked.

Everyone immediately laughed more, and when Norman described how Garth had said he had his notebook, we doubled up.

Garth showed us his leg which was badly skinned with blotches of tyre burn, and we all laughed again.

We drank tea from chipped enamel mugs and discussed the capture.

'I can't say I'm happy with the drugs,' Dr Harthoorn said. 'It's not what we want, but we must press on and do a few more because we are learning something about these beasts of yours.'

We went out into the Corridor in the afternoon and darted a half-grown bull below the Ncebe hill. As the dart plopped in, the rhino ran off at speed. Nick and Owen followed on horseback while Norman chased after it in his short wheel-base Land-Rover.

John Page was with me in my cumbersome long wheel-base Land-Rover and we could not keep up with the other vehicle and the horsemen. By following the tracks over the flattened grass we managed to track Norman's vehicle and caught up with him five miles on at the Nyalazi river.

'It was still running flat out when we last saw it,' Norman said pointing towards Hluhluwe Game Reserve. 'I'm sure he's gone right into my reserve.'

The horsemen returned an hour later and reported they had followed it for over ten miles to the Nqabatheki gate, one of the old entrances to Hluhluwe Game Reserve.

'It's obvious the dosage was too low,' Dr Harthoorn said, looking up from his red notebook.

The way he said it made me realise that he had kept the dosage low because he did not want to risk the death of another rhino.

The final rhino was darted early the following day, but it disappeared into the bush. Magqubu tracked it for hours, and found it feeding peacefully in a glade. The dart was still stuck in its shoulder.

'But it will come out the first time he has a wallow,' Magqubu explained to me later.

On Dr Harthoorn's last evening we got together and he spoke brilliantly about the pros and cons of the drug, and about everything else that had happened during his stay.

We sat drinking beer in my lounge. In the darkness outside a nightjar whistled and the wind blew softly under the thatched eaves. The buddleia still flowered in the garden and its heavy scent wafted into the room. After days in the sun Dr Harthoorn's fair skin was burnt a dark tan, and his blue eyes showed up clearly.

'Three deaths in ten animals darted is not good,' he was saying, holding a can of beer which he waved slightly to emphasise a point. The three could have survived if we had administered the antidote as soon as they went down. This might be possible with increased experience but when you think of the field conditions we've seen, the chances of giving an intravenous injection within three minutes of the rhino collapsing are small. No matter how good the horsemen are, some rhino will escape them and get lost.'

He drank from the can and was silent for a few moments. 'One of the interesting facts is the difference between the black rhino and the white rhino in their reactions to gallamine. The black rhino tends to develop respiratory distress soon after going down with large doses. The white rhino suffers respiratory arrest within minutes of only moderate doses of drug.

'Gallamine is generally tolerated better by the young animal than by the old. Maybe if we had darted young white rhino there would have been a greater range of tolerance than in the large bulls we have used in these experiments.'

He pondered this point for some time and drank slowly from the can of beer.

'No, the right drug for the large-scale immobilisation of your white rhino has yet to be found.'

'What do you think of our chances?' I asked. I had had just enough beer to clear my head and enable me to grasp what he was saying. It was a rare state of mind.

'It will be found,' he said. 'The white rhino, unlike many other mammals, may possibly be captured more easily with a centrally-acting drug. The principal difficulty will be to find a drug that in high concentration has no caustic effect upon the tissues. We have also got to find a way of bringing the animal round from anaesthesia. I'll start working on it when I get back to Uganda.'

I asked why it was that when a rhino was darted in the shoulder it tended to go down quicker.

'I suspect that the larger mammals show some difference in the absorption rates, from different parts of the body. This is possibly due to skin thickness or extent of fascial layers,' he replied, then added, 'No one can complain about our shooting, only twelve darts were fired. We had to shoot that one bull with the bird dung on its back twice, remember. Then you missed that shot when you fired across the wallow. It's always difficult to estimate distances across water.'

'Another question,' I said. 'All the rhino we darted in the morning survived while the ones in the afternoon died. Now why is that?'

He pulled his little red notebook from his light khaki safari jacket and flipped the pages.

'Numbers three, six, and nine were darted at three thirty-two p.m., three thirty p.m. and five thirty-five p.m. Yes, all these died, but it may be coincidental. On the other hand there may be a complicating factor, such as environmental heat and body temperature. We did some work on Carr Hartley's tame white rhino once. They underwent considerable fluctuation in body heat depending upon the surrounding temperature. The fullness or otherwise of the stomach may also play a part – gallamine is eliminated mainly by excretion through the kidneys. So the state of hydration could govern the absorption of the drug. On the whole it seems that the animal which goes down quickest has the best chance of survival. Some animals are inclined to fight the drug more than others. But if the rhino is swinging its head around with those nasty horns it's no easy matter to give an intravenous injection.'

We went in to dinner and spoke about music and books for the rest of the evening. He knew as much about these two subjects as he knew about physiology and pharmacology. I had developed a great affection for him and was sorry he was leaving.

'I look forward to seeing you back here soon,' I said when we shook hands.

'Don't worry,' were his last words. 'We'll find another drug and save these beasts of yours.'

CHAPTER 9

The Northern White Rhino in Uganda

In January 1961 Toni Harthoorn wrote saying that the Uganda Game Department intended moving the last of the northern race of white rhino from the West Nile district – the old Lado Enclave – to the Murchison Falls National Park. Poaching in the white rhino area was so bad the Game Department realised that if something was not done quickly, the Uganda rhino would be wiped out. Together with the National Parks Service they planned to translocate twenty white rhino. Professional game trappers had been asked to undertake the work in exchange for permission to capture young elephant in West Nile and hippo at Queen Elizabeth Park. Toni suggested I came up and watched them at work. 'You'll learn a lot about crating and loading,' he said.

I flew to Nairobi then to Entebbe where I was met by Toni's colleague, John Lock. Toni drove me north to Lomunga camp, where I met Ken Randall and Pat O'Connell, two professional game capture men. The stockades were already full of white rhino awaiting transport to the Murchison National Park. The heat was enervating and I was interested to note that elephant were sheltering in all the available shade.

The game ranger, John Heppes, offered to show me the catching area before he left for his home at midday, and I accepted with alacrity.

As we were having breakfast a herd of forty elephants passed our camp not more than half a mile away. Many calves were with the herd; it was a fine sight to see these great beasts with the grey dust rising near their feet pass us on their way to drink at the Nile. Framed by giant Borassus palms and the Nile in the background they presented a scene as ancient as Africa itself.

By 8 a.m. the heat was unbearable, but worse was to follow. Bouncing and bumping about in the Land-Rover, we made our way through dense patches of whistling thorn to a magnificent water-hole known as Moroki. Never have I been so glad to see water. In this desert of bush and grass a stream of crystal-clear water gushed from a hole in the hillside and trickled down into a pan. Big shade trees surrounded the oasis and game spoor of every kind was imprinted on the sandy soil. But until I was satiated with water I had no eyes for anything else. I stripped and had a wash but not for long for the tsetse fly lost no time in finding the new blood, as the Anopheles mosquito had the night before.

On our way back to the camp we passed five skeletons of recently killed white rhino, and many more that were older. All in all I counted forty skeletons in the area north of the game trappers' camp.

John Heppes said that organised rhino poaching was going on on a large scale and that one of the gangs was headed by an Arab. Poaching gangs of over five hundred were said to come in from the Sudan. A fantastic amount of white rhino horn had been coming in to Uganda from the Congo where it was fetching 114 to 120 shillings per lb on the legal market and 185 shillings on the black market. The Uganda Government had just stopped the importation of white rhino horn but it was still getting through and finding its way to Mombasa. One of the game trappers had recently seen twelve pairs of horns on the market.

We climbed one of the lava kopjes where the white rhino are said to move in the rains when the black cotton soil becomes impassable. I noticed many wallows dry at the moment but obviously used in the wet season, an indication that there was not as much rhino movement as made out.

Termite mounds with patches of bush similar to Umfolozi were common on the ridges above the Nile plain. The main grass was *Hyparrhenia* which is burnt every year during the dry season. Patches of unburnt grass over twelve feet high remained in many parts, a haven to birds like guinea fowl and francolins.

In the burnt areas patches of green grass were bursting through the rock-hard black cotton soil and buffalo, oribi, Jackson's hartebeest and Defassa waterbuck were seen feeding. I also noted hippo and white rhino tracks nearby. It was quite obvious that the white rhino travelled as much as five miles to get to water, but debatable as to whether they drank each day.

All the game we saw was very wild and I was not surprised when John Heppes told me that poaching and licensed shooting continually took place. He said that over one hundred white rhino had been poached in the last three years, to his knowledge.

Although the maximum fine for killing a white rhino was 20,000 shillings, poachers who had been caught actually skinning a rhino had been taken to court and fined 20 shillings. On the same day the same magistrate sentenced an African to six months' imprisonment for stealing a bicycle pedal.

The game capture firm consisted of Ken Randall and Pat O'Connell and two European assistants. Ken, the senior partner, began catching game as long ago as 1935. During his lengthy career as a trapper he had never had anyone killed during the capture of a wild animal. This was a real tribute to his skill for it is a dangerous profession.

Ken's attachment to the animals he captured was very obvious right from the start. He camped twenty yards from the stockade, fully aware that the camp would be plagued by flies. Care of the animals came first and sympathy for their captive charges was always apparent. It was in fact a moving experience to see these exceedingly tough men handle the very wild creatures.

The trappers' big opportunity had come when the Kenya Game Department decided to shoot some 400 black rhino in the Embu and Kitue areas. About 2,400 had already been shot in the area to open it up for African settlement. Ken Randall suggested that the animals be caught instead of killed, and was laughed at for suggesting it was possible to catch a mature black rhino. However, he persisted and the Game Department eventually agreed.

7. A charging white rhino.

8. A charging black rhino.

9. Black rhino capture.

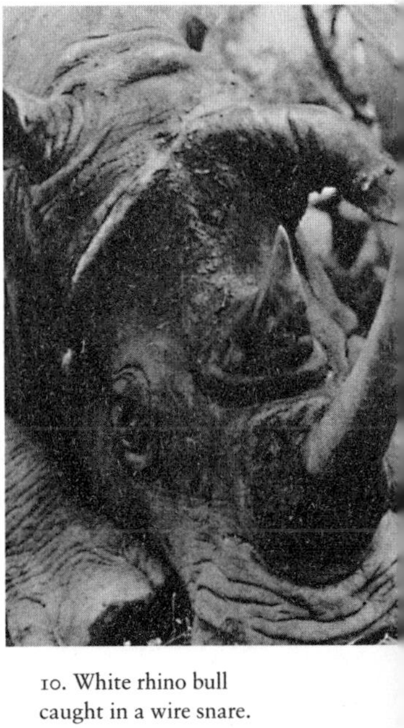

10. White rhino bull caught in a wire snare.

The one hundred and twenty black rhino caught had been taken to various parts of Kenya including the Nairobi National Park, Tsavo National Park and Meru African District Council Park.

As it does not get light until after 7 a.m. the next day's white rhino catching expedition started at 7.45 a.m. when we set off in the direction of a ridge running north-south and ending about five miles from the Nile. The white rhino usually lay up in the shade of large *Terminalia* trees or whistling thorn thickets until the evening when they grazed and made their way to water.

We travelled over miles of whistling thorn veld and except for one clump of dung there was not a sign of rhino. By midday I could hardly see, my eyes were so sore from the glare, dust and grass ash. The floor of the truck was almost red hot after the miles of low gear work and my feet felt as though they had been through a Hindu fire ritual. I forgot how many times I thanked God for the thick soles of the Parks Board boots. Every few yards the whistling thorns came crashing into the cab and ripped my bare arms and legs, but these discomforts were soon forgotten in the most soul-destroying thirst I had ever experienced. Then to make matters worse the hot wind from the Sudan sprang up and one had to breathe with care so as not to singe one's lungs.

It was with some relief I heard Pat O'Connell shout 'There's a cow and calf to the east.' Ken Randall swung the truck round, slipped into third gear and took off like a comet. By a series of hand signals the ropers on the back guided the driver towards the two rhino who were now running strongly. Trees crashed down left, right and centre, but within two minutes we were right next to the animals; Randall edged the cow away from the calf and then quicker than the eye could see the rope was over the calf's neck and the truck came to a halt. The calf squealed and struggled fiercely but every time it relaxed for a second the rope was wound in a figure eight on the upright poles bolted to the truck. I glanced at my watch – four minutes since the first sighting.

The calf squealed louder as it was brought closer to the truck. The cow looked round, heard the calf and came for us with her head lowered. I whipped onto the roof of the cab in a shorter time than it takes to tell.

Everyone screamed and yelled at the cow and she turned away. Two men jumped off the back of the truck and grabbed the calf's hind legs. One kick sent them flying. I busied myself taking photographs and avoiding everyone's eye.

A stream of foul abuse sent two more men jumping off the truck with short lengths of rope. Then the cow turned and came back with her horn held at a menacing angle, but a well-directed clod of earth turned her again. The team disappeared over the side of the truck, jumped onto the calf and threw her onto her back. Ropes appeared from all directions and in another minute she was securely tied. I looked at my watch again. Only ten minutes had passed!

I was rudely reminded that I wasn't at Billy Butlin's holiday camp and had to leap off and give a hand to lift the calf up and put her on the capture truck.

'Wait here!' someone shouted to John Buxton, the television cameraman, and myself. 'We're taking the calf back to camp and we'll come back for the cow. Don't lose sight of her otherwise you won't get any water!'

We spent an uncomfortable hour watching the cow and talking about beer in five-ton lorries. The whistling thorn veld provided no shade and the ground was so hot it burnt through the soles of our boots.

The cow circled us a few times but made no attempt to charge. She simply looked very puzzled.

An hour later the capture truck returned, cruised towards the cow and we hopped aboard.

The cow ran a few hundred yards then moved out into a small open plain. Ken Randall put his foot down and we roared up to her, I saw the bamboo pole come past the cow's head, then with a dexterous flick the rope was over her head. The truck moved on for about a quarter of a mile, the rope being wound in all the time, then Randall braked slowly and we stopped. The cow screamed with rage and swung her horn round viciously. Once again I lost no time in climbing onto the cab.

'Better photos from here,' I said to someone and got a rude word in reply.

There was yelling and shouting and some good army language and men jumped off the truck. By this time O'Connell and an assistant named Lu Wedd had ropes on the back and front legs. It only needed the few extra men to throw the rhino to the ground. No sooner was she down than ropes were twisted over and through, then a length drawing the front and back legs together. As the animal lifted her head to thump the ground a grass-filled bag was thrust under her head. The catching job was over in a mere seven minutes.

Had I not seen it I would never have believed it possible, let alone in seven minutes.

My tongue was swollen with thirst and I was sorely tempted to help myself to some of the rhino's milk, but the thought of never living it down restrained me.

We had to wait until the five-ton Mercedes caught us up. The Sudan wind howled around us, sending great billowing clouds of dust and ash into the air. I lay panting in the shade of the five-tonner as the gang dug into the hard black cotton soil. A sloping hole big enough to allow the truck to come flush with the ground had to be dug. This was by far the longest and most tedious part of the operation. It was late afternoon when this was finished.

The truck was then backed in and two sets of railway rollers were hooked onto the back. The cow, who had been quiet all this time, suddenly lashed herself into a fury of activity and in one backward sweep sent her horn crashing into the petrol tank of the capture truck. She had to be hastily removed before the petrol injured her eyes. When everything was ready she was hauled up onto another set of rollers and pulled manually towards the five-tonner, then a wire rope and hook were attached to the front leg ropes and she was pulled onto the five-tonner with the aid of a small jeep. A bucket of Nile water (undrinkable because of bilharzia) was sloshed onto the back of the truck to save her skin from being broken. (It is incredible how easily the skin is damaged.) A few more sacks of padding were placed under and around her head and she was driven slowly towards the camp. Three or four ropes were also slung over her to stop any movement.

I went in the capture truck and on our way back we came upon a cow and bull lying up under some trees. One of them had an ear missing and both were rather bedraggled specimens. Ken Randall looked at them critically and said they were too old for catching. I was not sorry.

A few hundred yards on a young cow with a very young calf broke cover. Everyone was alerted and we sped towards them but at the crucial moment the truck's carburettor blocked, then the following jeep hit a bump and the steering broke. Temporary repairs were effected and we made our way back to camp and arrived a few minutes before the five-tonner, so I was able to see and photograph the offloading of the rhino.

I estimated the age of the cow at between seven and ten years and the calf at eighteen months to two years. It appeared that this was the cow's first calf.

An offloading ramp had been dug at the boma, so the truck backed into it and the rollers were laid out. Ropes were attached and the gang pulled carefully under Ken Randall's direction until the cow was inside the stockade. Then Randall kicked everyone out and set about untying the ropes himself. The rhino lay prone except for an occasional death-like shudder at five-minute intervals. Working quietly and efficiently Randall slipped rope after rope off. He allowed no one to speak or move quickly during the operation and muttered some uncomplimentary remarks about the clicking of still cameras and whirring of cines.

I noted that the cow was sweating on the face, the back, under the neck, on the front flanks and underneath the back and front legs, and on the nuchal hump. Curiously enough there was no sign of sweat anywhere on the abdomen. This pattern of sweating was noted on all the rhinos captured, in distinct contrast to the rhinos darted at Umfolozi, who sweated all over, perhaps because of the extra exertion. The sweating of the cow attracted many multicoloured butterflies.

After all the ropes were off Randall climbed slowly out of the stockade and the rhino lay immobile until someone threw a bucket of water over her. She was on her feet in a flash and charged anything that moved outside the stockade. The calf was then allowed into her pen and immediately began drinking. A few hours later the cow was allowed water and drank about 30 gallons with only a few stops for breath. She had my sympathy.

Randall informed me that water was not usually given until about twelve hours after capture and that that all the rhino caught before my arrival drank no more than 10 gallons, very different from the black rhino caught at Embu in Kenya, who drank 50 gallons at once. He also mentioned the difference in temperament of the two species: when capturing black rhino the one-inch manila rope could not be used more than twice and was usually broken, whereas the white rhino, although obviously a far stronger animal, did not use its strength to any advantage.

While the cow and calf were roped and immobile I examined them carefully for ticks but could not find a sign of one. Masses of small flies were the only attendants. The absence of ticks was remarkable, for in Umfolozi the white rhino were usually covered in ticks, particularly around the anus and genital organs. This was certainly not the case with any of the rhino I saw captured in the Lomunga area of Uganda. I saw no rubbing stumps in this area either.

The white rhino at Lomunga were well attended by oxpeckers and piapiac birds which no doubt did a good job in keeping the animals tick-free. It was also noticeable that while walking through the grass at Lomunga one did not become tick-infested. A possible explanation for all this was that the tall *Hyparrhenia* grass was burnt every year and because of its height, thickness and abundance, must generate a great heat.

Despite a careful examination I could not see any really visible differences between our Southern White Rhino *C. simum simum* and the Northern *C. simum cottoni* with the possible exception of the ears of *cottoni* which appeared to be larger and the toes, which were perhaps slightly elongated.

Interestingly, many of the white rhino seen in the Lomunga area had ears missing. This provoked some discussion. The game warden of the area said he thought it was due to fighting, whereas Dr Harthoorn was of the opinion that hyena were responsible for they were perfectly capable of creeping up to a sleeping rhino and snapping off an ear. I agreed with this theory, particularly after one of the captured rhino died in Murchison and had one of her ears taken off by a hyena, in almost the identical place as the other white rhino with missing ears.

By the time the cow and calf had settled down it was dark, and we sat down to some beer. I came in for some ribbing because one of our fellow countrymen from a Transvaal Nature Conservation Department had been with the trappers in Kenya and after the first hour was telling them how to catch rhino. Needless to say he was sent packing, and South Africans were not very popular after that. I made it quite clear that I was far more interested in saving my own skin and learning from the trappers than in giving advice.

For the rest of the evening the television cameraman and I were regaled with tales of the Mau Mau emergency. All the trappers were in the Kenya Police Reserve.

There was very little sleep during the night for everyone in camp was periodically called out to quieten the rhino. I was awakened during the early hours of the morning by a tremendous commotion and looked out of the mosquito net to see Pat O'Connell perched on top of the stockade silhouetted against the rising moon and slapping the face of the rhino cow who was literally standing up on her hind legs with her front legs almost over the boma. The language would have made a sergeant major sound like a Sunday school picnic address, and only after considerable persuasion did the cow settle down again.

There were further interruptions when a large elephant bull walked up to the stockade and trumpeted fiercely. I could see his huge ears and head clearly in the moonlight. A white rhino came to the stockade and I saw him peering intently at the cow and calf. It was a strange and moving sight to see this picture of the captured and the free. Two leopards came within a few yards of the camp and woke everyone with their deep rasping, coughing grunts.

At first light the following day all hands helped get the two crates into position. Apparently the rhino only went in once and if the door was not closed behind them it involved a lot of work roping them in. If you wanted a rhino to go forward you tapped it on the face, if backwards, on the hindquarters. The cow walked into the crate without any trouble and the door was slammed behind her. The calf refused to budge and had to be roped. Two ropes were placed over the head and one across the rump. A pole was used to guide the animal and in a few moments it was jerked, albeit unwillingly, into the crate.

Shades were built over both animals and then they were driven two hundred miles away to the Murchison National Park.

The cow was let out first and ran to a patch of bush and stood panting in the shade. The calf was then released and walked around sniffing the air. When the cow saw the calf she ran towards it and they sniffed each other, then the cow gave the truck one charge and a jab, then both animals ran upwind to water.

I must admit that the first two days of unbearable heat were sheer hell and I lost count of the mugs of liquid I swallowed. The climate was not improved by hordes of tsetse and other biting flies in the daytime and clouds of Anopheles mosquitoes at night, not to mention the jigger fleas. When my eyes were not caked with sand, dust and ash I could hardly see the horizon for heat haze.

Pat O'Connell remarked after one very hard day that it was 'God's own country'. As everyone looked up in amazement from their mugs he added, 'No one else would have it.'

No two animals reacted to captivity in exactly the same way, and all the rhino were watched very carefully the whole time they were in the stockade or in transit.

I realised that when we decided to move the Umfolozi rhino from one Reserve to another or to other areas, we would have to ensure that they were released in an area where they could be watched, particularly if the area had carnivores and the rhino had been given tranquillisers. It might also be advisable to have a small boma at the release point where cows and calves could be put for a few minutes before being released. I also suspected it would be better to catch animals just before breeding age, although this had its hazards too. One bull caught at Lomunga crashed through the barrier separating him from a cow. After butting her to the ground he tried to walk all over her. It is possible that the cow was in oestrus, for this is the typical behaviour of the mating bulls at Umfolozi.

Calves usually took a long time to settle down to people approaching the stockade, but nothing stopped them from drinking from the cows. One adult cow tamed down very quickly. Put into a pen at 10 a.m. she charged everything that moved. When anyone came near she would take two steps forward, snort (this involved a quick inhalation and exhalation), lift her head and jab at the stockade, but by 5 p.m. she was so calm nothing would provoke her.

One female calf walked round and round the stockade, smelling every corner over and over again, and periodically scratched the ground and sniffed suspiciously. For a whole day she charged everything that moved and there were many small abrasions on her head from the battering she gave the stockade. It took her two full days to settle down.

One of the captured cows was a very calm animal and settled down within an hour of being put in the stockade. Two days later she was crated and ready to go when it was noticed she was looking seedy. Fearing that the long journey to Murchison might upset her, the trappers decided to release her and recapture her a week or two later. When the crate door was opened she stuck her head out and sniffed suspiciously, then took two steps forward. Television cameras whirred and still cameras clicked like machine guns. She reminded me of an actress making her debut. A minute later she walked right out of the crate and began grazing a few yards from where we were standing. Someone shouted and tried to make her charge but she paid no attention and continued grazing.

Gradually she moved away from the camp and I followed her until she disappeared into a dense patch of bush intersected by elephant tracks.

The following day at 5 p.m. a Game Scout reported that she had been found dead, speared by poachers not three miles from the camp. The television cameraman and I went to have a look at her. She had half a dozen spear thrusts in the throat and a dozen or more in various parts of her body. Only her horns had been removed.

Two nights later the hyena gathered round the carcass and set up a noise which I had never heard before, it sounded like a duet between two animals and had a greater variety of notes than I would have thought possible.

It was a sad ending to a lovely animal.

A cow and calf were captured at Lomunga and after one day in the stockade it was noted that the cow had a very bad foot. It may have been injured during the chase or it may possibly have been an old snare injury.

After resting for two days the pair were transported to Murchison

National Park and released, fortunately not far from the Paraa Lodge. The pair became separated immediately and the calf was chased by Land Rover for some four miles in an effort to make it rejoin the cow, but the sun set and the chase had to be called off. The calf wandered around for 36 hours by itself before re-discovering its parent.

Captain Poppleton and Colonel Trimmer of the National Parks Service reported that soon after the two were re-united a big bull elephant was seen making its way down a game path towards the rhino. The cow was in a bad way, and this was instinctively realised by the calf who stood up when the elephant appeared and without any warning charged furiously at the pachyderm. The elephant got such a fright it retreated with its huge ears flapping and then recovered its composure and made at the calf who ran behind the cow. The elephant then walked up to the cow and laid its tusks on her back. This was too much for the cow and she struggled to her feet and moved a short distance away and the elephant moved off. The calf was then seen to move up to the cow and begin feeding on the raw portion of the cow's foot – a phenomenon also observed with hippo.

I arrived at Murchison that afternoon and went out to see the pair. The cow was obviously ill and I suspected that something besides the raw foot was bothering her. A local Government Vet arrived with the intention of giving the animal an injection of penicillin, but after looking at her it was decided to leave her alone.

While we were looking at the raw foot through field glasses a pied wagtail arrived and began feeding on the flies that were buzzing around near the wound.

The following morning at 8 a.m. the Game Scouts who had been instructed to watch the rhino during the night reported that the cow was dead. They said that there had been an awful amount of noise at 4 a.m. which probably meant that the cow had fallen on her side and was unable to rise again. Then the hyenas arrived and the calf did a sterling job keeping the scavengers away, although they did succeed in tearing one ear off and eating some of the raw foot.

Alan Brooks, Biologist to the Uganda Game Department, was asked to come to Murchison and have a look at the carcass.

In the meanwhile the Warden of Murchison, John Savidge, decided to catch the calf and hand rear her. We had a battle royal to get ropes round her legs, for she must have weighed between 600 and 800 lbs and was terrifically strong. At one stage three of us were hanging on to her back legs and she was pulling us around without any effort at all. Then she turned and charged John Savidge and before he could get away she stood on his foot and he came crashing to the ground. It was the first time I had seen anyone try to do the backstroke on land. Fortunately she turned away otherwise he would have been seriously injured. It took us nearly half an hour to get her down and tie her up. She was then transported to a wattle and daub rondavel and put inside until a stockade could be built.

We then returned to the cow and watched Alan Brooks at work, cutting up and weighing the cow. Some of the weights and measurements were as follows:

Head	220 lbs
Heart	18 lbs
Uterus	7 lbs
Large intestines	255 lbs
Kidneys	5 lbs each
Lungs	40 lbs
Spleen	6 lbs

The total weight was 2,530 lbs, considerably less than any of the rhino weighed at Umfolozi.

Length from base of anterior horn along contour to tip of tail	12′ 8″
Length of tail	1′ 7″
Ear	10½″
Anterior horn	1′ 8″
Circumference at base	1′ 10½″
Posterior horn	7¾″
Circumference at base	1′ 6½″
Base of horn to tip of lip	10½″
Circumference hind foot	2′ 4″

Circumference front foot	2′ 6″
Heart girth	8′
Total overall length	11′ 6″

Ridge on lip serrated, probably due to thick grass grazing.

There was a large bruise 1′ x 18″ centred on the iliac crest and I believe this was the main cause of death. Rhino bulls that died after fighting in Umfolozi were found to have these severe bruises and no horn wounds.

I discussed this later with Dr Harthoorn and he said that when an animal is bruised it loses plasma through the blood vessel walls and as plasma is the fluid constituent of the blood, for every litre of plasma lost 2 litres of blood are lost. The remaining red blood cells harmfully thicken the blood, so there is an increased viscosity of the blood and decreased circulation, which results in dilation of peripheral blood vessels, resulting in stagnant anoxaemia.

Alan Brooks also remarked that there were small haemorrhages in the mesentery and that the adrenals appeared enlarged.

That afternoon I was taken up the Nile to see the Murchison Falls and when we returned we were told that the calf had escaped. Her rondavel looked as though it had been hit by a mortar bomb.

The calf was recaptured late that afternoon with old fishing nets. By this time the stockade was completed and the rondavel was reinforced with logs, so she was put inside again. We went down to dinner and came back an hour later only to be told that she had escaped once more, by pushing the stockade with her front legs. It was pitch dark, but we searched around and found her about 100 yards from the stockade, standing on the edge of a soil-eroded gully with a drop of about twenty-five to thirty feet. We drew closer to her and she went over the edge. Fortunately she went down a slide, nevertheless how she avoided killing herself is a mystery. She got up and walked away into the darkness. There was nothing we could do but hope and pray the lion, leopard or hyena did not get her in the night.

Early next morning John Savidge sent his Game Scouts out and they tracked the calf to the Nile, along the bank and up into another patch of eroded soil some four miles from the camp. The Scouts must have been first-class trackers because nothing was in their favour.

We caught her again with nets but she did not struggle much, the unfortunate animal was obviously exhausted, and while we were taking her back to the camp in the tractor I doubted whether she would survive. Her eyes were sunken deeply and her breathing was pitifully slow. John Savidge went ahead and mixed a bottle of milk, egg and brandy, and when she was inside the rondavel we fed her. She sucked greedily at the plastic water bottle and finished all the mixture, we then gave her a wash down and undid the ropes. She recovered in no time so we opened the door to let her into the stockade. She walked round the fence a few times, then instinctively finding a weak spot she climbed up using her front legs as battering rams. I ran forward to grab her horn, as I did so she belched and the brandy fumes nearly knocked me back. The situation was not without its humour.

Fortunately Dr Harthoorn arrived in the afternoon and was able to work out a feeding schedule for the young animal, which was named Obongi. That night we fed her porridge and she enjoyed every mouthful. The next day she was as fit as a fiddle and I hoped she would survive her trials. She certainly deserved to.

I spent three weeks in the field in Uganda and gained much valuable information. The team's experience of loading, crating and transporting animals could hardly be improved upon, but the capture of the rhino with ropes was an archaic method. The use of drugs would have to substitute this old method, or we would never be able to capture the quantity of rhino we needed to.

On the flight back to South Africa I had the opportunity of ruminating about my discussions with the game wardens and biologists. The wardens were very pessimistic about the future of wildlife conservation in East Africa. The political instability in both Uganda and Kenya and, to a lesser degree, in Tanzania led them to believe that wildlife conservation would get very little attention from the emerging governments. There would be too many other urgent priorities for politicians to bother about the fate of wildlife. Whatever the failings of the British administration of East Africa, they had done an excellent job in the establishment of the national parks. It seemed tragic that the dedicated work of men and women of all races was going to be destroyed, or certainly overlooked, because of other priorities. I thought that if the work of the western world in East and West Africa was to be maintained it would require a dedicated force, which I called the Green Helmet Brigade, to take care of parks until civil authority could be restored. It was quite obvious that once the colonial powers departed the internal power struggles would grow progressively worse and it could be many decades before there was stability. I knew too that South Africa would not be immune from political change, that apartheid was doomed to failure, and ultimately there would be a black government ruling the country. The civil disturbance that could so easily happen would again mean wildlife conservation would get short shrift.

I remembered the bleached carcasses of the northern white rhino lying in the sun in Uganda and I made up my mind I would do everything possible to ensure that if our Operation Rhino was a success, we would get breeding herds out of the country to guarantee the white rhino's survival in the event that there was a collapse.

CHAPTER 10

A New Phase

With squatter infiltration and possible outbreaks of anthrax, rhino and worry were synonymous. The effect of the rhino population explosion showed more each winter. Rhino eat a lot of grass daily, and every year the impact on the western area was clearer. This area had been cleared of bush in 1947 during a tsetse fly campaign. *Themeda triandra* (redgrass) grasslands had taken over, with the sweet grass, *Panicum maximum*, in the old shade patches.

The rhino had depleted the grasslands in the southwestern Ngabaneni area by 1954-5, and had now moved into the west. But other game was moving in too and the warthog population increased enormously. Fires started deliberately by the squatters complicated the situation. Much of the soil in the high density rhino range was poor and infertile. Dry years hastened the deterioration while good rains hid the truth and induced a false sense of optimism in those who could not see the danger signs – 'It looks so green,' they said. The fact was we had a serious overpopulation of white rhino; if the range was to recover we had to move at least a hundred rhino as soon as Dr Harthoorn had perfected his drugs and we had worked out all the translocation snags.

Early in June Colonel Vincent phoned to say that Toni Harthoorn and his family had arrived.

I was delighted to see Toni Harthoorn again, and to meet his family. There was no superior scientist air about him – in fact he always credited you with more sense than you had, and his calmness and certainty were a tonic. He brought greetings from Uganda and said that Obongi, the young rhino we had captured, was fit and well.

We all had dinner together and on the following day I got the rhino capture team together – Nick Steele, John Clark, and Owen Letley.

'What have you got with you, Doctor?' John Clark asked.

'Well,' Toni said, and smiled at John. 'You remember the last drug I brought was not suitable. This time I did a whole series of experiments at the physiology lab in Kampala. I've collected nine drugs. One of them must do the trick.'

'What are you going to use first?' Owen Letley said.

'Morphine – which is a narcotic – as a base, plus others. A cocktail, in fact,' Toni replied. 'We've got a lot of work to do. I'm only here for just on three weeks and we must do a series of at least twelve rhino.'

We discussed our plans and decided that John Clark and Magqubu would go out into the Corridor early every morning to search for rhino while Nick Steele and Owen Letley would take the horses out. Toni Harthoorn and I would test the Capchur gun and leave Mpila immediately John Clark radioed. This set the pattern – with slight variations as we got better equipment – for rhino capture; it still applies today.

For the rest of the day Toni spoke about his work with a formidable breadth of knowledge.

'Immobilisation is going to change the whole picture of game conservation. Previously, if an animal put its nose out of the park, there was only one thing to do; that was to shoot it. Now if the animal is valuable you can catch it and put it back. In the same way you can get animals out of pockets of contested land, load them up and take them to a game reserve.

'We've just done it with the Kenya kob,' Toni said casually. 'We've caught and transported them to a game park three hundred miles away. And we caught some buffalo in the Queen Elizabeth Park and vaccinated them against rinderpest. I think this would be possible on a large scale if necessary.'

'This could solve our anthrax worry,' I said to Nick.

'If a wild animal has a snare round it, or is stuck in a hole, or is wounded,' Toni said, looking at each of us in turn. 'There is the possibility of immobilising it and having a look to see if one could repair it. This opens up tremendously interesting possibilities for human interference with wild animals. We immobilised a large bull elephant in Murchison Park – Ian knows the place – a short while ago. It was lame. Unfortunately we couldn't do anything for it as it had been shot in the leg and the bone was splintered. If it had been a spear head or something sticking into it, one might have toyed with the idea of pulling the foreign body out and filling up the hole with sulphur powder and seeing if the animal would recover.'

Time passed swiftly as we talked about wild life problems. That evening Sven Persson and Jimmy Anderson, from the South African Tourist Corporation, came from Charters Creek where they were filming the documentary *Lake Wilderness*.

'My head office hasn't given permission yet,' Sven said. 'But I am determined to press on and film this darting of rhino. It's too valuable an opportunity to be missed.'

We began using the new drug on the 8 June 1961.

June weather in the Umfolozi Reserve is near to paradise; the days are warm, clear, and wind free, and the evenings are pleasantly cool. The mpafa tree leaves turn a vivid yellow among the purple-grey of the nthombothi trees. The White and Black Umfolozi rivers are lined by dark green sycamore figs and golden sandbanks as the water dries up. Wherever you walk the yellow-throated longclaw rises singing from the tawny red grass. On very clear mornings you can see the coastal dune forests in the east and the hill called Dingane's Seat in the west. It was worth suffering the blazing heat of summer for such perfect days.

Norman Deane came from Hluhluwe Reserve in his short wheel-base Land-Rover to help, and while John Clark looked for a suitable rhino I watched Toni fill the Capchur gun with the soda syphon sparklets and leave it out in the sun for the gas to expand slightly, for it then fired better.

I had just fired the third practice dart when John Clark called up. He had found a female calf estimated at fifteen hundred to twelve hundred pounds.

Half an hour later we met the horsemen and John Clark below Ncebe range in the Corridor. On the flat plain below Ncebe, John pointed out a group of four white rhino, one of them a young female.

Toni mixed Themalon, Sernyl, and hyoscine, shook the bottle and poured it into the dart barrel, then unscrewed the flight and put in acetic acid.

'Well, this is it, over to you,' Toni said, handing me the Capchur gun.

With Magqubu I trotted downwind through *Tarchonanthus* scrub into a grove of nthombothi trees with their sandalwood scent. A warthog scuttled out of its hole, looked at us, its head up, then ran quickly towards the sleeping rhino. It startled them and they were up, staring towards us, their bell-like ears straining for every sound. We froze and I heard Magqubu cluck, '*Hau, intibane* – the warthog.'

It was a long time before the rhino cow dropped her head and breathed a sigh like a breath of wind. The bull stood twenty yards away, still alert, then he too flopped down. The calf moved round the cow trying to get at a teat and whining softly. It is a pitiful sound. I was to hear it frequently at the yet unbuilt bomas and it always made me feel desperately sad.

Magqubu touched me and indicated we should go forward. I got on to my knees and began crawling. I had three hundred yards to go but rested behind grey boulders and rubbed my knees. Magqubu looked at me and smiled. I crawled another hundred yards and rested again behind an acacia tree. I could see Toni, Norman, and John Clark watching through binoculars. Nick and Owen stayed a hundred and fifty yards behind, both leaning forward on their saddles ready to move the moment I fired and raised my right hand to signify a hit.

I heard a bateleur eagle's weird cor-cor-corcor cry overhead. A reedbuck whistled downwind and for a moment the calf became alert.

It was a strain keeping the gun upright to prevent leakage. I pulled back the bolt and checked the dart. No sign of liquid. I started forward again, this time on my stomach, and kept going for fifty yards. Magqubu kept with me and we rested again behind a fallen log.

'Wait here now,' I whispered to Magqubu in Zulu.

I began the last twenty-yard crawl, at the same time searching for a tree to climb should the rhino come for me. At ten yards I clicked back the loading bolt. It was enough to get the rhino on their feet. The calf ran round to the other side of the mother. There was no chance of a shot yet. I dropped my head and lay dead still, my nose inches from powdered earth. I badly wanted to sneeze. The bull seemed to sense me and stared at me, its head lowered, but the wind was still in my favour so I knew I was safe.

One of the horses snorted and the cow trotted a few paces forward, leaving the calf exposed. Through the telescopic sight I took a bead on its shoulder and fired. The 'tonk' of the Capchur gun was matched by the thump of the dart hitting the shoulder. It was a perfect shot, but as the rhino ran forward it bumped against a tree and the needle broke. I raised my right hand. There was a good chance that the drug had been injected. The horsemen galloped past, one heading for the high ground and the other going after the rhino. I checked the time; 2 p.m. That stalk had taken nearly three-quarters of an hour.

Norman, John Clark and Toni drove up.

'The needle broke,' I said.

'I saw that but there was enough time for the drug to go in,' answered Toni.

He made notes in his book, then stood beside the Land-Rover, drumming his fingers on the bonnet.

Hooves clattered and Nick came galloping up a game-path. His khaki shirt was torn down the back and he was bleeding from a scratch on his forehead.

'It's down!' he said.

'What time ?' Toni asked.

'Two-thirty,' Nick replied.

Toni scribbled figures on his leg.

'Let's go,' he said.

We jumped into the Land Rover and followed Nick through the trees. The rhino had only travelled about three quarters of a mile. We came upon it lying on sand in a dry stream bed. Owen stood nearby, his reins looped over his arm.

'Hi, Doc,' he said. 'She grazed for about four minutes then walked here and flopped down. Her breathing is O.K. and she went down very gently in a normal sleeping position. She's been on her brisket all the time.'

I looked carefully at Toni and saw a flicker of pleasure in his eyes.

The sun was low by the time Toni had finished examining the rhino. We then measured her and Owen Letley sang out the measurements to me as I noted them in the book.

Anterior horn	9½″
Posterior horn	1¾″
Head	28″
Body along contour	76″
Tail	19″
Ear (inner measurement)	19½″
Heart girth	97½″
Standing height	51″

We tagged her right ear with a yellow and her left with a red tag. There was no flinching as the tagging machine crunched through the ear.

Owen examined the vagina and announced she was unbred. Norman made a ribald comment and Owen coloured.

I ran my hand along the body and felt the hair. This one seemed particularly hirsute. The third callous on the nuchal hump was well formed and there was very little sweating except for a few damp patches between the ribs. Toni rubbed his hands and looked very pleased.

'Is it the answer?' I said.

'Too early to say,' he said.

Nick came up and said, 'We must get the horses back and feed them well, if they are going to be any good tomorrow.'

'Certainly, you push on,' I said. 'We'll see this lot through and tell you about it later.'

We named the rhino 'Daisy'.

Toni had given the antidote Lethidrone intravenously after fifteen minutes, then again after tagging in case further drug was being absorbed. The breathing deepened, otherwise there was no effect.

'We can't leave until she stands up,' Toni said. 'And we must keep her warm.'

It was nearly dark as I sent John Clark with Magqubu in a Land-Rover to Mpila to bring sacks, a pile of grass, and food for us. It might turn out to be a long night. They drove off and I heard the Land Rover rat tling loudly as they crossed the boulders in the Tjevu stream. We waited another ten minutes and smoked a cigarette.

Then we started again, pushing, slapping, and shouting at Daisy, trying to get her on her feet. But she lay and snored. It was about nine o'clock when she slowly stood up and shakily began to walk forwards. We legged it for the Land-Rover, expecting to be charged. But she walked round in a small right hand circle, heading dangerously near a deep gully.

'I'll cut her off with the Rover,' Norman said.

He started the vehicle and we jerked forward. Daisy pressed hard against the side of the vehicle and Norman drove slowly forward, guiding her away from danger. Then he reversed. Daisy walked in another circle and came bang up against the Rover again.

'What on earth goes on, Doc ?' Norman asked.

'It has forgotten it is a rhino,' Toni said, chuckling quietly. He was delighted with the success of the drug combination.

On the next circuit Daisy got her horn against the front mudguard and pushed forward. It soon buckled under her weight. Her head and horn then slipped under the mudguard and the pressure she applied turned the wheels. We all laughed.

'It will be driving this thing next,' Norman said. 'Oh hell, there go the clutch pedal springs.'

Suddenly he sprang out of the driver's seat, ran round and grabbed the rhino by the tail.

'I've just remembered this vehicle is on my stock,' he panted. 'For goodness sake help me or I'll cop it from the Colonel.'

This was too much for us. We laughed until the tears rolled down our cheeks.

'You miserable bastards! Help me man, help!' Norman shouted as he hung on to the rhino's tail.

There was a splintering sound and Norman wailed, 'Oh hell, there go the brake pedals. Help me, please man!'

Toni and I were almost prostrate with laughter as the rhino slowly pushed the Rover back, various parts of the vehicle breaking with loud creaks and bangs. At last we clambered on to the bonnet and while Norman grabbed the horn we pushed the head from the other side with our feet. The rhino seemed intent upon getting its horn into the petrol tank, and this stopped our laughter. While Norman tugged we heaved and shoved, and freed the animal, but it kept on walking forwards. Whenever it headed for the donga we turned it by pulling the tail. In the pitch darkness with only the parking lights of the Land-Rover glowing, it was an astonishing scene.

We were now so unafraid and blasé that Norman leapt on to her back; this started us laughing again. Our laughter was also a relief from worry. There was no doubt about it, this drug really worked.

'This is a reaction which I have not seen with any other animal, with any other drug. She is not excited, she is tractable and we can do what we like with her. This is the most important aspect of the drug,' Toni said happily as he leaned against the Land-Rover and watched Daisy.

'She seems to have lost her dislike for human beings,' he continued. 'Doesn't mind smell, doesn't mind us talking – to say nothing of laughing. This really surprises me because I thought she would be particularly susceptible to sound.'

We heard a Land-Rover whining down Mpila hill and the lights flickered in the darkness.

'John Clark's coming – let's pull his leg,' Norman said.

We turned our Land-Rover round so the lights would blind him as he came up. Then we pulled Daisy's tail until she was behind the Land-Rover with her head facing the other way. She had stopped walking and simply stood, making loud chewing noises with her big square lips.

'When John arrives we'll lean on Daisy, call him over and hand him the tail,' Norman said, and we burst into a fit of laughing at the thought of it.

As John approached we switched the lights on and successfully dazzled him. He came towards us, shielding his eyes from the light.

'Did you see the rhino ?' I shouted.

'No. Has she gone?' he asked quickly.

Now he had reached us. Toni leant away from Daisy and Norman said, 'Hey, John, hold this a sec please.'

John Clark put his hand out and grabbed the rhino's tail.

'My God,' he said fervently. 'What has happened?'

We couldn't control ourselves any longer and burst into wild laughter. Norman and I had to support each other as John Clark stood there, a bemused look on his face, saying, 'No, oh no. I don't believe it.'

Magqubu and another guard came forward and stared at the rhino. They looked at Toni. 'This is witchcraft, witchcraft,' they muttered over and over in Zulu.

As we drove back to Mpila I reflected that, in spite of all the hilarity, history had been made today. In 1925 Dr Herbert Lang, an American naturalist, had urged the capture of white rhino and their translocation to former habitats. In 1927 another American named Harris tried to shoot a black rhino with a mercy bullet covered with a curare substance. Now at last immobilisation had been achieved and we were on the verge of something new and great in the long battle for the white rhino.

The following morning we drove out to Daisy and found her a short distance from where we had left her. She had her head caught in the loop of a liana monkey rope and her feet were moving in a walking motion.

'Look at the ground, it's beaten flat,' John Clark whispered. 'She's been walking all night!'

We approached closer and could see she was very much more alert. Toni clapped his hands and shouted. She broke through the vine and galloped off.

'This proves another thing,' Toni said, delighted. 'If you dart them and they get away, they can still recover unaided.'

John Clark and Magqubu went to scout for another rhino and soon returned to say they had found two young males, probably twin calves, about Daisy's weight.

I stalked them and fired at the nearest one, but the dart passed over the top of the shoulder. The second shot went into the ear and fell out in under half a minute. The rhino trotted a few yards then stood. After a quarter of an hour there were some signs of ataxia; it had difficulty holding up its tail. I crept nearer to shoot another dart but it ran off with the others. I took a chance and fired as it ran past me, but the dart bounced off.

Toni quite rightly ticked me off for the running shot. 'Both drugs and darts are in short supply. I had to clean out the whole of East Africa,' he said.

'Sorry Toni, it was my blood lust,' I said, cursing myself.

We brewed tea out in the veld while John searched for more rhino. All he could find was a very young calf on the north-east ridge of Ncebe near the Mcacaso stream. The cow kept getting in the way. The calf was suspicious and trotted towards me, the cow following immediately. I shot when the calf was ten paces away, hit it below the withers and ducked out of sight as cow and calf thundered past me. It was a stony area, difficult for the horsemen. Owen came back and said the calf had staggered after only eight minutes but had gone down near the junction of the two Umfolozis. We had to manhandle the vehicle to it. We found Nick sitting on his horse watching the young rhino which lay guarded by the cow.

'The old bitch has chased me twice. We're going to have trouble getting rid of her,' he said.

I walked forward, shouting and clapping my hands. The cow lumbered towards me, and I backed hastily.

We all threw stones and shouted, but it had no effect on the cow.

'This little Johnny is going to give us trouble,' Owen said.

So Johnny was the rhino's name. It had become a fetish which was to be permanent; not to name a rhino was to have bad luck. The name could come from an incident, the weather, the area, or a personality, but once named, it stuck.

'We've got to get at that little beast,' Toni said fretfully.

I asked Magqubu if he had any ideas. He loaded his .303 and we all moved forward, shouting. The cow came and Magqubu fired three quick shots into the ground. The cow hesitated and turned. We lobbed stones at her and Magqubu fired a shot into the air. This was too much for the unfortunate animal and she ran two hundred yards before she turned to watch us.

We reached the calf to find its breathing was quiet and shallow. 'A dangerous sign,' Toni muttered as he filled a syringe and injected twenty c.c. of the antidote intravenously through the ear. The breathing deepened at once, and we sighed with relief.

We later discovered it was possible to immobilise a full-grown bull with the same amount of drug that this little fellow got. Toni used 1¼ gm morphine, 375 mgms Sernyl and 60 mgms hyoscine. When we measured the animal we estimated the weight at only 1400 lb. Johnny had only two callouses on his nuchal hump, Daisy had had three.

Toni gave another 400 mgms of antidote in the caudal fold without effect. We slapped Johnny, shouted and pulled his ears to try to get him on his feet. We left him on one side for fifteen minutes, then rolled him over and found that the dart needle had broken off. John Clark tugged with a pair of sharpnosed pliers to get it out.

Toni then ran out of antidote and someone had to drive back to Mpila for a fresh supply. He quickly scribbled what he would need in my bird notebook while I told Adriaan Erasmus, a ranger who had recently joined us, that as he was the most junior, he would have to drive back.

Adriaan read the note, which said:

1. Small bottle of 5 grammes Lethidrone on top of cupboard in the hut.
2. Large empty 8 oz bottle near it.
3. 100 c.c. plastic measuring cylinder on the table.
4. Bottle of distilled water from the office.

Great care it is *all* we have.

'Don't worry, I will take care,' said Adriaan, and he was back within two hours.

Toni immediately injected 15 c.c. intravenously and the same amount in the tail. We tagged Johnny and he rose, a little unsteadily, then walked away. The following day he was tracked, found to have met the cow and gone to water, so all was well. We saw him many times afterwards trotting in front of his dam on the Ncebe plain.

The following day John Clark searched all morning and only after midday found a suitable rhino. I crept up to the calf and fired. It ran for a mile followed by the horsemen then the dart dropped out. Nick brought it back after the rhino did not go down. A piece of skin had blocked the needle. Nick said they had followed the animal into some thick bush then lost sight of it, but they tracked for half a mile and found it alert and unaffected by the drug.

We searched for another rhino but could only find a mature bull and that not until late afternoon. It was on the southern side of Ncebe at a point known as Kandelndhlovu – the Head of the Elephant.

The area was broken with boulders and encroaching acacia scrub.

'What's its weight?' Toni asked, squinting at me in the sunlight.

'Four thousand pounds.'

'I agree,' he said, and began mixing the drugs.

He filled the dart with the same mixture that Johnny had.

'Now we'll see the range of this drug,' he murmured as he screwed the needle into the dart and handed me the Capchur gun.

There was plenty of cover so it was an easy stalk, but as I fired the bull moved and the dart went into the left knee. It trotted a few paces then stopped. I motioned the horsemen to stay back for it was confused and probably would not run. I moved forward slowly to some boulders on the hill slope. I had darted it at half past three. Eight minutes later it was staggering amongst the rocks, swaying dangerously, but we could do nothing. It fell, rolled on to its back, and was wedged between two boulders. It lay there kicking its legs in the air and bellowing.

'Get him on his side,' Toni shouted.

Everyone rushed forward and tried to push it over, but it was impossible. Magqubu stood back for a moment then ran off. I asked him where he thought he was going, he said he would be back soon, and ran on.

Toni gave the rhino some antidote intravenously and we pushed again. John Clark grabbed one leg but was flicked off like a fly on a wildebeest.

Magqubu came back up the hill, his body bent double under the weight of two nthombothi poles.

'A wise man,' Toni said approvingly.

John Clark grabbed a pole and pushed it under the rhino's hindquarters. 'Bring some rocks,' he said.

We levered the rhino up a little, enough to slip a rock under it. We worked hard for an hour and slowly jacked him up. By now it was dark and the zebra were yodelling with their dog-like barks as they made their way down to the Black Umfolozi river. A reedbuck got our scent and whistled shrilly below us.

When the rhino was up and out of the boulders, we could not move its head. This was not surprising as the head of a mature bull weighs as much as six hundred pounds. Magqubu came to the rescue again by making a rope of bark. This gave us more leverage and we got the rhino out of the dangerous position and on to its brisket. Our nerves were on edge. Every time the rhino moved we would rush away, expecting to be charged.

'This country is so bad, one of us will be horned if he gets up,' Nick said.

There was no chance of running with all the boulders strewn about, some of them hidden in the grass.

Toni gave it more antidote and the breathing improved. By seven o'clock there was nothing we could do except give more antidote and leave it.

John Clark returned later that night to check, but the rhino had gone.

John Page arrived from our Pietermaritzburg headquarters. He brought with him all the drugs he had managed to find.

At ten o'clock next day I was stalking a calf the same size as Johnny, but the dart contained half the amount of drug. The cow with the calf was on heat and a mature bull was making advances which were repulsed with sudden charges and a low rumbling call. I lay behind a lala palm tree, watching the love play of the huge beasts. The bull was sweating a little and I was close enough to smell the strong tang of rhino. Then the wind changed and the rhino trotted off with their bouncy run, as though they were on shock absorbers. In spite of their bulk they are graceful creatures.

I ran round and down into the sandy bed of the Tjevu stream and used the high banks as cover to get close to the rhinos again. But I was at a bad angle and could not get a decent aim. The cow and the bull fought with rumbling snorts and the clash of horns and the thud of head hitting hard flesh. In typical fashion the calf ran behind the cow when the bull was close enough to mount. The bull would chase the calf a few yards then lumber back to the cow. There was more fighting and dust and the calf suddenly appeared out of the melee. I aimed but as I fired the bull rushed forward and collected the dart in the shoulder.

'Now that's really torn it.' I was so angry with myself I nearly forgot to indicate a hit to the horsemen. I waved them on and they galloped past, for the rhino was already out of sight.

'The big one, the bull,' I yelled.

Owen raised his hand in acknowledgment. His hair flopped over his forehead and his powerful back muscles bulged as he disappeared on his horse. There was a faint smell of horse dung and sweat which reverted to dust and the bush. It was quiet.

'That rhino is running,' Magqubu said, apropos of nothing, a habit of many Zulus.

Owen returned soon after half past ten. John Page finished loading his cine camera and we jumped into the Land-Rovers. The rhino had run some five miles.

We followed Owen. His horse cantered easily. He had trained it in the Drakensberg mountains when he was huntsman and he rode like a cowboy, with long stirrups. The horse stumbled in an antbear hole, but Owen kept his balance.

'The boy can ride,' I said to John Page.

We drove through thick *Acacia karroo* scrub and found Nick watching the still standing rhino. It looked very alert which was not surprising as it had only had enough for a calf.

'There is another rhino,' Magqubu said, pointing with a closed index finger in orthodox Zulu fashion.

A bull came from the shade of a dark green *Schotia* tree and slowly approached the darted animal which was shuffling backwards and forwards in a bewildered way. The second rhino charged with a squeal of rage and drove the darted rhino down a slope. It fell into a four-foot donga. John Clark ran forward, shouting and waving his arms, until the aggressor turned away.

It dawned on me that we had seen a territorial display, which proved that bulls did not only fight over cows.

The darted animal stood shivering and sweating in the donga. Rhino flies still clung to its wet back and flanks. We approached it cautiously but it took fright and tried to get out of the donga. Clods of earth and bits of grass and roots scattered as the rhino tried to pull itself up with its front legs.

'We must tag it, because it may not go down,' Toni said.

The rhino got halfway out of the gully and we ran for the trees. But the rhino fell back and stood, its body heaving and shiny with sweat. John Clark took the tagging machine.

'Forget it, John, it's dangerous,' I said.

'It's O.K., I'll get it in a jiffy,' John said as he ran forward.

His long pants flapped over his ankles and his shirt tails hung out. His black hair was reaching over his collar. He was lean and hard, with plenty of guts. He could trot after a wounded wildebeest for ten miles, barefoot, in rough thorn country. I had a great liking for him and as rhino capture grew he came to play an indispensable part.

He approached the rhino from the blind side and quickly grabbed an ear. The rhino shook its head and John sidestepped, the horn just missing him. He was not at all afraid. He grabbed the ear again and the tagging machine glinted. He moved round to tag the other ear but we bawled at him to come back. As he moved away the rhino snorted and with a mighty heave was out of the donga. It collapsed but rose and sent us running as we approached. It walked slowly into a thicket of spindly acacia. We followed in the Land-Rover as far as we could, then drove round the thicket. The rhino walked out unsteadily. It leaned against a tree and stood with drooping head like a city drunk leaning against a lamp post.

We got out and clapped, and the rhino started.

'Another small amount and we would have put him right down,' Toni said.

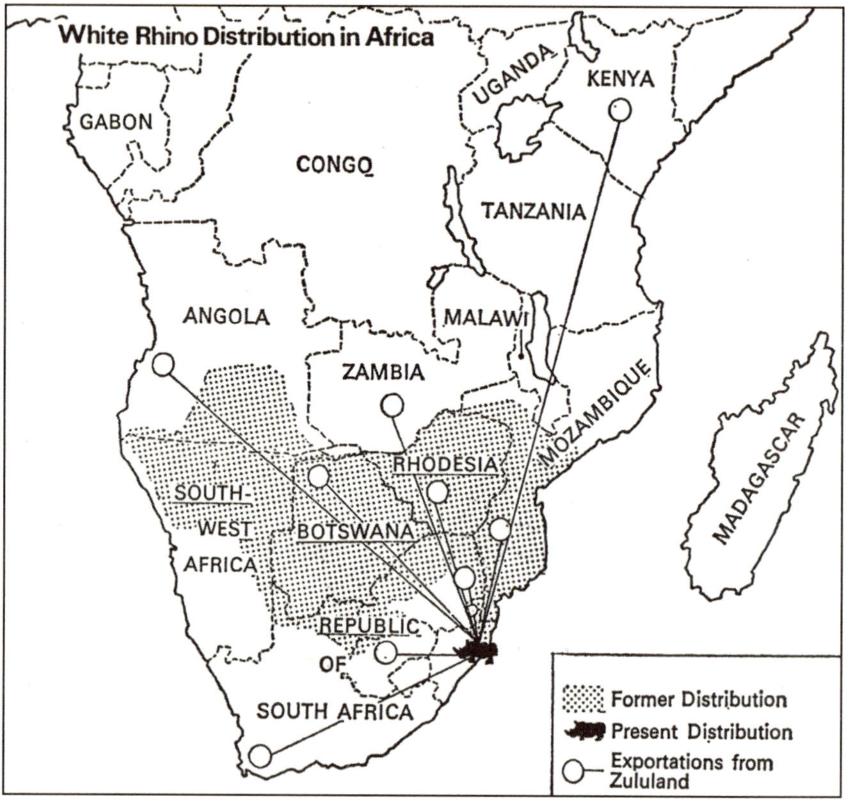

He had obviously learnt a lot from this animal: both his legs were covered in hieroglyphics.

John Clark followed the rhino in the vehicle. The rhino moved a little faster now and veered south. Nick cantered up to warn us there was a krantz ahead.

'If he goes over, it's tickets,' he said.

As he spoke the rhino crossed in front of us, heading for the donga. Stones and tree stumps prevented John from driving so he leapt out and ran after the rhino. Nick and Owen followed on horseback and they all reached the krantz just before the rhino. They drove the animal off in another direction.

The rhino was recovering every minute, so we left it and made for the Tjevu stream to brew tea. It was one of the few times we were all together and able to drink a mug without interruption.

CHAPTER 11

Crating a Rhino

We had for days been waiting for news about our first crate. The experiments had gone so well that Colonel Vincent authorised the removal of a rhino to Mkuze Game Reserve, a hundred miles away. But the carpenters dilly-dallied over how the crate should be made. We all fretted; Toni because he was due to go home soon and he desperately wanted to see at least twelve animals caught, the rest of us because we were terrified of the thought of Toni not being with us on our first journey.

We had successfully drugged our ninth rhino, tagged and released it, when the radio operator at Mpila called me up and said a crate had arrived at the rest camp. There was no time to lose. Nick and Owen unsaddled their horses; John Clark went out to look for a rhino; Toni Harthoorn mixed drugs and filled syringes; I drove to Mpila to collect the crate. John Kinloch the imperturbable camp superintendent had the one and only three-ton truck in the game reserve. I was back at the catching area an hour later.

'We've found a suitable animal,' Nick told me. 'It's a young female, about fifteen hundred to two thousand pounds.'

I studied the animal through binoculars. She stood grazing about eight hundred yards away among some young *Acacia karroo* bushes. It would be an easy stalk. I could use the Madhlozi stream bed then crawl a hundred yards through the grass. Magqubu agreed that this would be the best away.

'This is an important rhino,' Toni said as he mixed the drugs. He squinted at me and said, 'When last was there a white rhino at Mkuze?'

'A hundred years ago,' I said.

Toni poured the mixture into a 10 c.c. syringe and handed me the gun.

'Come, Magqubu, let's go,' I said and we walked east to the Madhlozi stream. It was hot in the valley and sweat soon poured down as we plodded through the sand, skirting the occasional pool of undrinkable water.

I kept nothing back from Magqubu and now admitted that I was sometimes afraid of the rhino. Magqubu and I had been very close for over three years and he had taught me more about the bush, about Umfolozi, and about game than anyone else had. We had crossed the burning plains, walked through the bush and over the shimmering hills of Umfolozi together, and we knew each other well. I wondered if he knew what fear meant. He had never shown it, and we had shared dangerous moments with black rhino, poachers, and a black mamba.

'Your trouble is you have only one and a half legs,' Magqubu said, referring to my wonky knee. 'In your mind you feel you will not run fast enough. This is not fear. You also want to do everything yourself. For ten days now we have been working. You are tired in your mind.'

The old Zulu was a good psychologist. He summed up a man quickly and his judgment was never wrong.

'*Wozan*i – let us go,' he concluded, and we walked forward at a fast pace. Abruptly he stopped and asked me if I wanted him to take the Capchur gun and shoot the rhino. I laughed.

'You old blighter – you can't shoot straight,' I said in Zulu, joking to hide my feelings. He had been shooting animals for forty years and was an excellent shot. He stared at me and giggled, his shoulders shaking with laughter. '*Lungile* – all right, you shoot it,' he said.

We had been talking for only five minutes but my fear had gone, as it often does if you talk it out.

Magqubu trotted along, his batats (sandals made from motor car tyres) leaving tracks in the sand. He leapt up on to the bank and jumped from boulder to boulder. For a man of sixty he was superbly fit.

We headed north for another two hundred yards, then he indicated that the rhino was just ahead of us. I looked over the Capchur gun, wiped the telescopic sight and rolled my sleeves down. My elbows were rubbed raw from all the crawling. As I slid off Magqubu tapped me on the leg and pointed south.

A mass of black cloud was moving. The old man had predicted rain, but I had not believed him. But he had been right.

'This will complicate matters,' I thought.

By this time the young rhino cow had grazed to the top of the slope and she was in open country. I crouched behind a spindly *Acacia karroo* memorising the clumps of grass, the boulders and the small trees on the way to the animal. I had to keep very low to remain out of sight. I heard Magqubu's breathing behind me. It was not easy for a man of sixty, even one as fit as he was, to slide on his belly like a snake. I motioned him to stay behind. He looked hurt, but obeyed.

I crept forward again, cursing the pepper ticks. There was no mistaking that burning itch. I longed to stop, pull them out of my skin and crush them between my fingernails. Some had already got between my toes, one of the worst places. I rubbed my veldskoen on a rock, scraping my toes to try to relieve the itch a little.

This faint noise was enough to alert the rhino. It stopped grazing, turned its head and stared in our direction, its ears swivelling to catch every sound. Magqubu gave a soft bird-like call. I turned and he indicated I should go off to the left and stalk from the rear. He was expecting the south wind to come up. I scuttled crabwise to a clump of *Themeda* grass then moved quickly uphill while the rhino faced the other way. Small thorn trees were invading this area of grassland too, and the hooked thorns of *Acacia caffra* ripped my shirt and raised red weals on my arms and chest. Sweat dripped into my eyes. I had to wipe the rifle's telescopic sight repeatedly to keep it free of dust and grass chaff. My shoulders ached from holding the gun in an upright position, to stop the drug pouring out of the dart.

I looked back. The tall figure of Toni Harthoorn was silhouetted on the skyline. Nick and Owen had ridden to the stream to wait in a position which gave them a clear view of both me and the rhino. John Clark was perched on the cab of a Land-Rover. Glass flashed as he lowered the binoculars. John Page stood holding a camera. They all seemed so remote, in another world.

I crawled forward, sliding over the small bushes and identifying them at close range: *Acacia caffra, Acacia karroo*, marula, *Schotia brachypetala, Acacia nilotica*; it was only when you were on your stomach that the extent of the scrub invasion became apparent. This was going to have a marked effect on the rhino grazing lands. Some of the shrubs bore old burn marks, but fire had no effect any more.

I was thirty paces away. The rhino had stopped eating and stood in a characteristic position, head drooping but ears moving all the time. At twenty paces I aimed but it was just too far, so I crept forward another five paces and loaded the gun. The rhino swung round at the noise. I had a perfect view of her right shoulder, I fired and the dart thumped home. The heat had warmed the gun up and it was working at peak efficiency. I raised my right arm and the horsemen cantered up the hill. This set the rhino off and it ran out of sight. My job was done, so I instantly pulled off my veldskoen and socks and scratched the tiny ticks out of their refuge between my toes. My blood lust wasn't satisfied until I had crushed a dozen or so.

The Land-Rover started up and approached along the Mhlopeni track. We walked across the veld to meet it.

'Nice shot,' John Page said. 'But what made you take so long?'

'Pepper ticks,' I said.

Everyone nodded knowingly.

We waited awhile then followed the road below the Mtunzini hills and saw Nick galloping back. He said the rhino was in a dry ravine a mile up the road.

'She staggered for five minutes before going down,' Nick told Toni, who jotted it down on his leg. 'I think you had better hurry, she's lying with her head down a bank.'

I shifted gears as he spoke. We covered the mile quickly and were flagged down by Owen, who told us to hurry. Toni grabbed his veterinary box and leapt out of the Land-Rover. He slipped a needle into the vein we had raised and injected the antidote Lethidrone.

He glanced at his watch and made a note on his leg. The rhino stirred, lifted her head and in one movement was on her feet. Everyone except John Clark and Magqubu scattered. Nick and Owen led their horses to safety.

The rhino began walking away. I ran to the back of the Land Rover and got a length of rope. John Clark snatched it from me. He ignored our warning shouts and tried to get the rope round the hind legs, but when he touched the animal she ran forward. At the third try the rope slipped round her legs and John rapidly tied it to a marula stump. The rhino struggled and squealed pitifully. John Page moved forward with a camera and tape recorder.

'What are we going to call her?' Toni asked.

'Well, she's an unbred virgin,' John Clark said after examining her.

'Forever Amber,' Toni said with a straight face, and so Amber she became.

Her whole body darkened with sweat as she struggled. She lunged and swung her head at anyone who came close. 'Seems to be coming round,' I said to Toni.

He nodded and mixed more drug. He gave her another injection and ten minutes later she quietened down.

We were all so intent on our purpose that it was only when John Page complained about the lack of light for his camera that we noticed how the sky had darkened. There was a rumble of thunder in the south and lightning flashed across the sky. Magqubu looked meaningly at me.

Minutes later John Kinloch's blue lorry came down the road. Toni examined the crate, criticised the open slats, but said that Amber would fit in.

It was now five o'clock. A strong south wind had sprung up, a prelude to rain. Darkness was falling fast. Black shadows stretched southwards from the Mtunzini hills behind us. Lubisana and Nqoloti hills to the south-west were caught in the glow of the fading light. The redgrass bent before the wind, changing colours until it too was as grey as the rest of the veld.

We manhandled the crate off the lorry and with much swearing and profanity carried it shoulder high to Amber and dumped it in front of

11. The 20cc dart; *left to right*: Magqubu Ntombela, Owen Letley, Garth Carpenter.

12. Black rhino – the final charge before drugs took effect.

13. 'Mpandhlana, the Great Bull'.

14. Rhino lorry and crate.

her. Everyone had a different opinion of the best way to get her into the crate. We argued so fiercely that only a squall of rain stopped us. There were too many senior officers present, so that each order was obeyed. At last the democracy of good sense prevailed. Ideas were put forward, discussed quietly, then accepted or rejected.

We had learnt that a drugged white rhino always walked forwards, albeit with a left or right bias so I insisted on having Amber's head lifted and put just inside the crate. Then John Clark tied poles to the side to act as guides if she veered one way or the other.

So our plan of loading developed, but we could not get the lorry into a good position. Nick, Owen, John Clark, and Magqubu took turns with a shovel to dig a loading ramp. John Page photographed the scene from every angle, cursing the fading light.

When everything was ready we called Toni. He filled a bright metal syringe with Lethidrone and injected Amber intravenously. We waited a few minutes then slapped and shouted at her to wake her up, like any patient coming round from an operation. She stirred, and everyone tensed. Then she sighed deeply and settled down again. Toni mixed more Lethidrone by the Land-Rover headlights and gave her another injection. When he pulled the needle out blood oozed in a dark stream down her ear and dripped on to her head.

'Will the penicillin you gave earlier be enough to keep infection away?' John Clark asked anxiously.

'Yes,' Toni said tersely. It was about the fifth time he had been asked the same question that day.

We had had nothing to eat or drink since breakfast and the cold rain sharpened our hunger. While we waited for the antidote to work I radioed Mpila and told the operator to warn my wife that we would be passing through and would need food.

John Clark began shouting and slapping her again. This time she stood up shakily. I glanced at the time, it was nearly six o'clock.

Amber took a step forward then stopped. There was a flow of bad language. Only Toni and John Clark did not swear. Even Magqubu was exasperated enough to shout 'bladyfool' when Amber refused to move forward.

She swayed slightly, took another step forward and we all rushed to push from behind, then she leaned to the left. We pushed again.

'Hang on, hang on,' John Clark shouted. He had his hand jammed on the side of the crate. No one on rhino capture escaped without having their hands jammed at least once.

Amber leaned drunkenly against the crate. I remembered Daisy and grabbed her tail and pulled. She swayed forward into the crate opening and we pushed hard. There was a pungent smell of sweating human bodies wet with rain and the rank smell of white rhino. Amber stumbled forward to the end of the crate. She wedged her horn in a corner and stood breathing hard. Over the years it was to become a far too familiar sight, but we were too busy bolting the door to take much notice.

In the few seconds' thankful silence that followed the tightening of the final bolt, we heard her strangled breathing. John Clark jammed a pole between the slats and levered her head into a better position and her breathing improved immediately.

We lifted the crate on to the bottom rung of the rollers with creosoted gum poles. It was incredible what could be done with poles. Without them rhino capture would have come to a quick halt, but we were constantly forgetting that the pitch burnt badly, especially if you touched your eyes.

The crate was lifted with two poles and more poles were put underneath to help its passage up the rollers. We then attached a length of cable to the U-bolt on the front of the crate, ran it to the top of the truck cab, and slowly hand winched the crate up the rollers. More poles were laid on the truck deck and the crate was jerked a few feet further. The cable was unhitched and the crate, with its heavy load, was manhandled the rest of the way.

The taut cable and the weight of rhino and crate had dented John Kinloch's lorry. I remembered his admonition and hammered it back into a semblance of its former shape. Arthur Nyawo, the driver, stood alongside, his tall frame stooped more than usual in the wind and cold, wringing his hands and muttering, '*Hau, nkosaan, hau*!'

It was half past six. It had taken us half an hour to get the crate on to the lorry. We stuffed grass into the open slats near Amber's head to try to prevent her wedging her head or horn again, then Toni and I left for Mpila to get a tarpaulin and to prepare for the journey to Mkuze Game Reserve.

Beyond Mantianna the road passes through more sandy country and the heavy rains made little impression here. We passed the turnoff to the rhino pans and drove slowly along the winding road to Little Mpila. The lightning display was at its height and for a few seconds the whole of the wilderness area was brilliantly lit. I saw the winding White Umfolozi, Nqabaneni, and Dengezeni hill. In the daylight it was a view no one could easily forget; in the lightning flashes it was like a photographic negative.

The wind howled over the gap between the two Mpilas and the rain fell harder. Umfolozi Game Reserve was in one of her wild moods. The Land-Rover slithered and the wheels spun. Water dripped on to me from gaps in the door and the wind was cold.

'What a night to move a rhino,' Toni said a little wearily.

'Do you think we should go on?' I asked anxiously.

'Can you imagine getting it off the lorry and letting it go again?' he replied sarcastically.

I dropped him at his quarters and we arranged to meet at nine o'clock.

I ran up to the house in the pouring rain. My wife met me at the door and my two young children played on the floor. The warmth of the house with the bright lights was a strange contrast from the wild scene outside. Even as I hurriedly changed in the bathroom I could hear the south wind whining, moaning and soughing past the house, and fierce squalls of rain lashed the window panes.

The rest of the men arrived and we filled up with thick, hot soup and coffee. I heard the lorry grinding up the hill to Mpila camp as we finished.

The crate was covered with a sail and lashed down with more rope. Arthur Nyawo had bad news: the truck starter wasn't working. It was too late to do anything about it, so we left as arranged. Toni and Nick were in my vehicle, John Clark was with the rhino, and the others went ahead to prepare Mkuze Game Reserve for our arrival.

Chapter 12

Travelling to Mkuze

Singie Denyer, the ranger in charge of Mkuze, was in his late fifties. He was originally from the mountain country of East Griqualand but came to Zululand when he was young. After running a trading store he joined the Veterinary Department and worked first in Umfolozi Game Reserve checking tsetse fly traps. He was later transferred to Mkuze Game Reserve, which became his spiritual home.

In the early days Mkuze was a hell hole of heat, drought and malaria. There were not many white men who lived on the eastern side of the Lebombo mountains by choice, but Singie Denyer and his wife Dawn adapted themselves to the isolation, the enervating heat and the attacks of malaria. He resigned from the Veterinary Department when the shooting campaign began. The butchery of the impala was too much. When it was over he and his wife were asked to rejoin and go back to Mkuze – the others who had been there had not lasted long. So Singie rejoined and went back to his Tongaland wilderness.

There were other worries besides the physical discomfort. Although Mkuze Game Reserve had been proclaimed in 1912, the threat of deproclamation was always hanging over it. The Denyers never knew from day to day what the fate of the reserve would be. Any official who visited Mkuze was always asked 'Is the reserve safe?'

The arrival of the first white rhino at Mkuze Game Reserve was a tremendously important occasion for Singie.

'When we have white rhino here the reserve is safe,' he said. 'Look how they saved Umfolozi. Everyone was afraid to deproclaim the Umfolozi Reserve in case something happened to the white rhino.'

His enthusiasm for the translocation of rhino was great, and he wanted to make sure the first white rhino came to Mkuze. He had the bomas built and the off-loading ramps dug in less than a week.

'I can't wait for the animals to arrive,' he repeated to everyone.

The road between the Black Umfolozi river and Masimba was bad and the lorry skidded on the corners. We peered through the wet windshield, anxiously watching the crate. Arthur Nyawo was driving at a good pace and we stayed just far enough behind to keep the crate in sight, our lights catching the back of the lorry in the rain.

Toni sat with his green canvas parka over his head, nodding rhythmically. It was a typical pose when he was deep in thought. It was also not a time to try to engage him in conversation.

We stopped at Macibini pans, undid the wet sail and looked at Amber. The air was warm but smelt strongly of urine and faeces. She had stopped sweating and stood in a good position. Her breathing was slow but Toni was satisfied with her condition.

By the time we reached Hluhluwe Game Reserve gate the rain had stopped and the journey up to the camp was uneventful, except that as we arrived there was great excitement among the staff. Everyone wanted to climb up and look at the rhino. The African staff were most impressed. They covered their mouths with their hands and muttered '*Hau!*' as Arthur Nyawo graphically described Amber getting into the crate and being loaded on to the lorry. A knot of visitors gathered round and began asking questions.

'Let's get out of here,' Nick said. 'These people will be cutting hunks off Amber for souvenirs if we hang around any longer.'

It does not take long for a gala atmosphere to spread and among a group of people there is always one who will behave badly. As we climbed into the Land-Rover one man asked us to remove the sail so he could take a flashlight picture. We ignored him and drove down the long winding road which passes Hlaza and Mkwankwa, then over the Mansimbomvu and out of the reserve towards Hluhluwe village.

Heavy rain began falling as we turned north on the main road. Cars, lorries, and buses had churned the road into a quagmire, and we were in for trouble. The lorry slid about and we had to stop and move the crate back into position. John Clark and Nick used long poles to get it on to a more even keel. Toni undid the sail, shone a light on Amber and peered through the slats. Steam rose, so she was warm enough.

We drove on following the blue lorry as it forced its way along the main road. A mile further on it slid into the left bank and within seconds was down to its back axle in mud.

'Have you a towing cable?' Toni asked Nick.

Nick looked in the back and swore. We had left it behind. 'It is something you might have checked on,' said Toni quietly. He never lost his temper.

Black rain clouds raced overhead and thunder echoed across the veld. The rain lashed us and an icy trickle had found its way down my neck. I pulled my beret on tighter. I couldn't do anything for a while in the lethargy induced by the heavy rain and cold.

Arthur Nyawo rattled around in the back of the lorry and brought out a pair of chains. He struggled to put them on while John Clark kept the engine running.

I took the other chain and with Toni's help tied it on to the front bumper of the lorry and the tow bar of the Land-Rover. John Clark got into the lorry, revved the engine and I jerked the Land-Rover forward. It moved the lorry a few yards then the engine cut out. The only relief was in bad language.

Twelve hours later the lorry was still stuck and the combined efforts of the two Land-Rovers could not pull it out.

We had gone on to Mkuze at half past two in the morning of 18 June for help, and at 11.30 had returned to find the lorry at a perilous angle and Amber's horn knocked off. She had to keep moving to keep her balance in the crate. I looked into the crate and saw very little blood. Amber appeared to be in no pain. It was eighteen hours since she had been darted and she was still drugged.

Nick was clambering over the crate and I heard him mutter. His voice was choked when he called me.

'Look at her back,' he said emotionally.

The sacral hump was raw flesh. With the crate at an uneven angle, every time she moved she rubbed her spine. I called Toni. He had a look and said: 'It's not doing her any good staying in this position. The sooner we get her into the boma at Mkuze, the greater her chances of recovery.'

Flies had come from nowhere and were massed on Amber's wounds. Blood oozed on to the floor of the crate where it mingled with faeces and urine. The stench was getting worse.

John Clark had driven to Hluhluwe to phone John Kymdell, the Parks Board road maintenance officer. He was to bring his caterpillar road grader and lengths of towing cable.

Another two hours of watching Amber moving up and down rubbing her wound, was too much for me. Peter Potter and I drove down the road looking for a farmer who might be prepared to help. It was still overcast though not raining, the farm roads were difficult to traverse even in a Land-Rover. Peter knew John Hassard who lived on a nearby farm. He said he would bring his tractor and with this to help us we dragged the lorry out of the mud and into the middle of the road.

Within minutes we were on our way again. We were soon overtaken by the grader. For safety's sake, we tied a towline from the lorry to the grader and kept going. It was dark by the time we reached the entrance to Mkuze Game Reserve. The road deteriorated. The grader moved forward slowly, its huge tyres scattering mud into the air.

Impala stood in groups under the trees and wildebeest snorted in alarm at the long convoy. A jackal then a hyena crossed the road, their eyes brightly reflecting the headlights. Half an hour later we drew up in front of Singie Denyer's house. He emotionally shook our hands, saying how pleased he was to have the rhino. But we still had a long way to go to the bomas.

Singie got into the Land-Rover with us. We started singing the old, nostalgic war songs. John Page and Toni led us with their fine voices, and the songs we did not know we hummed. Then as suddenly as the singing had started, it stopped, and we grew quiet. The windscreen wipers buzzed and the rain slashed down on the cab. Singie began to sing again, but no one took up the refrain.

'What's the matter with you chaps?' he groused.

'We're tired, Singie,' someone answered.

We waited while John Kymdell, who was driving with no cover except an old Parks Board hat and a weathered raincoat, reversed and manoeuvred to free the grader, then we drove through the bush to escape the sticky mud.

At ten o'clock we reached the bomas. A hole had been dug for the lorry so that the deck would be level with the boma. Arthur backed up and the lorry simply slid down. We all climbed out reluctantly, shivering in our wet clothes. Thunder crashed and the Lebombo mountains were lit by lightning.

'*Kom kêrels, kom!*' I shouted. 'John Clark, get the rollers off!'

Always willing and apparently never tired, John ran up to the lorry and organised the fresh Mkuze labour. In ten minutes we were all soaked to the skin. I noticed John Page standing shivering in the lee of the lorry. His face was blue with cold.

'Where's your coat?' I asked.

'Somebody's whipped it,' he said with chattering teeth. I saw a ranger beat a hasty retreat and start pulling on some ropes.

It took us two hours to get the crate off the back of the lorry. With no winch and inadequate rollers – the gaps were too wide – we had to manhandle everything. And the back of the lorry was higher than the ground. It was a frightful struggle to get the crate to the door of the boma. Everything that could possibly go wrong had gone wrong from the beginning and our morale was low. If anyone had told us that all this was valuable experience which would enable us to catch a hundred white rhino in two years, we would not have believed it.

When we had pushed the crate the last few inches to the boma gate, we made sure Amber would not escape by tying the crate to the gate poles. At last we were ready and with much grousing and spanner twisting we undid the bolts, the crate door was yanked up and we stood clear expecting Amber to charge out. But she stood quietly in the back of the crate and refused to move. We tried everything to get her out, but nothing worked.

An hour later we left her, in the crate. This was the final slap in our wet and muddy faces, but tragedy was still to come. The forty-four gallon drum in the boma had not been sunk deeply enough into the ground, and in the early morning when she staggered out, she cut her leg to the bone.

We drove back to Mantuma, the reserve headquarters, in a daze, dried our soaking clothes before a fire in Dawn Denyer's kitchen and collapsed for an hour's sleep.

At first light, we collected the lorry from the boma and returned to Umfolozi Game Reserve. Nick and I shared the driving while Toni slept sitting up. The Land-Rover lurched all over the road as we put our heads out to keep ourselves awake. I drove the final stretch and woke Nick outside John Kinloch's office. He staggered off for food and a change of clothing.

The following day we altered the crate. John Clark sawed an inspection hole for easy access to the rhino. We washed the congealed blood and faeces of Amber out – I was sickened by the bits of flesh on the wood where she had rubbed her back.

In the afternoon we had news that she was lying down in the boma oblivious of the mud and water. The wound on her leg was looking worse and she had not defecated all day, but Toni was more disturbed when I told him she had not had a drink either.

'Her inability to stand has probably got a lot to do with it,' he said.

Early the following day, we captured Charlie, a young bull, and by eleven o'clock that night he was in the boma next to Amber in Mkuze Game Reserve.

Toni examined Amber who still had not taken water or defecated. She had spent the whole day on her side, unable to move, her breathing laboured. Her wounds were smelling badly. Moving round in the boma up to the ankles in mud with only torches and a hurricane lamp for light, hindered treatment.

'We have got to get her up on to her feet, or she will die,' Toni said.

We floundered in the mud, pushing and rocking Amber to try to make her stand. Every time she moved we legged it for the boma walls and climbed up like monkeys. We knew we could expect no mercy from her.

Nothing we did could get her up. Her squeals of pain were heartrending, but nothing we did worked.

'There is only one thing to do,' Toni said. 'We must get ropes under her belly, tie them to the tree, and pull her up. There is no other way.'

John Clark at once took a rope, flopped on to his belly in the mud, and pushed it through. Amber made an immense effort and got on to her belly, but she could not stand. John persisted until the rope was through. We passed two more under the front and the back legs, tied the ropes to an overhanging *Acacia mossambicensis* and with everyone pulling, we got her up. She bellowed in pain – the rush of blood to the wounds must have been agonising.

Toni could now get at her wounds, clean them and fill them with antibiotics. I had to turn away from the leg wound where the flesh hung in rotting strips. There was a severe laceration under her jaw and her bottom lip was cut too.

Her stomach was swollen by intestinal gases. The hours in the crate and the foul weather conditions had left their mark. There was little else we could do except ask Singie Denyer to replace the ropes with slings of wildebeest hide in the morning.

We had news of Amber the next day. The wildebeest hide slings had not been a success. They stretched in the damp and their smell attracted blow flies. They had rubbed her skin and the abrasions were turning septic. She had been given Prostigmin as a purgative, but had violently thrown her head from side to side. Part of the boma had to be pulled down so she could not injure herself. But she had been given twenty gallons of water with a garden hose and had sucked the tube.

'That at least is good news,' Toni commented.

But Singie Denyer said her condition was weakening all the time.

It poured with rain again on 24 June. I got through to Norman Deane at Hluhluwe Game Reserve on the phone, an achievement in itself as it was a party line loud with mission hospitals, storekeepers and loquacious Zulus interrupting. I asked him to go to Mkuze to see how Amber was getting on. She was much on our conscience and we worried about her constantly.

Norman phoned later with a dismal report. 'It was raining cats and dogs when I got to the bomas,' he said. 'That poor animal has had one hell of a time. I had to get all of Mkuze's labour force to turn her on to her right side so I could examine her injuries. The wound on her leg is far worse – it's as big as a saucer now, if not bigger. There's another cut below this which is down to the nail and is rotten. The cut on her lower jaw is half an inch deep and there's another one on her lower lip.'

He was interrupted by a storekeeper arguing with the mission hospital about a patient. Norman asked severely if he didn't realise that a white rhino was much more important than any human being. There was a flabbergasted silence on the other end and Norman continued listing Amber's injuries.

'Her belly is an unhealthy white colour with several hernias caused by grass in the intestines. She has only defecated once since we gave her the Prostigmin. There are pink raw bands left by the ropes and she has multiple bruises. It grips your guts to see all this and to hear her whimpering. She doesn't seem to mind human beings near her any more, which shows what condition she's in.'

I asked him what he thought we should do.

'I can only recommend that we shoot her, we can't continue to let her suffer like this. The rain is the last straw – that boma is a stinking mass of mud and there's no protection for her,' he replied.

Toni was sitting near me and I explained the position. He shrugged his shoulder.

'Norman's right. There's nothing we can do but put her out of her misery.'

Reluctantly I said to Norman, 'Tell Singie to shoot her.'

The old man would be terribly upset. This was his rhino, the first in a hundred years, and in his eyes an insurance against the threatened deproclamation of Mkuze Game Reserve. Amber had become a symbol of safety and now we had to tell him to shoot her. I felt desperately sad about it all. Singie couldn't bring himself to do it and sent a young ranger.

There was a depressing sequel to it. A few days later this ranger was told in Mkuze village how lucky he was to have the distinction of shooting a white rhino.

Chapter 13

Consolidation

We caught our next rhino in the Cigqayana area of the Corridor. Sven Persson and Jimmy Anderson from the South African Tourist Corporation were with us to make a film of rhino capture.

I went after a young fifteen hundred pound male we nicknamed Billy.

I walked down the eroded bed of the Mcacaso stream stripped to the waist in the heat. There was almost no wind, which made stalking difficult. Billy and his dam moved into thick bush. Vision was so poor I had to get seven paces away before being able to aim. I was about to fire when the cow roared loudly and made a rush at me. She had probably smelt the horses or thought I was a bull. As she charged I fired quickly at Billy, saw the dart go in, then fled. Billy ran, bumped against a tree and broke the dart needle. I climbed the hill and told Toni.

'Let's hang on a while, perhaps he got enough of the drug to knock him down,' Toni said.

We lay among the boulders at Itsheamabunu (Dutchmen's Rocks) and watched the rhino. They moved out into a clearing and began grazing, unconcerned by the earlier disturbance. On calm, windless days and nights it took a lot to disturb the rhino. Scent played so important a part in their lives that a man's scent on a windy day was like a physical blow to them.

Three quarters of an hour later, Toni gave me another dart. I banged the gun while creeping up to Billy – this must have set the dart off. When I fired there was a spray of drug and the dart missed. This was the last 10 c.c. projectile we had.

Toni made up a 5 c.c. dart and I shot Billy in the leg. Eighteen minutes later he was down. He only ran a hundred yards so the horsemen had an easy day. The cow ran off making that strange call peculiar to the white rhino. She circled and came back to the calf. She smelt it all over and became agitated when it wouldn't rise. One of the horsemen went near but she swung round and charged.

'Great, great,' I heard Sven Persson grunt as his camera whirred.

The presence of the cameraman had subtly changed the atmosphere of rhino capture. Hair was slicked back, and people seemed to be taking more chances. Willing hands were in evidence wherever the camera focused and everyone worked furiously while the camera churned. But within a week the glamour of being film stars quickly waned. The continual re-takes irritated everyone. Sven Persson had become deeply interested in the whole capture but as soon as he approached with his huge Ariflex 35 mm camera slung across his chest, there was an exodus of rangers. Then we drove him to distraction, by hamming it up unmercifully. 'You blady swines,' he shouted angrily in his Swedish-American accent, 'I hafn't efen got permission to make the film yet. You nearly get me killed and now you act like hams.'

The heavy camera slowed him down and twice he was nearly horned as we headed for the trees. But his film gradually took shape. In time, he became part of the rhino team, repaired vehicles, radios or guns – the only thing he would not do was ride a horse and carry his camera at the same time.

It was a beautiful, clear day, ideal for photography and Sven got some outstanding shots as Toni gave Billy the Lethidrone. Billy rose almost immediately and everybody clung to his tail as he moved off, but he flicked them off one by one. John Clark shouted for a rope. Nick slipped the halter off his horse and it was used with a stirrup leather to tie Billy's hind legs while a rope was being fetched. Billy stood after being tied and was easy to handle. He treated us as though we were a herd of rhino and grazed calmly while his statistics were noted. We guided him into the crate without any trouble. Toni gave him an injection of Largactil, a tranquilliser, and 3 mega units of procaine penicillin while we smeared his anus and the inside of his legs with tick grease. We loaded the crate on to a tip lorry and Norman Deane left with it for Mkuze Game Reserve.

An hour later he was back. Billy was dead. He had jammed his head in the corner and fought the crate until he died.

We were all depressed. Everything had gone so smoothly, but Toni softened the blow.

'There's no need to feel low,' he said. 'We can be glad that this drug is particularly suited for the translocation of rhinos. The way the animal goes down without struggling is so important. Also when it comes round it doesn't bang its head on the ground, doesn't hurt itself, is not excited and is very tractable. Usually the animals which come round from a neuromuscular blocking agent suddenly become wild animals again and rush off or at you! These rhinos after being given the antidote are very easy to handle. There is also no pain, they don't even flinch when you put the ear tags in. They seem to have lost their dislike for human beings and don't mind the smell or the talking.'

Early the next morning I darted a young female rhino. The horsemen took off after it.

We waited half an hour but there was no sign of the horsemen. Toni and Norman Deane went round Ncebe hill by vehicle while I went with Magqubu as he tracked the rhino. I could see no tracks or signs but his short thickset body moved with an irregular rhythm through the trees and over the maze of game paths. He would hesitate for a moment, retrace his steps ignoring me and my questions, grunt and move on again speaking softly to himself. We came into an open heavily grazed glade. Here the tracks were more obvious and Magqubu began jogging, his head darting from left to right following signs I could not even see. A rhino path wider than usual, began at the end of the glade and wound past the eastern foot of Ncebe hill. The spoor was much clearer here. Magqubu increased speed and looked further ahead instead of at his feet. The path forked, Magqubu turned left. He ran fast downhill, stopped, and pointed to the opposite slope.

'*Nango* – there,' he said.

Owen was leading a white rhino calf up the hill by its small front horn.

'*Hau*, this doctor,' Magqubu said. 'This stuff that he has brought this time is *umthakathi kakhulu* – great witchcraft.'

Owen led the young rhino which took small steps forward like a blind man walking to the edge of a cliff.

We crossed a stream bed. Magqubu pointed to flattened grass and blobs of mud and said the young rhino must have fallen into a pool we had skirted. Owen confirmed this when we caught up with him.

'She was staggering down the path and she stumbled into the pool,' he said. 'I managed to get her head above water and gave her fifteen c.c. of antidote. But if she'd been another minute coming round I'd have had to drop her. Her head weighs a ton.'

We named her Babs. She was photographed and Owen rode her to demonstrate her docility under the drugs. Toni made many notes and looked very pleased.

'Curious, curious,' he said, suddenly looking serious.

'What's up?' I asked anxiously.

'Haven't you noticed she has a decided bias to the left?' Toni said.

'Yes,' I replied.

'Well, isn't this likely to get her into trouble in South Africa ?' Toni laughed.

The lorry came jerking up the hill, its engine coughing spasmodically.

'We're taking a chance with that damned wreck,' Norman said, pointing to the lorry as it moved erratically over the veld.

Toni said he was concerned about the age of Babs. She seemed too young to be taken away from her mother.

'The lorry has no brakes and no starter, and if it stalls in any of the dongas we might have difficulty starting it again. Let's let the animal go and send the truck back to Hluhluwe for repairs,' Norman said in his blunt way.

I wanted to get as many rhino to Mkuze as we could while Toni was with us, but it was too much of a risk, especially after what had happened to Amber.

The question now was what would happen if we painted identifying marks on the young Babs.

'Being a painted lady will chase the boys away,' suggested John Clark.

Someone said heatedly that the cow would reject her calf, then there was a chance of its starving to death. To stop an argument developing, I asked Magqubu.

'A calf is a calf and a mother is a mother: what difference will a little bit of paint make?' he said.

Babs was painted on the ears and forehead but we left two guards to observe the cow's reaction. She returned an hour later with a bull which prevented her from going near Babs. Normally a calf interferes with the bull trying to copulate. This time, thanks to science, everything was in favour of the bull, and the guards gave graphic descriptions of the copulating, with sound effects.

At half past two that afternoon I stalked a mature bull and darted it in the right flank with an eighteen c.c. dart. It took off at a gallop with the horsemen following fast. In six minutes ataxia set in and it could not run straight. It had already covered two miles.

In the distance, I heard the riders shouting hoarsely. Something was wrong. We sped towards the shouting. I hoped no one was injured. There was always a fear in my mind of a black rhino catching Nick or Owen unawares; there were so many things that could go wrong. We stopped to listen and hooves pounded in the distance. A herd of wildebeest and zebra ran towards us with Nick galloping behind. The game veered off at the sight of the vehicle, the zebra yodelling loudly.

Nick pulled up Zoom and said anxiously, 'For Christ's sake come quickly, the rhino's gone over the krantz.'

We hurried to the spot and saw where trees and boulders had been ripped out in the rhino's plunge. He lay squealing on his back.

'God, it was grim,' Nick said as we slid down to the rhino. 'The poor devil was balancing on the edge and we got him away, then he turned and went tumbling down. The sound the body made thumping against the rocks made me sick in the stomach. This one is a real Jonah.'

Toni avoided the flailing legs and gave the rhino an intravenous injection of antidote. We waited for it to take effect.

'Get a rope,' Toni said curtly.

John Clark ran up the steep slope and was back in no time. He made a slip knot and lassoed one of the front legs. When Jonah jerked his leg it pulled four of us about like a tug of war team. We tried for a quarter of an hour to right the animal but the angle of the slope made it difficult for us to move, and soon we were drenched with sweat. The antidote had taken effect and the rhino was thrashing about and calling pathetically.

We rested a while and Nick told me how he had avoided colliding with a reedbuck ram while following Jonah. 'We'll be lucky if someone isn't badly injured,' he said.

There was a flurry of movement and Jonah rolled over and heaved himself on to his feet. We scrambled for cover. John took a few steps forward and slipped the rope off the front leg.

'Good man,' Toni said.

John shook his head and laughed. Bravery was a matter of course to him. Sometimes he had to be reprimanded for the risks he took.

Jonah stood up again, breathing heavily, his body dark with sweat and his muscles trembling. In the half darkness of evening, with long shadows thrown by the trees and upturned rocks in the silent bush, it was a primeval setting. He walked forward a few steps, lost his balance and fell heavily. He tried to get up and rolled completely over, dislodging loose stones.

'Look out, grab him! He's going to roll down more!' Owen yelled.

It was too late. Jonah was down and rolling. He crashed into a boulder with a deep thud and was wedged against a strangler fig growing from a crack in the rock face. He breathed in short gasps and a trickle of blood ran from his nose. Toni shook his head and I knew Jonah didn't have long to live. He reared his head, shuddered and lay still.

'Sorry about this,' Toni said sadly. 'But this illustrates a hazard that besets all animals released after immobilisation; misadventure is always likely before all faculties are fully recovered.'

I made arrangements for John to come out early the following morning and chop the horns off the skull. The human hyenas would not take long to find the remains and the horns would be stolen and sold to an eager market always on the look-out for this supposedly powerful aphrodisiac.

It had been a long and tiring day and to take my mind off the day's tragedy during the return journey I spoke to Toni about early attempts at immobilisation.

'When were the first animals darted?' I asked.

Toni described how in the United States in 1953 a twist drill coated with a mixture of honey and miotus had been fired from an airgun, and deer were actually immobilised. Then in 1957 Crockford invented the dart-syringe. This changed the whole course of immobilisation because it was now possible to deliver a measured dose. The Palmer Chemical Company became interested commercially and mass-produced the syringes and got the Crossman Company to make the gun, now known as the Palmer Capchur gun.

It was, as always, a pleasure to hear Toni speak. His enunciation and pitch were perfect and his text to the point. He gave a clear resume of our captures to date, listing our successes and failures and outlining the direction we would have to follow when he left in a few days' time. He cleared my mind of the clutter of emotion, fatigue and worry; our purpose came into focus and our future course distinct.

'One more rhino with you chaps tomorrow, then I will be on my way back to East Africa. So we must make sure that this one gets to Mkuze Game Reserve. It had also better be a female companion for Charlie,' Toni said.

At half past one the next day I stalked and darted Minnehaha in the right shoulder. We had found her grazing in the open on Mhlopeni flats. A strong north-east wind was blowing, which made darting much easier. The horsemen followed her for two miles then she slowed down and stopped after twelve minutes. She staggered a little then ran across a dry stream bed and got her head against a tree. We were able to walk up to her and pull the dart out.

'How are we going to get her to the lorry?' Owen asked.

'Walk her there, like you led Babs,' Toni said calmly.

'But do you reckon we'll get her up that bank, Doc?' Owen said. He pointed to a steep ledge between us and the oncoming lorry.

Toni nodded his head. He gave Minnie twenty c.c. of antidote. She flicked her ear, spattering blood on my shirt.

John Clark tagged her yellow in one ear and red in the other.

Minnehaha stirred and John slipped a thick rope round her head. She persistently moved forward so Nick and Owen chopped the tree down. She stumbled but Toni pushed against her flank, turned her and we all grabbed the rope and pulled. She came along quietly but with jerky footsteps, dragging her toes through the coarse sand.

We led her to a semblance of a path made by small antelope. John Clark hacked footholds for us with a cane-knife. The smell of dust, human sweat, crushed grass, and the tang of rhino lingered in the confines of the stream. Minnie took the first steps up the bank with ease but then balked. She was at an awkward angle. As we pushed her backside she leant against us and we slipped down. Norman got the giggles and we became weak and helpless with laughter. John Clark hung on to the head rope, pleading with us to hurry as his arms ached. Nick clambered up, jerked her tail and she moved uphill again, but collapsed at the top. Someone kicked her on the neck to try to revive her.

'Now don't be unkind,' Toni said.

Nick said later, 'One doesn't expect this expression of concern from a scientist. His attitude to the rhino right from the beginning really impressed me. I saw anguish on his face every time a rhino died.'

We measured Minnehaha and Toni administered an antidote and five c.c. Largactil. At half past two Toni injected more Lethidrone but she was very sleepy and in a few minutes she quietly lay down and fell into a deep slumber. We got her moving after three o'clock but it took nearly half an hour to get her into the crate.

John Clark had nailed a strip of masonite over the slats at the front of the crate. She could not jam her horn in the corner but she fell on her side. When the crate tipped she scrambled to her feet and kept her balance for the rest of the loading operation. We passed two ropes through the crate under her chest to prevent her lurching forward when the lorry went through dongas.

Six hours later she was in Mkuze Game Reserve.

That evening we discussed the merits and demerits of sending the white rhino to zoos. We all had a horror of captivity but I felt it was important to have our rare animals all over the world, as well as in their former ranges.

Toni backed me up. 'You are right,' he said. 'I think a hundred rhinos ought to be sent to zoos : this will ensure the establishment of breeding units. The question of national prestige connected with special animals is catching on all over the world. In Europe they are going to tremendous lengths to recreate the European bison. They have only been able to get a small nucleus by buying animals from zoological gardens.'

He gave us other examples of breeding nuclei being established from zoos, and said, 'I hope that all the nations in Africa will become extremely conscious of the special animals they have got and which exist nowhere else in the world.'

'How long do you think we would have to keep the rhino before it would be safe to send them to a zoo?' John Clark asked. He seemed to sense that he was going to be responsible for this aspect.

'This is something you chaps will have to work out,' Toni said. 'As we have demonstrated, a rhino can be taken over a hundred miles straight from the field. If you were going to send them overseas you would have to condition them to artificial food; this may take time. They need at least a fortnight in captivity to stabilise them completely.'

On the morning of 30 June 1961, as we prepared to catch our first rhino alone, Toni left for Uganda. He explained to me in detail how to mix the drugs and left enough Themalon, Sernyl, Largactil, and hyoscine to capture two more rhino. Toni had become one of us and I pleaded with him to leave his job in Uganda and return to South Africa to direct the rhino saving operation.

'It's completely unnecessary,' he said. 'I may come back in September to start off the large-scale translocation, but all you need is a better gun, more syringes, needles that really work, and enough drug. It will take a few months to stock up then you can quite easily operate on your own.' His parting words were, 'Send me a telegram on how you get on with the twelfth rhino.'

At a quarter past twelve after carefully mixing the drugs I stalked a two-thousand pound female we named June after the month of our success.

She was grazing calmly on the western side of the Madhlozi stream when I crawled up and darted her at ten paces. She ran north for three hundred yards then turned towards the Madhlozi. The horsemen galloped towards us, whooping loudly to try to stop her crossing the stream.

'If she crosses the Madhlozi we won't get the truck across,' Magqubu said.

June ran towards the banks, which were twenty feet high. The drug had not taken effect and she hesitated, charged back to a game path and disappeared. The two horsemen collided as they kicked and urged their horses after her. She had gone upstream, I could tell by the swarm of flies hovering above. Horses' hooves knocked against stones and Owen shouted, 'Turn her Nick, turn her!'

John Clark came running barefoot down the hill slope, his long trousers flapping against the grass and his shirt tails streaming behind. Magqubu grunted. He was always impressed by John's tough feet. John ran to the edge of the Madhlozi and shouted to draw my attention to June who had emerged eight hundred yards upstream followed by the horsemen.

Reedbuck scattered, whistling shrilly, and four little warthog piglets, their tails straight in the air, trotted after their mother.

June was running strongly towards the foot of Nqoloti then she stumbled.

'This is it,' John shouted happily. 'The drug's working.'

June slowed to a walk and even from our position we could see the glint of sweat on her back. The horsemen cantered nearer, Owen's long hair rising and falling against his neck. Four passing red-billed oxpeckers landed on June's back and set up alarm cries as the horsemen approached. She took no notice of their calls but plodded forward jerkily. Nick and Owen followed slowly on foot, leading the horses which swished their tails to chase off the horde of rhino flies. June stumbled and stared fixedly at a boulder shiny after generations of warthog scratching themselves against it. Her tail curled and uncurled and she splayed her legs like a drunk on the point of keeling over. Urine dribbled down her legs and she sweated heavily on her head, ears, flanks, and along the ridge of her back. I turned to speak to John and she was down.

We slid down the stream bank and ran upstream till we found a game path to climb out. John beat me to the horsemen.

'Well, this is our first rhino,' John said proudly.

'It's not going to be easy getting her across that lot,' Nick said. He pointed to the wide depression of the Madhlozi.

We discussed a plan of action and decided to give her a little Lethidrone then lead her across.

'Sounds easy,' Owen said. 'But it's a mighty long way.'

'Well, let's get started,' Nick said.

He led the horses to tether while I mixed a bottle of antidote. I followed Toni's injunctions as though my life depended on it, even shaking the bottle as he did.

Magqubu guided the lorry to the nearest point on the opposite bank. June rose suddenly and stood with quivering limbs, then collapsed on to her brisket again. We measured her as she lay there breathing noisily, mucus trickling from her nostrils. This alarmed me but John had seen it with other rhino. I was far more alert today and noticed things I had not seen when we were with Toni. This was always the case when one did a job alone for the first time. It was the best way to learn.

Nick Steele smothered tick grease around her anus, vagina, under the hind legs, and around her teats. The tough tortoiseshell ticks crawled on their long brown legs into the grass. They were a menace to animals and caused large sores on horses and dogs that were not frequently de-ticked.

June breathed six times to the minute, a healthy sign. The rattling noise in her throat that worried me was only mucus. The sweating pattern was constant, starting on the head and front legs in the folds of the skin, then along the belly and underneath to the teats. It was always the side to the sun that started first.

'It's damned interesting that the white rhino don't have any of the erosions on their sides that the black rhino have,' Owen observed.

'Well I'd rather be dealing with the white ones right now,' Nick laughed. 'But I look forward to catching the black rhino, they're such dramatic beasts.'

We lowered the crate off the lorry, gave June a small injection of antidote and she walked calmly into the crate. Half an hour later she was ready to go. John Clark offered to go with her to Mkuze and he delivered her there safely at half past nine that night.

Next morning I sent a telegram to Toni that must have puzzled the postal officials a little. It read: 'To Mkuze a 2000 lb girl called June. Delivered fit and well.'

This ended the experiments with the drug combination of Themalon or morphine, Largactil, Hyoscine, and Sernyl, names that had become household words. Toni had proved that not only were the drugs a success but that after training, field men could use them without fear of losses. The whole concept of rhino removal had changed dramatically. Conservation had taken a stride forward; it was the beginning of the end of the professional trappers who captured rhino by rope. Dr Hubert Lang, the American scientist who visited Umfolozi Game Reserve in the 1920's advised the removal of the white rhino in 1930. It had taken thirty-one years for a proper technique to evolve.

As I lay in bed that night looking out into the starlight with the wild sounds of leopard, nightjars, dikkops and hyena calling, I thought how pleased Vaughan-Kirby, the first game conservator of Zululand, would have been. There were days when he wondered if the small herd of rhino would live to see another dawn. I thought of Captain Potter too, and his efforts to get a few rhino into the Hluhluwe Game Reserve in the 1930's. Then there was Sir Charles Saunders, a man who had done much for the reserves. People had accused him of being a fanatic because he proteced the white rhino. He would have been pleased with what we had done. Umfolozi Game Reserve would never be the same, but we had a lot to be thankful for. The white rhino were on their way to being re-established.

CHAPTER 14

Another Taste of Wilderness

The experiments with the new drugs had been outstandingly successful. The Natal Parks Board now agreed to Colonel Vincent's request for a hundred white rhino to be sent to areas where they had occurred in the historical past. It was decided that the Kruger National Park would be the first recipients. But we were told that there was to be a four-month delay before further supplies of drugs reached South Africa. Our large-scale movement of rhino could only begin in October.

This gave me a chance to catch up with other work that had been neglected in the past month. But the first thing I did was to go on a two-day foot patrol with Magqubu. I felt I had to get away from the sense of urgency that had prevailed over the last month. I needed to taste the wilderness again and refresh my body and mind with the sights and sounds of Umfolozi. Remarkable though the capture of the rhino had been, it had also upset me to see these magnificent beasts humbled by a silver dart and a few c.c. of liquid, and close contact with the animal had robbed it of some of its wild beauty.

So Magqubu and I set out on a walk. It was before the spring rains when the north-east wind blows hard and every succeeding day gets hotter. The bush shimmered in the burning sun and the horizon was blurred in palls of smoke from a hundred veld fires in the surrounding tribal reserves. It was on days like this that the game came panting with thirst to those pans still holding water.

We made our way along a rhino footpath to a pan below Mantianna hills. It was always fascinating to sit in a tree overlooking the pan and watch the game come down to drink and wallow.

Throughout the Umfolozi Game Reserve there are pans, shallow depressions where rhino and warthog wallow. Tourists in the reserve often reported seeing red rhino and warthog, thinking they were different species. The animals had merely wallowed in a red clay pan.

The origin of pans has been the cause of much speculation. On one occasion I observed how a pan began.

A warthog had been killed in the western part of the reserve and the carcass lay on top of an antbear hole. Vultures settled around the dead animal and during the pecking of the carcass flattened the grass nearby. The summer rains fell shortly afterwards and a small pool of water formed where the dead warthog and the vultures had been. Wandering warthog rolled in it a few times, then one morning I saw a white rhino bull wallowing. The pan grew larger over the years, deepened by rhino and warthog wallowing, then emerging with large blobs of mud adhering to the skin. But it is mainly the rhino who are the creators and maintainers of the pans.

The behaviour of white rhino arriving at a wallow differs, but a pattern does emerge. The hotter the day – and in Umfolozi temperatures rise to 110°F in the shade – the more the white rhino come to wallow in the pans. They usually have a lengthy drink first, then enter the pan to lie in the water for as long as two hours, moving their position slightly every ten to fifteen minutes, then later moving to the shade of trees.

In the afternoon they begin sighing and snorting loudly then get up and go back to the pan. They walk at a leisurely pace and invariably stop at a dung heap to defecate or urinate. The rhino then enter the pan. If the water is deep, they might go in backwards. Their next action is to stick their horns into the mud, often submerging the head up to the eyes in water. After the horns are well covered with mud the rhino lie in the wallow and begin to roll from side to side and at times right on to their backs with all four legs sticking up in the air. The accompanying *Stomoxvs* flies move off until a dry patch appears then try to buzz back and settle. Terrapins swim up to the rhino and pick off the thick bloated ticks near the anus and scrotum.

If the water is deep the wallowing about in the mud will take place on the edge, in this way enlarging the pan. After moving about in the mud for three to five minutes the rhino get up, move to another muddy section and repeat the performance. Then depending upon the temperature they either stay in the mud for a few hours or go to the shade again. When undisturbed, rhino go straight to a rubbing post after wallowing.

Rubbing stumps are usually a firmly-anchored boulder, a termite mound, a tree stump – normally a hard wood like nthombothi (*Spirostachys africanus*) – or a tree. Many of the trees surrounding the wallows have been ring barked by the rubbing of animals over the years and polished as smooth as the best piece of household furniture.

Although rubbing and wallowing rids the rhino of ectoparasites, particularly ticks, it is the red-billed ox-peckers that perform that function most efficiently. Sometimes as many as twenty of these small tick birds run all over the rhino, even going into the ears and nostrils without disturbing their host. I once followed a white rhino bull all day and watched its behaviour when ox-peckers were about. While they fed on the parasites the birds made a variety of different calls and the rhino took no notice. Then I raised my hand and waved it about, and the calls of the ox-peckers changed to a high pitched shrill twittering. The rhino was immediately alert and stood up, looking around. I kept quiet and it lay down again. A troop of baboons came over the hill and the ox-peckers' call changed to a hissing sound. The rhino lifted its head and listened but as the bird call did not change, it relaxed again.

I have been grateful to ox-peckers many times because their shrill alarm call in dense bush was a sure indication of black rhino. Horses learn to react to the alarm calls too.

But ox-peckers have declined drastically over the years because they feed on ticks of cattle that have been through arsenical dips; one more result of 'progress'.

White rhino occasionally like to sand-bathe and resort to special spots to do so, but this is in the winter when there is no water in the pans. Except for three pans filled artificially, all the pans in the Umfolozi Game Reserve rely on rainfall or the flooding of the rivers.

After a very dry season at least an inch of rain is required to fill the pans. If it is a year of average rainfall, pans remain full until the end of March, then the majority dry up rapidly. The pans Dadethu (named because the sister of an Mtetwa chief was taken by a crocodile), Mgizweni, and Ingwenyeinqina (The Hunting Place of the Crocodile) usually retain their water for most of the year because they are filled with the overflow of the two Umfolozi rivers. The Mpafa water-hole also holds water for long periods.

These pans are not, however, favoured by white rhino for wallowing purposes. They prefer the shallower pans, probably because there is less chance of their getting bogged down. They have an intuitive fear of deep water. This fear was illustrated when a white rhino bull that lived on a small reed island upstream from the Mdindini drift on the White Umfolozi river, decided to vacate his home when the river rose two feet. It took him nearly three-quarters of an hour to cross the seventy yards of river. He took advantage of every sandbank, stepping very gingerly whenever he approached a deep channel. He stuck in the sand and only pulled himself out with tremendous exertion. When he was nearly across he fell into a deep channel near the west bank. He disappeared for a few seconds then surfaced and after a hard struggle got his head on to the bank. He rested then heaved his bulk out of the water. If the river had been a few inches higher he would probably have drowned. A black rhino would have trotted across without fear of trouble.

In the hot, dry months from August to October when all the central pans are dry, white rhino do lie in some of the shallower river pools, but always on the edge. I have never seen them carry out the same wallowing motions as they do in the pans. Sometimes after floods a muddy depression is formed near the reed beds and both rhino and warthog will wallow normally.

The deep pans with clay bottoms hold water for much longer than the shallow sandy ones because these are soon emptied by desiccating days of sun and animals flocking to drink.

At the height of the dry season even the deep clay pans become dry and only one or two pans over a wide area hold water.

It was a pan such as this I overlooked from my perch in the tree. Magqubu lay hidden nearby in the grass.

An old warthog with enormous tusks came out of the bush and took a few hesitant steps towards the water. Although I was well hidden behind the green boughs of the *Schotia* tree, it gazed in my direction, aware with the superior quality of animals, that danger was near. I was only armed with a camera and could not communicate that I had no intention of harming him.

Eventually the smell of water and his own driving thirst overcame his suspicions and he trotted the last few steps to the water. He lowered his head and drank long, deep and silently except for a few sucking noises. After drinking he looked around then flopped into a pool of thick mud. The delightful, all-encompassing feel of the mud erased all his fears and he uttered little squeaks of joy, and clicking sounds.

He rolled on to one side and over on to the other, then sat on his haunches like a dog and pushed his anus into the mud, squirming with obvious enjoyment. After completing a number of circular motions he sat for a full minute like some old philosopher contemplating a profound thought. Then as the ticks bothered him he moved, scraping his anus through the mud again. When the mud bath was over he walked to a flat rock and began rubbing, first along the neck, then he straddled the rock and vigorously rubbed his stomach along it. The daily toilet over the old warthog trotted into the bush.

Half an hour passed and the pan was deserted except for two brilliantly coloured scarlet-throated sunbirds and a flock of glossy starlings.

An isikehle bush francolin called raucously in the valley and overhead a yellow-billed kite swooped and dived after insects. Twice it dived low and whistled its fluting 'inhloeeewa' call. Then it was still again, until like a tall guardsman on parade, a most magnificent nyala bull stalked through the shadows, bringing colour and grace to the pan.

There was a low grunting from behind a clump of trees and a sow warthog with three youngsters trotted straight to an isolated pool just in front of me. Then another two warthog came from the opposite direction and the pan was alive.

Both the nyala and the warthog trusted each other's ability to detect danger. Only when my camera clicked did they all freeze and stare silently in my direction. The nyala took a few steps towards me, its head jerking up and down and the white mane on its back flowing in the wind. I heard its hooves crunch through the sand, then it stood near the water, its reflection a mass of colour.

I was unable to contain myself and said aloud, 'God, you are a beauty.' In a flash the pan was deserted. The sun was going down and long afternoon shadows spread over the veld. The wind died and there was a strong smell of mud and rhino dung. This was so much part of the bush and age-old Africa.

I had climbed down from the tree when Magqubu whistled softly. He pointed and I heard the loud rumbling of two rhino fighting. We crept through the bush to watch, and sat like spectators at a professional prize fight, thirty yards away from the two fighters. Half an hour later it was too dark to see, and we left. The evening was full of the smell of rank sweat, dust, and acacia buds coming into flower.

As we walked to a grove of trees where we had our camp, Magqubu talked about white rhino. He said the young white rhino males that approached too close to a bull are frightened off by the aggressiveness of the adult. They run away with their tails curled in a posture similar to that which announces or accompanies defecation. I wondered whether in the case of fear this posture was only a displacement action. Similar behaviour is not unknown in man and finds expression in a number of slang phrases. With the white rhino the tail curling could also be a mechanism which inhibits further aggression by the attacker. Magqubu said that when the white rhino runs, the head is in a lowered position almost touching the ground. The black rhino carries its head up. The difference is most marked.

White rhino react with fear in two sets of circumstances, firstly in the presence of man or a moving vehicle, and secondly, aggression by another member of the species.

Immediately danger threatens the head is raised and the ears keep in constant motion. If more than one rhino is present they will all stand facing different directions with buttocks touching. They take a few nervous steps and once suspicion has been aroused they will run away, tails curved over the back. Often the sound they make is like a barrel of water being shaken – a 'humping' noise. They usually canter for the first few yards, then change to a trot. This is an extraordinarily graceful gait and the rhino appears to bounce across the veld. The rhino run away from where they expect the danger to be. In many instances they unwittingly run towards you. Unless you are accustomed to these apparent charges, they can be very frightening. The clapping of hands, or shouting, is usually enough to make the white rhino realise its mistake and it will swerve away. Black rhino can also be frightened off on occasions by making a loud noise, but it is better to be up a tree.

The white rhino died in strange ways.

Some were caught in flash floods because in the early summer months they lie on the sandbanks of the two rivers.

Fighting between males, and between male and female, took a toll. We kept a log of rhino deaths and there appear remarks such as: 'Female died from injuries in a fight. Front leg broken.' 'Male found rotten, with horn stab marks on body.' 'Male near Nqabaneni died from gore wounds sustained in fighting. Large hole 8 inches by 3 inches on back just behind withers. Cuts on neck and chest. Later washed away by floods.'

There were many spectacular battles. One took place on the krantz overlooking the Mandhlagazi caves. The two bulls fought for hours, their low bellowing roars rising to elephant-like screams. The smaller of the two slowly retreated to the cliff where it slipped, somersaulted on to a rocky ledge and broke its back. The next day I watched from above as the vultures circled a few feet below. With a hissing and a swishing of wings they hurtled out of the sky, circled, then landed on the rocks and strutted to the carcass.

White rhino mate and calve throughout the year. As a female is coming into heat a bull does everything it can to keep the cow in its territory. If another male challenges the bull the fighting is always in deadly earnest, the loser frequently dying. Very few bulls escape injuries.

When fighting, the rhino aim their horns behind the foreleg or at the

15. The author firing a dart at a white rhino.

16. Closing in on mother and calf.

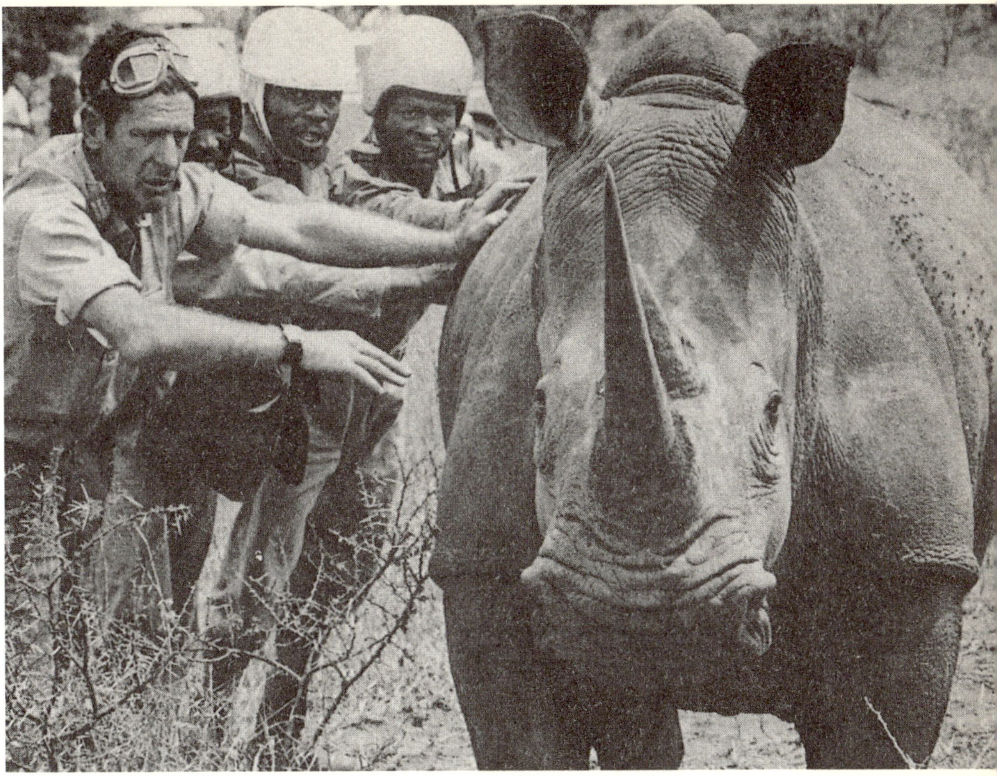

17. John Clark and Game Guards with drugged rhino.

18. 'Hyoscine dilates the pupils'.

base of the neck. They also rush at each other like two huge battering rams on a battlefield of trampled bush and grass. This type of attack leads to extensive internal rupture and haemorrhage which accounts for some dead animals having little sign of external injury. But the majority of antagonists have deep horn punctures in vital organs. If one of the fighting rhino should fall or be knocked over, the other is upon it in a flash to inflict the coup de grace.

No quarter is given and the fighting goes on until one of the combatants runs away. Throughout the fighting, rumbles which rise to screams echo through the bush. The noise attracts other rhino and probably acts as a guide to other males unaware of a female in oestrus. The fight sometimes goes on for hours while the two adversaries charge each other, panting for breath and their whole bodies covered in an amber-coloured sweat.

The triumphant male then moves off with the female who during the fighting indifferently continues grazing. After signifying his intentions by nudging the female in the buttocks the male places his front legs on the female's back and copulates. Some males have been observed to stay mounted for an hour.

The gestation period is sixteen to eighteen months and the cow moves off to thick bush just before giving birth. When the calf is born the pair remain in the same area for a few days. It is during this very early period that the calf will follow the cow if they are disturbed. Once the calf has developed proper co-ordination it always precedes the female, whereas the black rhino calf always follows its dam.

If a cow is not on heat and a bull comes near, the female will charge it and sometimes wound it mortally. The calf frustrates the male by getting in the way of the bull. Sometimes it is killed.

Like most grazers, white rhino spend as much time as possible feeding. Their behaviour during daylight hours is also governed by the weather. On hot, sunny days they move to the shade of trees and bush, usually on ridges where there is a breeze. Here they rest and sleep either lying down or standing up. In the late afternoon they will begin feeding again, and at dusk go to drink from the pans or the rivers, depending upon the season. On a cool day they will continue feeding throughout the day. They avoid the open plains in cold or windy weather, preferring to take cover in the thick bush.

During dry periods, white rhino usually drink once every twenty-four hours, but can go longer without water. In the rainy season there is water in every depression, waterhole, stream, and in the two main rivers. In the winter the pans dry up and only the Black Umfolozi and some of the small secluded streams have water. The White Umfolozi river dries up completely but water can be found just below the surface. Antbear and warthog dig in the bed of the river and the white rhino take advantage of the small holes to drink. The supply does not last long because the bulky rhino soon force sand into the holes and cover them up.

The white rhino bull urinates backwards, the urine squirting out in great sprays between the back legs. Before defecating the tail is curled over the back and when the act is completed a few vigorous scratching movements are made with the hind legs. The black rhino, however, scratches so vigorously it spreads its dung.

White rhino dung heaps are a familiar sight throughout the Umfolozi Game Reserve. Some observers have tried to assert that the rhino return regularly to the same dung heap each day, but the behaviour is not so rigidly determined.

Dung heaps are formed for several reasons. Individuals are stimulated to defecate and urinate by the very presence of a dung heap. Throughout the game reserve there are steep and stony hills. These areas are not inhabited but they are regularly crossed. White rhino (and other animals) always climb by the easiest route, so over the course of time well-worn paths are made. Scattered along the paths are large dung heaps, many of them on the crest of the hills. The long hard climb makes the animal want to defecate. Although they are large, these particular dung heaps are only used infrequently by the passing rhino. Water points have well-worn paths converging from all sides and as long as the water remains, large and regularly used dung heaps are found. In thick bush, the rhino makes paths for protection against heat or cold. Dung heaps litter this type of area. Dung heaps also play a part in territorial demarcation.

White and black rhino sometimes use the same dung heap but there is a big difference in the composition of the dung. The black rhino dung has a slight reddish tinge from eating the nthombothi tree. It is also full of twigs and thorns. The fresh steaming dung of the white rhino is greenish but soon turn a dark brown and becomes chaff.

The dung heaps provide life for an assortment of insects, birds, and animals. The most common of the invertebrates is the dung beetle which can be seen hurrying along the rhino paths rolling a small ball of dung in which it lays its eggs. It is most active after the first spring rains and the dung heaps seem to be alive with heaving and pushing beetles. Harvester termites move along in a continuous stream carrying away undigested grass stems to their nests. A terrestrial species of the *Isopoda* is also common in the dung heaps.

The banded mongoose and other insectivorous mammals move about scratching and feeding. Crowned guineafowl, crested francolins, European rollers, and tchagra shrikes also feed and dust bathe in the heaps. Even the two monitor lizards, *Varanus niloticus* and *V. albigularis* have been seen digging, all proof of nature's continuous cycle.

Chapter 15

Poachers

It took Magqubu a few minutes to get a fire going. I laid out my sleeping bag then collected water with a billycan from a dun-coloured pool. Frogs croaked nearby, first the bullfrog, then the tiny tree frog with its loud rattling cry. In the distance I heard the successive grunts of our lone lion.

'The King is calling for a mate,' Magqubu said and then imitated the loud roars of a lion.

A leopard coughed as though in reply and a jackal took up the refrain with a long drawn-out scream. We sat close to the fire absorbing its warmth. Magqubu cooked sqamba – hard maize meal porridge – and cut thin strips of impala meat which we roasted over the wood coals. The billy boiled over and I threw in a handful of coffee. It was a very simple meal but one I enjoyed more than restaurants in Europe could provide.

Magqubu and I sat talking for hours, his white teeth glinting in the firelight when he laughed. We spoke about poaching.

Poaching had always been a problem but when I first arrived at Umfolozi there were only four game guards to look after an area of seventy-two thousand acres. Poaching gangs fought with each other in the game reserve over the right to hunt in the best places. White poachers roared through the Corridor shooting reedbuck, kudu and other game by dazzling them with lights. It was murder on a large scale. But we persisted and when we caught a few policemen and chased a magistrate, everyone knew we meant business. I was warned that certain local people had started a fund to pay the legal fees for the first man to assault me. There were also some unpleasant social experiences when some people were so angry at their sons getting caught that they spat on the ground when I walked by. It left me unmoved for I had been warned by Colonel Vincent when I joined the service that it would be necessary to have 'a hide as thick as the pachyderms for which we are responsible'.

By winter 1958 we had nearly eliminated white poaching. The new Ordinance, which imposed heavy penalties – the loss of vehicle, rifle, and a fine, and lawyer's fees, left only the diehards.

Tribal Africans, however, were a different story; to them the mere existence of the game reserve was a challenge to their hunting instincts. Magqubu recalled the serious incident he was involved in late that July.

Nick Steele and I had gone out on a patrol to the Nqoloti area. Hugh Dent was with us. We left Magqubu behind on duty at the office ready to rush game guards to any troubled area that a poaching gang might move into.

We walked to the Nqoloti foothills and camped the night near a game path. It was not long before we were rolled in our blankets and asleep. I woke at eleven o'clock to stoke the fire because a cold wet mist was rising from the river. I had just dozed off again when a crocodile grabbed a buck in the Munyawana stream; there was a most fearful scream then a splash. A little later some jackals passed on the opposite bank and set up their alarming yelps. Sleep was impossible. There seemed to be a stream of animals on their way to drink. The fire went out and there was no more wood gathered to stoke it up. I lay shivering for half an hour then dozed off once more. In my half-awake state I thought I heard a vehicle and I wondered if some European was on his way through the southern buffer zone to hunt. I woke with a jerk when a vehicle stopped at the edge of the river on our side. It was our tractor.

I heard voices then saw Ken's young brother, John Tinley, loom into sight.

'What's up, John?' I asked.

He sat down near the fire and said slowly, 'There has been a ghastly mess.'

I waited for him to continue then saw Magqubu, his son Khonamangele, and another game guard, Mnugeni, approach the fire.

'A man has been shot,' John said.

'Dead ?' I asked.

'Yes.'

Hugh and Nick sat up in their sleeping bags and blankets.

'What's up ?' Hugh asked.

'A poacher has been shot at Mcetshwanene,' John said quietly.

'Who did it?' I asked, looking at the guards.

'*Gima nkos* – it was I,' Magqubu answered firmly.

'Thank God for that,' I said aloud. Magqubu was not the sort of person to kill for no good reason.

While Hugh Dent translated, Magqubu described how, after receiving a report, he went out on patrol with Khonamangele and Mnugeni in the Sokwezela area of the game reserve. They saw eight Zulu poachers chasing a family of warthog. The guards stalked them until they were fifty yards away, then they stood up and challenged the poachers. The leader of the gang shouted, 'There are the game guards – let us stab them!'

Magqubu loaded his rifle. Khonamangele rushed in and tried to close with the leader who immediately stabbed at him with his assegai. The point went into Khonamangele's shirt, scraped his body, and came out on the other side. Viewed from behind, it looked to Magqubu as though the spear had gone right through his son's body. Khonamangele fell to the ground and Magqubu rushed at the man he thought was his son's murderer, and they scuffled. The gang leader, a tall, strong Zulu, broke loose, lifted his assegai and stabbed at Magqubu. Magqubu said he was warding off the thrust when his rifle went off. The poacher staggered back and ran towards a small ravine. Magqubu chased him and caught hold of the man as he slipped into the gully. The poacher lay still and Magqubu saw he was dead.

Hugh finished translating and we all sat quietly. A hyena wailed in the distance and the bush stirred for the false dawn. The guards piled wood on the fire and we moved closer for warmth.

I broke the stillness to ask John how long it had taken to reach us.

'Five hours,' he replied.

This was to travel twelve miles, but it was the first time in three years the track had been used. The thought of going back on the tractor was appalling, but there was no other way. We climbed aboard the trailer and rattled into the darkness.

We reached Mpila at seven o'clock and I had to go seven miles to the phone at the old tsetse fly outpost of Masimba. I got in touch with the South African police who said they would come at noon. I returned to Mpila and spent four hours getting statements and going over the points again and again. Magqubu was most distressed and said repeatedly that he would get the rope. I did what I could to reassure him.

'My heart is troubled,' he said. 'I am a Shembe, and it is against my religion to kill human beings.'

The CID detective did not arrive until half past three and it was nearly five o'clock before we reached the donga where the corpse lay. It was not a pleasant sight. The man's hands and legs were stretched out and his eyes were staring.

Magqubu described the whole incident to the detective. His story tallied with footprints, body wound, and everything else. I came away happy that Magqubu's story was obviously true.

The corpse was placed across the fork of a fallen nthombothi log and we walked back to the Land-Rover. The sun had already set and as the guards climbed over the last hill with the log on their shoulders, I watched the corpse's head silhouetted against the fading light. Death is so final.

Nick came up behind, dragging a warthog shoulder. The police and the game guards were horrified. Nick laughed and asked what difference would it make to the meat.

Months later the case was held at Mahlabatini court house. The building of red brick and grey stone had been used as a fort during the Anglo-Boer War. Slots in the upper walls were spaces to rest a rifle. Tall gum trees with strips of peeling bark grew in the grounds. The small flowers of the gum trees attracted bees and there was a steady hum as the insects collected nectar. Groups of Zulu men and women sat in the shade of the trees talking quietly amongst themselves as they waited to see the police or the Bantu Affairs Commissioner. For many of them the court house and its cases were a source of entertainment, a social occasion.

The magistrate came out of his office and the Zulu men rose to greet him. 'Nkoos' (Chief) they said. Magqubu's case was called and he walked into the court room. The case dragged on for hours. Witnesses tried to infer that Magqubu had fired without warning, but his honesty and the direct way he gave his evidence soon convinced the magistrate. One witness contradicted another, and there was a perceptible change in the attitude of the court officials. Even the local Zulus who came to court for entertainment, stirred in their seats. An old, grey-bearded Zulu shook his head.

Brendan Cullinan, the Natal Parks Board legal adviser, summed up the case in concise sentences and asked for Magqubu's acquittal on the charge of culpable homicide.

The magistrate went out. He returned to declare Magqubu not guilty. The interpreter translated and Magqubu lifted his hand in salute to the magistrate.

'*Nkoos, nkoos!*' he said with deep relief, voicing the Zulu term of respect for their elders.

Later in the year Game Guard Ntoyana, a slender man with a sensitive face from the Ngubeni guard camp near the junction of the rivers, came running into Mpila. He told me that while he was on patrol that morning he and the other guards from his camp had seen a group of twelve poachers. Seven of these poachers were armed, five with .303's and two with .22's. At fifty yards range the poachers opened fire. One shot hit the tree Ntoyona was hiding behind. The guards were hopelessly outnumbered so they scrambled down the steep slopes of Iqaqaleimpisi krantz four hundred feet above the White Umfolozi river. The poachers kept on firing and the guards had to run for their lives.

Nick and Ken Rochat were away so I sent Magqubu out to other camps for reinforcements and left immediately on horseback for Ngubeni camp. I had been ill for the past few days with bad stomach trouble, and the ride was a nightmare. Every half mile I had to get off the horse to defecate until I was so weak I could hardly climb into the saddle again.

Fortunately I was riding behind Johannes, the donkey handler. The donkeys were not fast walkers, and Johannes could keep his eyes open for black rhino.

We passed a herd of twenty waterbuck which stood at the side of the track watching us go by. Usually this would have thrilled me, but that day I just kept riding and praying I would last to Ngubeni camp. When we got there I had to tell the guards I could not go out with them. I lay down in one of the huts and fell asleep at once, waking only at intervals when the gripes were too bad.

I got up in the late afternoon with a mass of pepper ticks crawling over my arms, legs, and chest. They dig their heads in and are hard to locate until the bites itch so much you draw blood scratching them, then the sore often turns septic.

I heard the guards splashing through the river when it was dark. I stood up near the fire and they saw me.

'We've caught one,' they shouted jubilantly, and one of them held up a shotgun.

I felt murderous when Ntoyana said he had been shot at again. The guards had seen the man and three others stalking and shooting reedbuck. One of the poachers had a .303 and another had a shotgun. The guards crept along until they were twenty yards away before they charged. Two poachers ran but the man with the shotgun turned round and fired. The guards took off their hats and showed me tiny holes; it was a miracle none of them had a face full of shot. Before he could reload the guards were on top of him and he was beaten to the ground with the butt of a rifle. He grabbed one of the guard's legs, drew a knife and tried to stab, but a kick in the face stunned him temporarily.

The guards removed the knife and were taking off their handcuffs when the poacher came to and grabbed Ntoyana in the genitals. He had to be cracked with a knobstick before he would let go. The others got away.

I looked at the poacher who stood sullenly in the firelight. There was a thin trickle of blood running down his cheek. 'What is your name?' I demanded in Zulu.

'I am an *Mtewa*,' he answered insolently.

One of the guards moved up to hit him but I waved him away.

I told him I understood why he was poaching. Many of his people poached. 'But why do you try to kill my men?' I said.

He looked away.

'This man works for the road grader operator,' Ntoyana said.

Philip, a guard who the following year had half his face blown away by a poacher's bullet, said, 'I gave you meat on Monday, now you come in here and try to steal, and murder a guard. What have we done to you?'

The poacher cleared his throat and spat.

Ntoyana leapt forward and grabbed him by the throat. I jerked him away and said the man was now our prisoner.

We questioned him about his companions; who were they? The firelight flickered on the faces of the guards round me.

Angasi – I don't know,' the poacher replied.

'Do you think we are that stupid?' Ntoyana said. 'You were two people today and one had a .303 rifle. Who was he?"

'A man,' the poacher said.

I had to restrain the guards again.

'You have tried to kill my guards. Do you know the law can hang you for this?' I said.

'It is thick rope they put about your neck, then you never see the sun again,' Ntoyana said softly, with a twisted smile.

The man looked up into the night sky and shrugged his shoulders. I had to admire his courage. Grilling people was not my line at all, and after four hours' questioning I gave up and went to bed.

Late into the night I heard the guards' voices droning monotonously. They were angry at being shot at twice and they were determined to get some information from the prisoner. Bright moonlight filtered through the nthombothi trees where the guards had made their kitchen boma. The reedbuck the poachers had shot swung silently from one of the dark branches, the blood already black and congealed.

Early in the morning I woke with more stomach cramps.

This time I heard the poacher talking and the guards saying '*Ehe!*' and '*Yebo!*'

At first light Ntoyana came to me and reported that they had the names of all the men who had carried fire-arms on the two occasions.' I looked at him and he laughed quietly.

'No, nkosi, we did not beat him – you can come and look for yourself.'

I gave the man some of my coffee and bread.

I was too weak to move until the afternoon when I climbed on to Cherokee, my horse, and rode across the river to look at the attempted murder sites. We found one of the game guard's hats where it had fallen when they fled. The tree Ntoyana had hidden behind was barely three inches thick. The bullet had only just been deflected; a millimetre more and Ntoyana would have been killed. I made sketches, paced out the distance then rode slowly back to Mpila.

The South African police located all the fire-arms and the owners were charged. The poacher with the shotgun got off a charge of attempted murder but was found guilty of assault with intent to do grievous bodily harm. For a few months the area was quiet, but poaching trouble started up in another area.

I first saw him in 1952 and old man Foster, who understood the Zulus, said, 'There's a good man.'

Philip Mtetwa was the best man who ever worked on the fenceline. Nothing was too much trouble for him. He would gladly run back a mile to fetch a forgotten pair of pliers, or stay at the camp and make tea, or act as a bearer. It was only in 1958 that he shyly approached me and asked to join the game guard force. I took him on immediately. Tall and slenderly built as he was, he always looked smart in his pressed khaki uniform. He knew bushcraft too, and before long caught an impressive number of poachers, soon qualifying for his laurel wreath, the game guard award for capturing a poacher's rifle. It was always a pleasure to see his handsome smiling face and the pride he took in his work. I looked forward to seeing him on the next pay day. I wanted to promote him to corporal.

But at eight o'clock on the night of the 23 April Game Guards Mzulwini and Msikeni ran twelve miles from Domba camp to report that they had been attacked by poachers and Philip Mtetwa had been shot in the face. George Duby of the South African Tourist Corporation was with me at the time, and I gladly accepted his offer of help.

I gathered a few medical supplies, filled my Land-Rover and made for Domba camp near the junction of the two Umfolozi rivers. The track had deteriorated badly and it took three hours to reach the guard camp. We left the Land-Rover and crossed the White Umfolozi on foot. The two guards guided me to three men huddled round a fire. Philip was lying near them, covered in an army coat. He was in an extremely bad way, half his face a raw wound. He was saturated in blood and moaning for a drink of water. It was obvious that only immediate hospitalisation would save his life. I did my best to stop further bleeding then had him carried to the vehicle. He moaned at every jolt on the unimaginably rough track. We made slow time until we reached the main gravel road then I drove over the Black Umfolozi river causeway. The splashing sounds made Philip ask again for water – '*amanzi, amanzi*,' he cried. I stopped and scooped some in a hat, he sucked at the water in dreadful agony. We drove through the darkness up into the Hlabisa hills, and reached the hospital at two o'clock in the morning.

An African nurse asked if the case was serious enough for her to call the doctor. I drew the overcoat back and let her look at Philip. She ran to the phone. Dr Hall, the mission doctor, came into the foyer looking drawn and tired. After his examination he said he did not hold out much hope that Philip would live, but that he would do his best.

Before he left for the operating theatre Philip croaked a request. Game Guard Msikeni leant over him.

'What is it?' I asked.

'Philip asks that his little boy be brought to see him in case he should die.'

I promised to have the youngster sent for at first light.

Dr Hall roused another medical man and they operated until after dawn. They told me that Philip would live but would be terribly mutilated. One eye had gone as well as most of one ear. They could not tell what damage there was to the brain.

When he was wheeled into a ward, I sat on a chair next to his bed. The part of his face that remained was drained of its usual black glossy healthy look. He breathed slowly with little choking noises in his throat. I held his hand and whispered in Zulu that he was my friend and a man. An hour passed before he came round from the anaesthetic.

He called out a name. I told him Madolo was with him. He stiffened in an attempt to salute then murmured my name, 'Yebo Madolo, yebo Madolo.' I found it hard not to cry.

When we got back to the game reserve the other guards told me what had happened the night before.

On the Wednesday evening a group of poachers slipped across the White Umfolozi river. They waited until it was dark then began shooting in the dense riverine forest at the junction of the two rivers. The game guards heard the shots but there was no hope of finding anyone in that tangle of bush, so they waited until the following morning. Before first light they crossed the river at Domba and went quietly along the game path through the reeds. They climbed the highest point in the southern buffer zone, known as Ciyane. Here they waited.

They had barely settled themselves in the lush red grass when a shot was fired in the game reserve. They knew the main footpath from the reserve came up the Iqaqaleimpisi (Ridge of the Hyena) so, led by their corporal Anias, they ran to the ridge where they planned to ambush the poachers in a narrow defile. It was not until after midday that they saw ten poachers splashing across the Umfolozi river. Some were armed and the others were carrying game meat tied to poles.

The hunters stopped in the southern buffer zone and made a fire. They obviously thought they were safe. The guards could see the smoke rising above the reeds. If they had known how long it would be before the poachers moved they would have sent for reinforcements from the Makamisa camp, but as the poachers were well armed, they were reluctant to reduce their own numbers.

The shadows of the April afternoon were growing longer when the poachers left their small fire and started up the footpath of the Iqaqaleimpisi. Corporal Anias peered over a boulder and saw that four men were armed, with one .22, one .303, a Martini Henry lever action rifle, and a shotgun. The other six poachers were carrying the meat. Anias noted a reedbuck and a bushbuck among the carcasses, both specially protected animals. Just before the top of the ridge and a short distance from where an attempt was made on Game Guard Ntoyana's life a few months previously, the poachers stopped. They hesitated and spoke hurriedly to one another, then the men with the meat started off in a northerly direction.

The guards stood up and challenged the hunters. The four armed men came forward and the one with a .303 rifle aimed and fired at Game Guard Mdiceni. The bullet hit a rock and ricocheted among the guards. Then Philip Mtetwa shouted a warning, telling them not to be fools. They kept on coming and Philip fired a shot but he had been shaken by the unprovoked attack and his bullet went wide. The poachers ducked into the bush fringing the path and opened fire at random with all their weapons. Philip who was out in the open was shot in the face before he could take cover.

Anias fired back, and this time he meant to kill. The guards kept on firing until the poachers retreated. They could not follow with Philip lying badly wounded in a pool of blood. They helped him down to the river. By now it was dark and Mzulwini and Msikeni ran the twelve miles to Mpila.

Major Curt von Keyserlingk, the District Commandant of Police at Eshowe, came to the actual scene of the shooting so that he could have first hand knowledge of the whole affair. There were not many senior men who would have taken the trouble.

Sergeant Charles Marais of Empangeni, the best detective in Zululand, was assigned to the case. Six days after the incident he sent me a note saying he had arrested all ten poachers. Four firearms were also recovered. Although a charge of attempted murder was brought against one of the poachers he was found not guilty. This was a hard blow but there could be no dispute with the court.

At the end of my report to Colonel Vincent I said that more bad poaching was expected since the drought had ruined crops. I pleaded again for radio; we could never really combat poaching until we had proper communications. Colonel Vincent wrote persistently to the Postmaster General and eventually got permission for our radio link up. We were equipped with radio before many other civil service departments. It came in time to save the lives of many guards, and it seems impossible that we ever managed without it.

Philip Mtetwa was in hospital for a long time and when he was temporarily released I sent a driver to take him to his kraal to recuperate. Six months passed before we met again. Then one morning on my way to the office, a bent figure walked down the path. He stopped a few yards from me and saluted. It was Philip, his face unrecognizable. He greeted me, trying hard to hold himself erect. I asked him how he was and he replied stiffly and correctly. While we stood there other guards and labourers passed us, and quietly greeted him, '*Sabona* Mtetwa,' (I see you Mtetwa).

Philip replied softly each time, '*Yebo*,' (Yes, I see you too).

We walked to my office and he told me of the continuous pain, the throbbing headaches and the constant dizzy spells. He could not concentrate and kept on pathetically apologising for his inability to hear properly. It was a blazing hot day but he kept his heavy khaki overcoat on, because he felt cold. He was obviously troubled by something else and I pressed him gently to tell me what it was.

Would I continue to employ him as a guard? he asked. He needed the money to feed and educate his son.

I explained that there was no need to worry, that he had a lifetime of service, that he was one of us and we would always look after him. He sobbed quietly.

It was eighteen months before he could work again. He had a job on the wilderness trails on full game guard salary. He did his work faithfully and with the old conscientiousness, but there were days when he had bad spells. The blast from the bullet had affected part of his brain, but he insisted on working for another nine years. Hundreds of wilderness trailers met this slim, quiet man who was always courteous. He would sit huddled near the burning nthombothi logs and talk without malice of the men who shot and disfigured him for life.

In early 1970 he asked me diffidently whether he could now go on pension. With the courage and loyalty of men like Philip Mtetwa, I thought, the wilderness of Umfolozi Game Reserve would always be safe.

CHAPTER 16

Squatters

The first squatters moved into the western buffer zone in October 1944. Two huts were built near the Hlungwana river. I reported this immediately to the magistrate. He said he could do nothing because the land was under the control of the Lands Department. Colonel Vincent took the matter up with the Lands Department in Pietermaritzburg but was told that the Bantu Affairs Department was responsible – the usual departmental buck passing. For us it was the beginning of a long struggle, with the future of Umfolozi Game Reserve and the white rhino in the balance.

With the coming of the squatters, poaching increased a hundred fold. The game guard picquet stationed at Madhlozi (The Place of the Spirits) reported that a group of thirty men had been hunting along the Mtunzini hills. They wiped out an entire herd of mountain reedbuck.

Our relations with most magistrates and some members of the junior ranks of the police were not good in those early days. They considered our cases trivial and, after the game extermination campaigns, they were sceptical about our protective activities. The public prosecutors said our guards gave poor evidence. This was true at times, but mistakes occurred through incorrect or slovenly interpretation by African court interpreters, who were hostile to conservation. They made the guards look untruthful and stupid and this irritated the magistrate, who then imposed fines which were ridiculously low, such as R1 or one week for serious offences.

By the early part of 1956 the whole west bank of the Hlungwana river was occupied and fields had encroached onto the eastern side. The position worsened because some officials turned a blind eye to the infiltration. So the squatters continued to pour in with their cattle. The land west of Mtunzini hill deteriorated quickly. The squatters chopped down trees, ploughed up and down hills, and planted mealies (maize) and sorghum.

When I remonstrated with one magistrate he acidly replied, 'But good God, man, these people have to eat.'

'Quite right,' I replied. 'But their grandchildren will be eating stones if you don't take the trouble to understand land management principles.'

Our interest was not altruistic. We knew that when crops failed in the inevitable drought, poachers would stream into the reserve. In fact the future of the game reserves was bound up with the way the Bantu Affairs Department tackled its urgent land management problems. In some of the tribal areas adjoining the game reserve, soil erosion and overstocking were obvious. Officials would gloss over this, but should a rhino or a hippo wander through a mealie field, these same men would create an uproar.

Some magistrates were aware of the serious land problem, and they tried to get more staff to teach the tribesmen contour ploughing and soil conservation methods. It was a losing battle. Every year more cattle and goats were brought into the area and tons of valuable topsoil went down the Umfolozi rivers to the sea. There was very little chance of ever putting it right until there was a complete change in land management.

In 1956 it was already a proven fact that lowveld areas next to the game reserve could, in terms of game, provide more protein than cattle. But this was not acknowledged. In fact most Bantu Affairs Department officials laughed loudly when I suggested a tribal hunting area next to the game reserve, yet such an area would have been an outlet for the hunting instincts of the tribesmen and would have at the same time provided valuable protein. It could have been continually restocked by the overflow of game from the reserves. Instead, squatters were allowed to fill the vacuum.

I had much sympathy for many of the squatters who were victims of forces which they did not understand. Overpopulation on farms and some badly eroded African tribal lands incapable of carrying more people caused the exodus. Then, too, they were being exploited by their own people who charged exorbitant sums for permission to squat in other tribal areas. It was a sad, serious, and complex question, but my duty was clear. I had to try to save the last white rhino habitat from being overrun by human beings and their stock.

We very nearly lost the fight because of the weight of numbers against us. In no time two-thirds of the former southern and western buffer zones was inhabited by the squatters, a solid phalanx of humanity circling the last sanctuary of the white rhinoceros.

I could foresee great bitterness which in the end could erupt into violence, but officialdom as always followed the line of least resistance. The root cause – overpopulation – was overlooked because it was expedient to do so.

I had been away for two years. On the morning of my return in May 1958 I looked out from the house and saw that the squatters had now reached the Mandhlagazi footpath boundary. More squatters came in daily, encouraged by some chiefs, and they arrived on foot, by bicycle, car and bus. Some came from Msinga, an area of tribal unrest even when Natal was a British Colony. These warlike people infiltrated the ranks of the local tribesmen and had their own aggressive indunas appointed.

There had been drastic changes to the veld. Where once redgrass stretched for miles there was now soil erosion. Trees were being hacked down and livestock grazed in the game reserve.

The years went by. We watched the land daily and saw in the changing ecological conditions a clear warning that bad land management and squatter explosion meant the loss of valuable top soil.

To have the squatters removed was a continuous struggle. Colonel Vincent tried to get various senior officials to take action and Mr Douglas Mitchell, M.P., pursued the matter in Cape Town with cabinet ministers. I never lost an opportunity of lobbying anyone who would listen to me. Many times I stressed to Bantu Affairs Department men that it was their responsibility to see that the land was properly cared for, but they were so wrapped up in the tribal structures and personal problems of the African that they could not see the deterioration in the land.

In December 1960 I met the magistrate from Mahlabatini and a representative from the Department of Lands. It had taken nearly two years of phoning, writing, and personal visits to get people to agree to meet and view the problem *in situ*. We stood on the slopes of Mtunzini hill and looked at the squatter huts which were still springing up like mushrooms after rain. New lands were being ploughed in the heart of the rhino range. Two days before I had come across a group of squatters a mile inside the 1897 boundary of the game reserve. I chased them out at the point of a gun.

This had been reported to the magistrate and he now took me to task. Indecision, I said, was going to cause endless trouble and possible bloodshed. I explained that informers had told us that the local chief was accepting bribes and allowing more warlike tribesmen from the Msinga district into the area. Our game guards had been threatened and told that it would take not one, but five hundred policemen to move the squatters. There were rumours of a hunt that would wipe out every wild animal on the Ukuku ridge. It was said that the hunters would storm into the game reserve and burn down the Thobothi guard camp and rangers post. It was vital that the boundaries of the game reserve be resolved. Privately both officials agreed with me but each blamed the other department for the indecision. It had been this way since 1955.

As I drove back towards Mpila camp I saw a pair of white rhino bulls grazing near a hut. Some dogs appeared and the rhino rushed across the boundary road into the game reserve. Minutes later a herd of cattle came pouring over the skyline near Ntaba-amanini. I wondered how many were diseased.

The situation deteriorated even further when squatters penetrated deep into the southern buffer zone. Huts were built on Mdindini fist below Mpila camp. I rode out with Owen Letley one morning to see the infiltration. It looked hopeless. We rode to the Mahlabamvu ridge and saw huts going up all over the country. Senior Game Guard Mzwabantu Masuku rode with us and he pointed out cane knife marks on trees indicating the beginning of a kraal site. Some tribesmen had crossed the White Umfolozi river and staked out areas inside the reserve at Dadethu pan.

To us the issue was clear. Other land had to be made available for the squatters and part of the buffer strips must be proclaimed game reserve if Umfolozi was to survive. Mdindini fist was like a dagger pointing into the heart of the Umfolozi Reserve. Future control was impossible if the squatters occupied it.

On one occasion Owen and I heard chopping in the Maunzi bush. We found two squatters cutting hut poles. They were miserable looking, unfortunate men, pushed out of their homes, and they were hostile and refused to listen when we told them to move out.

We rode away from them. I wondered desperately what to do. I felt sick and depressed about the whole business, worse than I had ever been. The guards were depressed too, and moved listlessly ahead of us. Only Mzwabantu Masuku, Nick's head game guard, looked expectant. He seemed to be hoping I would be able to do something.

We rode for miles. Everywhere it was the same story: squatters moving in.

'We can't sit back and let this happen,' Owen said despondently that night.

We camped on the White Umfolozi sands at Makamisa. We sat for hours staring into the campfire as the guards talked quietly about the day's events.

'Surely if we had some sort of demarcation we could keep these people on the other side of the line,' Owen said.

So was born the idea of putting in a road. There could be little departmental objection and it would give us a breathing spell.

We saddled up early next morning and rode back to Mpila camp. The road and a newspaper campaign might have results, I thought, and I decided to see Colonel Vincent who was at Lake St Lucia with some VIPs. He appreciated how urgent it was. We got in touch with the *Natal Mercury* who sent one of their best reporters up the following day. The Colonel agreed to phone Major von Keyserlingk and ask him to try to prevent further infiltration.

'Have no fear,' the Colonel said reassuringly. 'We will leave no stone unturned to bring attention to this business.'

I returned to Umfolozi feeling much happier.

On the tenth day of July the Roads Maintenance Officer began the new road. On the eleventh Nick Steele reported over the radio that the road from Mfuyeni stream to the junction of the Umfolozis at Siyembeni had been completed and the squatters were moving south of the road. A group of squatters had asked the guards why the road was being graded. The guards said the army was coming to throw them out. It was effective propaganda.

The newspapers were making the most of the situation and the *Christian Science Monitor* representative came for a story. 'History Corners the White Rhino' appeared in his paper on 10 August 1961, and it was one of the fairest newspaper articles that had appeared on the whole problem.

I was called to Pietermaritzburg by Colonel Vincent who told me that negotiations were under way with government officials and that we would be getting only a portion of the western and southern state owned lands.

'If they don't act with the squatters, there will be even less, I suppose,' the Colonel said.

While we were talking Norman Deane phoned from Hluhluwe Game Reserve. There had been four black rhino deaths and he suspected anthrax. Later some paralysed nyala and crows were brought in and there was a suspicion that the waterholes had been poisoned.

'And some people think we have no problems,' the Colonel said.

This bad news upset our morning and we discussed it until Mr Douglas Mitchell arrived. He was taking up the squatter question with the Minister of Bantu Affairs, and he wanted more information from the Colonel.

On 8 September 1961 I noted in my diary, 'There is a smell of drought and trouble in the air.' Nick had called up in the morning to say that squatters were once again pouring into the southern buffer zone. 'So far they haven't crossed our road but one tin shack is being built right on it,' he said.

I told Nick to chase them off in any way he could, before they did any more building. We were barely holding our own, and the future didn't look good.

Within a month more squatters had come into the western and southern buffer zones and there were rumours of a big raid that was going to sweep right to Thobothi and Mbuzane camps.

All through the month we heard of a big hunt that was going to take place in the western buffer zone and penetrate into the game reserve. Guards were warned that anyone trying to stop the hunt would be dealt with.

On 5 May Owen Letley radioed me urgently. He had just received news from an informer that the poaching mob would be hunting the following day, 'Three hundred of them,' he said.

That afternoon a message came from the South African police at Mahlabatini. We must expect trouble the following day, they said. They would be arriving at nine o'clock.

We had to prepare. I phoned Paul Dutton at Charters Creek and told him to bring John Tinley to Umfolozi Game Reserve. Then I got in touch with the Chief Conservator, Peter Potter, and asked that Bob Murray, one other ranger, and three armed guards each with twenty rounds of ammunition be sent to Umfolozi immediately. I spoke to Hugh Dent, the Wilderness Trails Officer, and asked him to come with me, as it looked serious, and it might be vital to have a fluent Zulu linguist with us. Hugh made arrangements to hand over his wilderness trail to John Clark.

At nine o'clock I gave out ammunition to game guards and supervised the loading of the Land-Rovers.

Paul Dutton, John Tinley, Bob Murray and Garth Carpenter arrived at half past nine. I explained everything to them, emphasising the need for restraint and discipline amongst the guards. We had to make it clear that our aim was to prevent trouble, not to cause it.

We left for the Madhlozi guard camp on the western edge of the game reserve at ten o'clock, and drove without lights from the Mpafa stream. A jackal and two white rhino crossed the road and a nightjar appropriately chanted its 'Good Lord deliver us' dirge.

As we offloaded our bedrolls at the guard camp there was a strong smell of maize meal, boiling coffee, and woodsmoke. It brought back memories. In 1953 I had camped here because of the mviti tree (*Boscia albitrunca*). The guards had taught me how to make coffee from its roots, a good standby for a young bachelor. Later, in 1955, I had established the game guard camp. This was the heart of the white rhino range and there had been no protection along the seventeen mile western boundary. It became our taking off point when we patrolled the western buffer zone.

We sat round the fire for a while and spoke to the guards of the Madhlozi camp. They had heard about the impending raid from some women who were cutting grass near the western tourist road.

We turned in early. There was going to be a long day ahead.

At four o'clock in the morning of 6 May I sent Graham Thomson and an armed guard to the top of Sokwezela hill with a portable radio. They were to report every quarter-hour.

At half past five we paraded the game guards. We told them that no shot was to be fired, even at a dog, until they were given an order. Game Guard Gqakaza Ntombela, a short, well-built man, gazed at me under his heavy eyelids and smiled slowly. Like his famous relative Magqubu Ntombela, he was a tough person.

'I pity anyone who gets in his way,' Paul Dutton said.

At six o'clock Peter Potter flew over Madhlozi camp in a light aircraft with Boet Badenhorst, a local sugar farmer. I spoke to him on the radio.

'We're over Ukuku now,' Peter Potter said. 'But there's no gathering anywhere.'

He contacted control at Mpila a little later – he had just seen six tribesmen on the south bank of the Black Umfolozi. Then his radio went dead.

At eight o'clock Graham Thomson on Sokwezela hill reported that two shots had been fired in the Mcetshwanene area near the Black Umfolozi river. We went by Land-Rover to a ridge overlooking the area. We stopped to listen and soon heard a .303 rifle shot.

'So they've got rifles too,' John Tinley grunted.

Another shot went off just north of us.

'*Ngebe* – a shotgun,' Magqubu said.

At nine o'clock six tribesmen appeared on the hill opposite us, moving slowly northwards.

Fifteen minutes later Graham Thomson's voice crackled over the radio. 'I can see a group coming down the Ukuku ridge,' he said.

Bob Murray pointed them out. There were thirty-seven.

A five-minute silence was broken by more shotgun blasts and we saw over fifty men moving slowly along a ravine northwards. It looked worse than I had expected.

'This doesn't look too good,' Paul Dutton said calmly.

I looked at the men around me, these rangers and guards. God forbid that any of them should get hurt.

'Norman Deane will be cursing that he wasn't here today,' Bob Murray said. 'So will Nick Steele.'

'There's still plenty of time,' I said. 'Nick will be here this afternoon.'

Head Constable van Zyl of the South African police at Mahlabatini joined us at half past nine. I was very pleased to see him. We had first met some years ago at Ndumu when I was ranger in charge of the game reserve. He was one of the fairest policemen I had met, always restrained, and the Zulus respected him for his bearing and manner. I explained what had happened so far, then pointed out the various poaching parties.

Soon Graham Thomson was on the air. More men had been seen moving down the Ukuku hills. Owen Letley and Adriaan Erasmus went forward two hundred yards to a high vantage point. Just after ten o'clock we heard more shots. A lone man on horseback came down the proposed boundary ridge.

'That must be the Chief,' Hugh Dent said, pointing.

Almost at once four tribesmen came out of a patch of bush. Two were armed with rifles. Five minutes later we saw two more armed Africans. The noise of massing men was on the increase. Dogs began barking and there was a scream.

'*Mpunzi* – a grey duiker,' Magqubu said.

'I think we had better send a message to the District Commandant at Eshowe and to the Hlabisa police,' Van Zyl said.

I called up the radio operator at Mpila from my Land-Rover and asked him to send for John Kinloch, the imperturbable camp superintendent. Van Zyl dictated his message slowly. John Kinloch repeated each line.

'To District Commandant, Eshowe. One hundred and fifty Bantu near

Black Umfolozi in western crown lands. Bantu are approaching us. Seven shots have been fired at game by Bantu hunters. We have eight white rangers, two white South African police, two Bantu South African police constables, four revolvers, and one sten gun. We are watching the situation. They are now one point five miles from us. Would request police be on standby but no assistance required yet.'

Another message was sent to the Hlabisa police:

'Please come immediately fully armed to Umfolozi Game Reserve.'

The sergeant at Hlabisa was out in the Land-Rover and was not expected back until the afternoon. So the Mtubatuba police were contacted and they promised to send out a party as soon as possible.

While these messages were being passed, Peter Potter arrived by vehicle. He had landed at Mtubatuba when the radio gave in. He was given a rifle and joined the party.

By eleven o'clock the early morning mists had gone and a heat haze was spreading over the hills. Game guards took their dark khaki overcoats off and wrapped them into bundles. Some smoked while others chatted and laughed. Magqubu sat a little apart, staring towards the dry hills already changing to their winter colours.

'What do you think, Magqubu?' John Tinley asked.

'It can be very bad,' he said flatly. 'These people want trouble and will not listen today.'

Van Zyl said, 'Let's move down the road, get onto that Mcetshwanene track and try to arrest some of these people.'

Five minutes later we were a few hundred yards away from the mob. We parked on a slight slope in a bad section of the road enclosed by thick bush.

'This is unhealthy,' Paul Dutton commented dryly.

Poachers' dogs were running round near us. I nodded to Game Guard Gqakaza and he shot two with his .303. There was a sudden hush, then a cry rose from the main mob. Three men, one carrying a bushbuck doe with its throat cut, passed close to us.

'Shout to them to come here,' I said to Hugh Dent.

Hugh called to them but they ignored him and ran to the main group in the bush. By this time rangers, game guards and police were all out of the vehicles and milling around. If we were going to be attacked we were in a vulnerable position.

The poachers began chanting and stamping their feet, and there were loud cries of '*ozana ngamandhla*' (gather in strength). Whistles blew and the chanting grew louder. I had a quick discussion with Peter Potter and Van Zyl, and we decided to withdraw as we could be attacked at any minute.

Our new position was unsatisfactory, but better. We formed the vehicles into a rough laager with the men in the hollow space. But I knew we could not repel the poachers if they attacked us in a body: they were hidden from us in the ravine below by the dense bush which lay sixty yards beyond our chosen flat piece of ground.

The mob had grown to two hundred or more and the noise was rising. The slight north wind which had been blowing earlier had stopped, so sound carried far and we could hear their threats. I was very worried; worried for the game reserve and the adverse publicity which could wreck years of hard work; worried because I felt lives lay in the balance of a decision.

Our position was not at all safe and we had made no plan about when to open fire. Peter Potter and I talked to Head Constable van Zyl and we quickly agreed we would fire only if we were attacked in force.

By now the chanting of the mob had deepened and they were so close to us we could hear clearly the Zulu phrase, 'The burning hills, the smoking fires; we defeat them by being fully armed,' repeated again and again. This was like Isandlwana. These men were worked up to kill.

'Let's get to another position and wait for reinforcements,' Van Zyl said.

The familiar phrase was reassuring, and we moved to just below Sokwezela hill where we collected Graham Thomson from his observation post.

Van Zyl sent a message to the District Commandant, Major von Keyserlingk, at Eshowe: 'We're about to be attacked by two hundred plus Bantu. Have withdrawn to another position.'

Peter Potter suggested he should go back to Mtubatuba and fly over the area again with Boet Badenhorst. I agreed, and this move probably saved our lives.

At a quarter past one the Mtubatuba police – three Europeans and some Zulu constables – arrived. Nick Steele returned from leave and joined us immediately. It was good to see him.

Soon after two o'clock we had a radio message from Mpila to say that the Hlabisa police were on their way, and that Peter Potter and Boet Badenhorst were about to take off.

I heard more rifle shots and the thump of a bullet striking a body. A lot of game was being killed. Then we heard the yelping of dogs in full chase. I searched the nearby hills with binoculars and picked up at least ten dogs streaking after a kudu bull. The kudu ran full tilt along a ridge, laying its horns back as it ran beneath thorn trees. Some poachers burst out of the bush. One aimed, and seconds later came the report. The kudu turned east, making for the game reserve. One lean, greyhound type dog had kept up with it. I fired at the dog, using a .375 telescopic sight. The bullet whacked the ground in front of it, so that it veered off and the kudu disappeared into the bush.

At half past three the light plane flew overhead and I spoke to Peter Potter on the radio.

'The poachers are breaking up and moving off,' he said. I asked him to get the pilot to dive on the biggest group to show us their position.

The light plane banked steeply and dived towards a patch of bush, swooped up then dived at the same spot. Rangers, police, and game guards ran in the direction of the bush.

'There's a huge mob now,' Peter Potter shouted anxiously, his voice fading in the howling of the aeroplane.

By the time I had finished speaking to him, some men were over a mile ahead. I ran after them but going up the steep hill along a narrow footpath soon tired me. I caught up with Sergeant Spammer of the Mahlabatini police who had run out of breath and was resting at the foot of Mcetshwanene hill. Together we hastily searched nearby squatter kraals; hardly one did not contain at least half a dozen game skins, mostly of mountain reedbuck, one of the rarest antelope in Zululand.

We heard the aircraft zooming and its engines whining in a dive; it was concentrating on one spot. Sergeant Spammer and I climbed to the top of Mcetshwanene and in the distance, on the slopes of Ukuku hills, we could see a big crowd of Zulus with some guards and rangers near them. The plane was sweeping low over the crowd, again and again. It was obvious that they were doing their best to break up the dangerous mob.

I remembered an old track leading to the ridge where the Zulus and our men were, so Sergeant Spammer and I ran back to the Land-Rovers. It was a mile-long, exhausting run, but we had to join our people on the hill. Some policemen who had not been able to keep up with the younger rangers had also returned to the Land-Rovers. I gathered everyone together and we raced down the Black Umfolozi track, round the back of Mcetshwanene hill and up the southern ridge of Ukuku, somehow without knocking out the sump or breaking a spring.

We could find only a few stragglers. Inwardly I had a horrible fear that our men on top of the hill had been slaughtered that afternoon. We searched and shouted, and fired shots into the air, but there was no answering sound to break the stillness. Any moment I expected to stumble on a heap of bodies. Darkness was coming swiftly. I strained to hear a human shout or whisper, but only a jackal screamed. It was too dark to search any more, and we stumbled back to the Land-Rover. Suddenly, out of a nearby bush, a lone Zulu broke and ran. I could just see his tall, lithe body, naked except for his bechu and bead bracelets, leaping, jumping, and running over boulders into the gloom. We shouted at him, hopelessly.

In the darkness it took nearly an hour to get down the track we had sped up earlier. We met Graham Thomson and Magqubu, who had come to call us. Everyone had returned safely. Nick Steele told me that he, Hugh Dent, Garth Carpenter, a European police constable, and some guards led by Magqubu, had caught up with the main mob of poachers.

'We saw we were in a dangerous situation,' Nick said. 'One wrong move and there would have been a lot of killing. I called Hugh Dent forward and we handed our rifles to someone to hold and walked forward. The Chief saw us and did the same thing. The Chief said they had no intention of letting themselves be arrested.'

While they were talking Owen Letley came forward and said that a police party under Major von Keyserlingk was on its way. Owen suggested that the mob sat down and awaited their coming. But the mob would have none of this. The plane kept swooping overhead, and this probably prevented a massacre. Nick's and Hugh's bravery in going forward unarmed also made a great impression on the crowd.

Later Magqubu told me, 'When our two white men went forward, I slipped a bullet into the breech of my rifle. If anyone had lifted a hand, I would have shot the Chief dead and then kept shooting until I was killed.'

Major von Keyserlingk, one of South Africa's finest policemen, arrived later that evening with a strong force of South African policemen. His father was a policeman, first in the Natal Colonial police and subsequently in the South African police. Major von Keyserlingk had served with distinction in the 1939-45 War, and was respected by the black and the white people of Zululand. He decided to have a show of force in the area.

Two days later Head Constable van Zyl spoke to me on the radio. He said they had caught forty men and taken possession of four fire-arms, many assegais, and much game meat and skins. He asked me to contact the Bantu Affairs Commissioner at Mahlabatini and ask for a three-ton lorry to be sent to a nearby dipping tank to collect the prisoners.

The Commissioner was horrified. He had had enough of this trouble over the crown lands, he said. He asked that I stress the urgency of settling the crown lands affair.

'We have been doing that for nine years,' I said.

The massed raid made its impact in official circles and it was at last realised that the situation was getting out of hand. Something had to be done to settle the boundary question.

Another year passed before it was settled, and then the tribesmen got three-quarters of the available land. But the quarter allocated to the game reserve enabled us to put up one of the finest game-proof fences in the world.

But this is running ahead of the story.

My report to Colonel Vincent ended : 'With the extremely important high density rhino range bordering the trouble areas, indescribable havoc would be caused if a mob as large as Saturday's actually penetrated the game reserve.'

On 26 June 1962 a big force of police and military moved into the western area of the Umfolozi Game Reserve to begin the removal of the squatters who were now five thousand strong. High ranking police, military, Lands and Bantu Affairs Departmental personnel directed the removal. Curt von Keyserlingk, now a Lieutenant-Colonel, was in charge of the field forces. The Zulus knew and respected him and when he warned them that any violence would not be tolerated, all opposition crumbled away.

That night a long convoy of police and army vehicles rumbled through the reserve and the next day huts next to our boundary were demolished and the people removed to a settlement on the Ukuku hills. It was the end of the squatter problem we had struggled against for nearly six years.

The ridge of Mtunzini hill, part of Unoma, and the Ukuku were added to the Umfolozi Game Reserve and later proclaimed, in area only ten thousand acres, but a vital part of the rhino range. While squatters dominated the heights the guards could never go out on patrol without being seen. A week after everyone had gone I saw a rhino cow and four mountain reedbuck feeding on the skyline of Mtunzini, safely in the reserve.

This sight alone was sufficient reward for all the talking, writing letters and lobbying people, the countless dinners we had given, trying to persuade persons of varying influence how important the western and southern buffer zones were to the saving of the white rhino and Umfolozi Game Reserve.

As the mountain reedbuck, their russet colouring blending so perfectly with the landscape, stalked along the path, I saw before me the long parade of men I had spoken to. The petty politicians – some who said that soil erosion was God's will and if the rhino became extinct it did not matter. The officials from Government departments in the flush of liquor making vain promises and others cruelly taunting us with threats of taking all the land away from the game. I experienced again the violent anger repressed into a smile and offers of more wine, of biltong or of views to be seen, whereas all the while I wanted to smash my fist into their miserable uncomprehending faces, grab them by the throat and shake some sense into their thick heads; tell them how I had seen rangers work day and night, prepared to give their lives to the cause of the Umfolozi Game Reserve and the white rhino, prepared to die for a piece of land they could never own, prepared to be maimed or blinded, not for a pittance of a salary but for love.

Well, dedication and honesty of purpose had paid off. We now had just enough land to ensure the survival of the game reserve. In an emotional gesture I saluted the reedbuck and the rhino and said aloud we had done our best for them – it might have been silly but it made me feel happy.

A little while later I sent Nick Steele a copy of Proclamation No. 53 of 1962, the official legislation entrusting the land to our care. A game guard in a clean khaki uniform and mounted on a well-groomed horse took him the document in a pouch.

Nick sent a note back: 'I can hardly bring myself to believe that after years of the most terrible suspense this land and its wild life are safe in the hands of conservation.'

CHAPTER 17

Repopulating the Kruger Park

The capture of rhino for Kruger Park was due to start on 3 October. It would be an historic occasion.

The last white rhino in the Kruger Park had been shot in 1896 and for the past forty years there had been talk of re-establishing a herd. The American scientist, Dr Herbert Lang, recommended in a report to the South African Government in 1925 that two separate colonies be transferred to the Kruger National Park, but advised that 'the Zululand troops should not be weakened or even frightened, yet enough rhinoceroses should be transferred for breeding purposes'.

Various capture methods such as nets and pits were considered. Nothing came of the suggestions and as time passed, they were deliberately forgotten. The Natal Provincial Administration had realised that the white rhino was a trump card in preventing any deproclamation of Umfolozi Game Reserve.

In the 1940's two young white rhino – Zuluana and Dengezi – were caught with ropes and taken to the Pretoria Zoo, otherwise no white rhino had left Umfolozi Game Reserve.

Among some of the staff there was still a lingering fear that if the white rhino were taken to Kruger Park our game reserve would be lost. I pointed out that the publicity following the capture of rhino would forever ensure the survival of Umfolozi Game Reserve, as it would be regarded as a reservoir for restocking all former white rhino habitats from the Cape to the Zambezi. The four going to the Kruger Park were only the beginning, but it was important that they arrived alive, as it was the first public demonstration of translocation.

The distance to the Kruger Park was over three hundred miles so I decided to catch the rhino, tame them down in the bomas then crate and transport them by truck.

But first I had to select a site and build the bomas.

One afternoon when the white blossomed *Acacia gerrardi* were coming into flower and their lovely scent hung in the air, I drove slowly round the game reserve wondering where to establish the bomas.

Water was a problem. We couldn't build them too near either of the rivers for fear of floods, and it was bitterly cold in the river valleys on winter nights. But I soon found the site I wanted. It was near enough to Mdindini to cart water from the White Umfolozi river and within sight and sound of my home. John Clark ruefully said that I had put the bomas where I could watch him through my binoculars.

Ranger Adriaan Erasmus started work on the bomas the following day. A gang of Zulu labourers went out into the reserve and cut thick nthombothi poles, the wood least affected by termites. Another gang went to the Black Umfolozi river to cut loads of reeds.

The pens were thirty feet square with one gateway each. Poles were placed close together in a trench two and a half feet deep and wired at the top with a cross member to stop them from parting when a rhino pushed against them.

From my office I could hear the shouts of the men and the stamping of earth as the poles were put into position. Magqubu came in later and together we watched the progress from the top of the hill. Adriaan Erasmus was stripped to the waist working alongside the gang who chanted as they dragged the heavy poles into position. The clanging of a cane knife echoed up the hill. I told Magqubu that the day would come when our rhino would go all over the world.

'How will they get there?' he asked, smiling, his head cocked to one side.

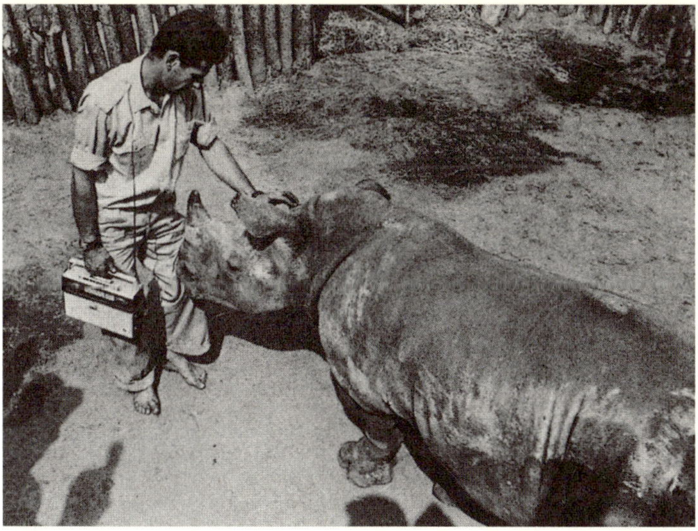

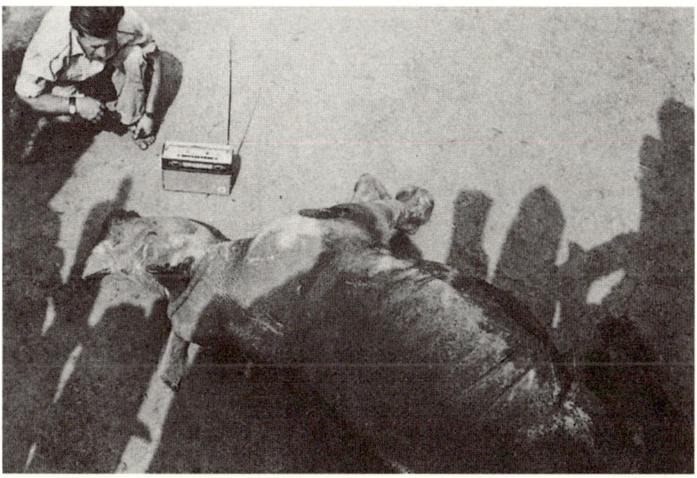

19, 20, 21. Downing the radio-tamed rhino.

'By boat,' I replied.

He laughed and said what would the rhino eat on the water because they had to have food, even I must know that. I explained that the boats could carry enough grass for months if necessary. Magqubu covered his mouth with his hand, Zulu fashion, and looked dubious.

It was overcast and chilly on the morning we left for the western section of the game reserve. The white rhino stayed out on the plains feeding on this sort of day and we soon found a group below the slopes of Mtunzini. Three bulls walked southwards following the line of the old Mandhlagazi footpath.

'If you get one of those, let's name it Mandhlagazi in honour of the old tribe,' said Nick.

The approach was easy and the dart hit the young bull squarely in the triceps. It stood for a moment then headed east at a canter. The horsemen followed but Owen went a little too close and the rhino stopped, swung round and lunged at his horse. Owen cantered away casually and the rhino ran off again.

I watched it slowing down as the drug began taking effect. Its steps became shorter and its head jerked from left to right, then its back legs splayed and it stopped.

Four pied crows fluttered on to its back and pecked near the dart wound. They flew off when another mature bull came out of the Madhlozi stream and walked up to the darted rhino. We thought we were going to see a territorial fight, but the darted rhino merely leant against the other bull for a few moments, then dropped. We drove up and Nick said, 'That was the easiest chase we've had.'

We moved forward shouting loudly to drive the other bull away. John Clark quickly tied a rope to Mandhlagazi's hind legs but he got up and ran thirty yards, dragging John behind. Five minutes later he went down properly. We measured him and injected procaine and sodium penicillin while the lorry came up with the crate. At six o'clock we triumphantly deposited him at the bomas. John Clark slept the night in his Land-Rover in front of the pens.

With Mandhlagazi safely deposited in the bomas, our capture

techniques improved, we were ready to make sure that the capture of rhino for Kruger Park got maximum publicity.

The press arrived later and Sven Persson and Jimmy Anderson, the South African Tourist Corporation men, came for more film material. It was almost a gala occasion as we left in a fleet of vehicles early the following day.

'Might as well have a little bit of glory while we can,' I said to Nick.

'It's like a circus. I wonder how many people are hoping to get a photograph of you being crushed,' Nick replied gloomily.

The resultant publicity, which reached even the London *Times*, put Umfolozi Game Reserve on the map, but we soon learned to forget about everyone around us and concentrate on the work.

We went out to the Madhlozi area again and I stalked a young female on foot. News photographers followed, and Arthur Bowland of the *Natal Mercury* hid under a bush and got an outstanding picture of the dart in flight, but the dart, by some incredible coincidence, landed in the sole of the animal's foot. I ran back to the Land-Rover and John Page hurriedly mixed more drugs and filled a dart. I carefully stalked the same rhino, moving the last twenty yards on my belly. This time the dart whacked into the shoulder. There was no immediate reaction but the rhino, perturbed by the Land-Rover and the hubbub of voices, ran over a mile and joined a cow and a young calf.

We stalked her with a rope in our hands but six people moving through the bush at the same time make a lot of noise, and she moved nervously. I slipped the rope round her right leg and was about to wind it round the other when a camera clicked. This was enough to set her off again. The rope tangled round my leg and I was dragged on my backside until Nick and Magqubu came to help. Then Owen darted in and grabbed the rope too. But our combined strength was not enough to hold Mpila, as she was already named by Magqubu, who ignored our English names. She dragged us through a thorn bush, ripping off half my shirt. Then she turned slightly and I saw bits of *Panicum* and *Urochloa* grass drop from her lips. I tried to point this out to Owen who was keen on grasses, but as I opened my mouth she kicked some sand into it. By this time my eyes were so full of dust that I could hardly see where we were being pulled.

More labourers raced up and Magqubu in his thick army overcoat, his hat over his eyes, shouted orders. Several minutes and five hundred yards later we managed to get the rope round a tree, but Mpila still showed fight and John Clark had to rope her front legs too. She tried to rise repeatedly but we pushed her head down by her fourteen and a half inch horn. Eventually she gave in and we pulled the dart out.

We had her tethered. The cameramen joined us. Nick nudged me and said, 'Look at Magqubu, he's pulling his hat straight, he's also got the camera fever!'

The old man was making sure he was presentable.

The lorry backed up and the driver, who was nervous with all the pressmen and cameras about, nearly dropped the crate on Mpila. We put the crate in position and I gave her ten c.c. of antidote intravenously. She rose like a prima donna and gracefully walked into the crate. Even the newsmen were impressed by the performance.

By half past three we had the crate at the second boma. Mpila lay quietly on her brisket and did not move until I had injected another ten c.c. of antidote intramuscularly. Once she was in the pen there was very little fighting. She charged us twice, banged her head then lay down and fell asleep, her ears flicking slowly.

John Clark bedded down in his Land-Rover again but was woken in the middle of the night by bellowing and thumping in Mandhlagazi's pen. He bent down in the darkness and shone a torch between a gap in the poles. All he saw was a large navel, and was nearly brained by one of Mandhlagazi's front feet. The rhino was trying to climb out of his pen and stood with his front legs on top of the gate pole. Having reached so far he was afraid of going further but was reluctant to return to the pen when escape was so near. John Clark picked up a stick and gave him a gentle tap on the nose. Mandhlagazi dropped back and fell into his waterhole, a shallow trough in the ground.

Thinking the rhino might be hungry John dropped a bundle of succulent green *Panicum* grass over the poles. Mandhlagazi hooked the grass before it landed, spread it all over the pen and sent some of it back over the gate on to John's head. So it went on all night. John arrived tired and haggard at the capture point next morning. We listened to his description of Mandhlagazi's goings on.

'I tell you, there's a big difference between those two rhino,' John said.

'Well, they are male and female,' Owen said laughing.

'That's not the point,' John said heatedly. 'Each rhino has unmistakable characteristics. Mandhlagazi is put off by the constant attempts to try and get him to eat, and I think he will only eat in the dead of night when he isn't disturbed.'

I went down to the two rhinos in the bomas. They had recovered fully from the drugs but were not yet eating. In spite of Toni's warning we had foolishly supposed they would begin eating at once. Already the place had begun to smell of stale, drying urine. Flies buzzed over the heaps of faeces and both rhino had turned their small drinking pools into muddy wallows.

John Clark asked for labour to clean the place up and cut grass to put into the pens for food and bedding. I asked him if he would live at the bomas and look after the rhino. It was obvious that he had a knack of handling them. They knew his voice and became calm when he approached them, talking softly. John agreed without hesitation.

That evening, men from the Kruger National Park arrived, led by Lappies Labuschagne, their Deputy Director, and Andrew Brynhard, then Park Warden.

We were out early on 6 October and I darted a three-thousand-pound female we named Madhlozi after the area we had been working in. She ran off with a bull, and at one stage the horsemen had more than twenty rhino running all round them. After two miles fast running she came to a halt. The horsemen chased the bull away, we got the lorry to the site and began our routine measuring. I noticed she had been mated, her hindquarters being covered in semen. This explained why the bull was reluctant to leave.

We had developed a new way of loading. Instead of hand-winching the crate up inch by inch, we pulled it with a steel cable attached to the Land-Rover and running over a pole on the cab of the lorry. This was John Page's idea.

Madhlozi stood shivering and sweating in the crate. There was something dreadfully pathetic seeing a wild animal incarcerated and I felt sad as we drove her to the third boma. She recovered sooner and more completely than the other two rhino. She had been darted in the leg and the drug took effect quicker and seemed to wear off more rapidly.

We got four white rhino in four days; the fourth we called Mfohloza after Vaughan-Kirby. We were very proud of our efforts but desperately tired and frustrated by the innumerable mechanical failures and lack of proper equipment. I was apprehensive too about the next stage of the operation, getting the rhino into the crates and making the long journey to the Kruger Park.

A list of auxiliary equipment was drawn up; cane knives and axes to chop through bush when necessary, ropes to tie down and sails to cover the crate, towing cable, pliers, funnel and hosepipe to give rhino water, four-gallon jerry cans for water and petrol; sacks to wedge in rough corners, old tyres to put in crates, crowbars and poles to lift the crate on to the rollers.

A drug box was fitted with syringes, pliers (to pull darts out of rhino hide), tape measure, penicillin, and special compartments for the narcotic, the tranquilliser, and the hyoscine; ear tags and applicator, terramycin ointment, distilled water, CO_2 cartridges, citric acid, and tablets; dart bodies and spare needles and a thermometer. As a precaution against the far too fallible human memory, I pasted a list on the cover. A notebook and a spare ballpoint pen completed the drug box equipment.

John Clark took to resting in the day when the rhino slept. At night they came to life, viciously horning everything that moved or standing on their hind legs and bashing the stockade. I could hear the thumping of the rhino and John's frantic calls to the labour for help from our house, a mile away. In the morning when I went down to John, he was trying to repair the gaps in the pens with thick rope and cable. The bomas looked like a spider web with the walls strengthened by ropes crisscrossing from the top of the corner poles.

Then new complications arose. Mandhlagazi's dart wound turned septic and began swelling. Next day John Clark met me on the path, unshaven and red-eyed from lack of sleep.

'Mandhlagazi hasn't defecated since we brought him here,' he said. 'The dart wound is giving him a lot of pain.'

From observation I knew dung heaps often stimulated defecation, so we collected fresh lumps and threw them into Mandhlagazi's pen. We watched hopefully as he smelt them, but it did not have the desired result. As Nick so rightly said later, 'It's bad enough having a constipated child, but when a rhino won't shit what the hell do you do?'

That afternoon we roped him and after a furious struggle gave him an injection of Prostigmin which caused muscular cramps. He bellowed loudly and his mood stayed vicious.

The two females were far more tractable and they would feed from John's hands after only four days in the pen. But the only grass they would touch was *Panicum maximum*, buffalo grass. They refused every other grass we offered them, including lucerne, even when we sandwiched it between *Panicum*. When all the rhino were eating, John had to cut enough *Panicum* to fill four Land-Rovers.

A sense of urgency filled us. The rhino had to be tamed and made ready for the long journey. On 14 October the National Parks Board intended unveiling the memorial to Colonel Stevenson Hamilton, and the arrival of the rhino was intended to be part of the ceremony.

Constipation and dart wounds began bothering the other three rhino. Mandhlagazi made dummy charges and sent mud flying when anyone walked past his pen. He knocked the hosepipe from a Zulu's hand when it was put through the reeds to fill up the waterhole. A tractor bringing a load of poles made all the rhino nervous. When the engine backfired it sent them crashing round, banging into the sides of the bomas.

Mpila was the only one who became tame enough to come forward to have her horn rubbed. She took no notice when her water hole was filled, and quietly drank her forty-four gallons a day. She tried to widen her wallow by knocking down the edges with her feet, then walking round in circles as the edges crumbled in.

Mandhlagazi's agitation became more marked as his dart wound festered and the thin dribble of pus attracted hordes of black flies. He learned to move the gate poles to one side and nearly escaped twice. His constipation worsened and he walked round the boma through the wallow, squealing pathetically.

We put grass in the corner and he would lie on it like a huge dog, then get up squealing to push against Mpila's pen. Nothing we did would stop him putting his forefeet on the gate and battering it with loud shrieks of rage. The day before we were due to load the animals Mandhlagazi's constipation was so bad he rubbed his anus against the rough poles and removed layers of skin.

When the crates from the Kruger Park arrived we put them in front of the bomas and tried to get the rhino to feed inside, but with the exception of Mpila they were far too wary. They made moves in the evening when they were undisturbed, but we could get nowhere near to push poles across the door to trap them inside. Our attempts to lure the rhino into the crates next morning were futile. They were due to leave that afternoon; there was only one thing to do and that was to rope them in like the trappers in Uganda did. This was a harsh method which we had hoped to avoid.

I took the job in hand and made myself unpopular by asking everyone to leave the area. All the available Zulu labourers were summoned from Mpila camp. A rope was threaded through a hole in the front door of the crate with a running noose on the end. Then we took turns to lassoo the rhino. They soon learnt to flick the rope off but Owen dropped it over Madhlozi's horn and when she moved her head back the noose slid over her ears.

'Pull, pull!' Owen yelled hoarsely. 'We've got her!'

The excited Zulus dropped the rope to run and look, and there was a pandemonium of shouts and curses. Nick and John Clark jumped off the boma, pulled the rope taut and called the labourers to drag her into the crate. She dug her feet in firmly and shook her head from side to side, but the combined strength of twenty men was too much for her. She was pulled squealing into the crate.

The next was Mpila. John enticed her to the door of the crate with a handful of green grass.

'I love this animal and it's a damned unfair way of getting her,' he said, scratching her forehead.

The noose dropped over her head and the tug of war against twenty sweating, chanting Africans began. Mpila viciously horned her crate as she was slowly dragged in. While the straining labourers held the rope taut, John Clark leapt into the pen, lifted the door, and bolted it into position. Then, surprisingly, both Madhlozi and Mpila defecated. The strain of being pulled in worked when nothing else had done.

With two rhino in the crates I felt happier. It had been easier than I expected. We winched the crates on to the waiting lorries and the first two rhino were on their four-hundred-mile journey to the Kruger Park by three o'clock.

Mandhlagazi's wound was syringed with permanganate, he was roped and drawn, kicking and squealing, into a crate. The strain burst his dart wound open and he also defecated, but he had by no means given up the struggle. He turned turtle in the crate. Nick Steele battled for an hour to right him, and was about to pull him out and release him in the veld when he righted himself. The other rhino, Mfohloza, fought too, kicking bits off his crate and rolling over inside.

The first part of the journey was chaotic. The transport was separated by fifty miles, and met later that evening at Mkuze drift where we tried to give the animals water. Mpila was the only one who did not knock her plastic baby bath flying.

Andrew Brynhard and I discussed arrangements for the rest of the journey. We decided that Nick and I would lead the convoy with our radio switched on, while the two film men, Sven Persson and Jimmy Anderson, would bring up the rear with one of our portable wirelesses. Sven called us up when there was trouble with a rhino, which was roughly every hour. Mandhlagazi was the main cause of trouble. He repeatedly jammed his anterior horn in a corner of the crate, and one of us would have to hang by our heels, get a rope round his neck and pull him free.

We reached Gollel, the Swaziland border post, at two o'clock in the morning, at which point Mandhlagazi chose to twist himself round and on to his side. Bleary eyed and irritable as we were, we tried for an hour to get him on his feet. We used rubber pipes, ropes, anything to right him. At three o'clock I decided it was hopeless and said either we shoot him or take him back to Umfolozi.

Andrew Brynhard and Lappies Labuschagne said they would wait with the rhino for a little longer and suggested we drive on. As the truck jerked forward, Mandhlagazi stood up as though nothing had happened and we sped over the Swaziland roads.

'Just like bloody sheep,' Nick said. 'Always looking for another way to die.'

The Lebombo mountains, the hunting ground of Baldwin, Drummond, and Leslie, lay on our right. They had seen the white rhino in all its glory on the flats we were now driving over, and I wondered what they would think of our rhino translocation.

Nick and I took turns driving. Thick dust poured in through every crack, settled on the windscreen and turned to mud when the dew fell. The radio crackled and the lights of the convoy flashed in the rear view mirror. The Southern Cross dipped in the south.

Dawn broke over the Swaziland lowveld, on the tall knob-thorn trees and red *Themeda* grass stretching into the distance. Long-tailed shrikes perched on the telephone wires and glossy starlings and European rollers flashed in the early morning sun.

We reached the Mbuluzi river, foaming crystal clear over the rocks, at eleven o'clock. The lorries crossed the low concrete causeway and stopped on the north bank. We lowered the baby baths into the crates and filled them with water. The two cows drank placidly but Mfohloza and Mandhlagazi smashed the baths to pieces. We dropped grass in the crates but they refused to eat.

We washed and shaved but as we moved, Mandhlagazi wedged his horn in the crate. This time it was so tightly jammed we had to prise one of the planks out to release him. Once we reached the tarred road the animals settled down, but there was a delay when a traffic cop stopped the convoy and asked for papers. Andrew Brynhard soon explained the situation and we entered Kruger Park at Malaleni gate. The last thirty odd miles to Pretorius Kop were a pleasure to drive – any game reserve was like home to Nick and me.

A crowd of people, including the Administrator of the Transvaal, watched the unloading. The original plan was to release the animals in the paddock, but with all the people about this would have been disastrous, so the rhino were put into bomas. A battered Mandhlagazi thumped his crate as it was let down the rollers. He entered the boma and drank deeply from the pool, then proceeded to turn it into a wallow.

The following day Nick and I were ceremonially opening the boma doors, and there was Mandhlagazi lying prone on the ground. For a moment we thought he was dead, but as we approached him he leapt to his feet and chased us round the boma. He had the last laugh.

Thol Pienaar, the biologist of the Kruger Park, wrote to me later to say that the four rhino had settled down well in their new surroundings. Mandhlagazi, true to form, had charged the fence but had made no impression. Thol said: 'Mfohloza was a bit anti-social but during the last few days he has joined up with the other three and they spend most of their time on the new burn either grazing or lying up in the shade.'

These four were the vanguard of the hundred white rhino which were translocated to the Kruger Park. Thol Pienaar, Andrew Brynhard and Henry Wolhuter – a ranger and old school friend – kept us informed about the rhino. It pleased us to find others as enthusiastic about the white rhino as we were. Thol mentioned that he had caught hippo with the same drug, and Toni Harthoorn wrote to say he had immobilised buffalo.

A few days later I received a personal note from John Page, which was much appreciated by the rhino team. 'Thank you and congratulations on a first class job successfully completed. I feel you and your Umfolozi team have achieved a tremendous objective. I am certain no one will ever achieve more for this Board and I would like you to know it. To have been allowed to play a small part with you all was more than a pleasure – it was a privilege I shall long remember.'

Although we had moved four rhino simultaneously we knew there were many problems to be solved before we could ship rhino overseas. No rhino would survive a three-week sea journey if it behaved like Mandhlagazi.

Chapter 18

White Rhino Mating

While John was working at the bomas, Nick Steele patrolled the southern buffer zone and Owen Letley returned to his outpost at Thobothi.

Owen radioed me early one morning and reported he had seen a new bird which he suspected was a martial eagle. He asked me to come out to identify it. I rode out to the headwaters of the Thobothi stream where Owen proudly showed me his 'new bird' sitting on the top branches of a knob-thorn tree. He was rather disappointed when I told him it was a white-hooded vulture.

We rode back via the Nyamagwatengwa stream and after we off-saddled the horses, Owen showed me where he had witnessed two white rhino bulls fighting and the victor copulating with a young cow. One of the bulls was Onehorn, a rhino we successfully darted with gallamine triethiodide during Toni Harthoorn's first visit.

Owen said he was out on patrol and while crossing the Kandalenyati stream (Buffalo Head) he heard a rhino squeal. He sneaked quietly through the grass and came upon One-horn, another bull and a young heifer. The time was seven in the morning. As Owen appeared, Onehorn put the other bull to flight and chased it for fifty yards, squealing crossly. Onehorn then returned to the young cow making a low sobbing, choking noise like an unfit man after a long hard run. He varied this with a noise not unlike a very young eland calf wanting to nurse. Onehorn walked up to her, rested his chin on her rump for a minute or so then resumed grazing.

It was obvious that the cow was ready to accept him but the interfering bull was persistent and kept returning to voice his dissatisfaction loudly. Onehorn replied to this with a deep rumbling growl and charged the other animal. The clash of their horns reverberated in the bush. These skirmishes occurred again and again, ending each time with Onehorn walking after his cow and the other bull following. There was a lot of movement but they remained in a relatively small bushy area which they seemed to prefer to the more open ground. The cow constantly kept her tail curled up or over to one side and as she walked she discharged a trickle of pale yellow liquid.

'She had a very strong rhino smell,' Owen said, pointing to where he had been hiding. 'An interesting fact,' he continued, 'was that at one time they were joined by another heifer and neither of the males objected to her, but she moved off after a few minutes.'

Onehorn tried to mount once but was foiled by an overhanging branch. The cow made no attempt to move off though she staggered a bit under his weight. Owen was very busy keeping himself a few yards upwind of them to watch what was going on, and staying out of reach of the battles, some of which were uncomfortably close. After an hour the wind changed and they ran off. In the chaos Onehorn was separated from his mate.

'His agitation really amused me,' Owen laughed. 'The urge to reproduce in rhino must be very strong. He ran round and round in a circle with his nose to the ground, trying to pick up his cow's scent. I think it must be the fluid she discharged that made him able to follow her. He nearly knocked me flat twice, but he took no notice. He finally found the scent and galloped off with me following. He found the cow with the other bull who obviously believed in making hay while the sun shone.'

Onehorn uttered his low, rumbling growl and launched himself at the other bull, who flattened his ears and backed away with loud rumbling noises. They clashed repeatedly, their horns rattling. A haze of dust hung overhead.

Onehorn returned to his wayward cow triumphant and full of affection, making his calf-like noises. They grazed along for a while then the other bull reappeared making the usual hiccuping noises followed by the deep rumbling growls. They fought once more and when the dust cleared Onehorn went back to his mate, placed his chin on her rump, and this time mounted her. He remained in the mounted position for three to five minutes, then slid off. They moved into some shade and rested for half an hour, their hides damp with sweat. Onehorn got up and tried to rouse his mate by pushing her and making his soft calf-like noises, a pitiful sound. This had no effect so he started to mount her while she was lying down. As she got up the other bull came back, so they fought again.

The cow moved off and the contestants followed, fighting every so often. Onehorn and the cow stopped in a patch of shade. The other bull walked to a nearby wallow and rolled in the mud. After a short rest, the courting rhino took to a path, and Owen followed at a safe distance. They met another pair of rhino coming from the opposite direction. The oncoming rhino stopped abreast and refused to move. Onehorn rumbled and growled but gave way and left the path.

Owen showed me where the four had met.

'I was so busy looking ahead I didn't see the muddy opposition bull coming in on the run. He wasn't welcome and got a licking for his troubles,' Owen said. 'Soon after this Onehorn mounted his cow again and after three minutes in the mounted position he started to erect his penis. This took a full two minutes – there must have been close on three feet of it. He couldn't seem to get his penis more than a few inches into the cow. She sort of moaned, it was like a low gurgle, and moved about the clearing, reversing, going forward, then backing again very slowly. Onehorn tried desperately for a quarter of an hour, but he couldn't complete the siring act, and when he was dislodged his penis immediately folded back. They were breathing heavily and they both lay down under a tree.

'I had temporarily got shot of the opposition while all this was going on. I stood right in his path and as he moved towards the couple I hissed at him to '*voetsak*' (go away) and let him have it on the nose with a stick. It worked – he trotted off with a lot of snorting, but he didn't disturb the others. He came back later to fight again. I had to jump behind a tree and they brushed past in a cloud of dust with the cause of it all leading the way. That was the last I saw of them!

Owen and I returned to Mpila along the Mtunzini ridge. It was a disheartening ride. We passed a mass of goats and cattle, and saw some reedbuck running away from the noise of shouting herdboys. The squat ters had begun ploughing along the road near Sokwezela hill.

Later we investigated the report of an injured white rhino bull near the Kandaledube pans. We found the poor old beast struggling along with a broken front leg. It was able to move only by pushing its jaw along the ground. The guards said squatters' dogs had chased it over a krantz. It had to be shot.

CHAPTER 19

Black Rhino: A Death

In 1961 thirty-seven black rhino died in a short period in Hluhluwe Game Reserve. Senior veterinary officials from Onderstepoort examined the carcasses but could find nothing wrong. Norman Deane was anxious that we capture some, so the vets could examine them alive. On 6 November, we went after our first black rhino. Nick sent the horses over to Ntabamhlope in an old crate which had been used years before to transport giraffe from the Transvaal. He and Owen rode to Hlogohlogo (Weaver Bird) hills. The horses had become an indispensable part of the capture – 'the unsung heroes' Nick called them.

Norman Deane organised a search for black rhino in the morning and Rangers Bob Murray and Garth Carpenter found seventeen in the Nomagetcha valley. I reached Hluhluwe in the afternoon as the guards reported seeing two black rhino near Gunjaneni gate. We left immediately and I mixed the drugs. We had run out of Themalon again so I was forced to use morphine, 1.25 grammes of it, enough to kill a lot of human beings. No Sernyl was available so I mixed the morphine with Largactil tranquilliser and added 100 mgms of hyoscine.

We later found Sernyl was essential in the drug mixture for black rhino because it stopped them fighting. It was the reverse with the white rhino; we had no more trouble with them fighting their crates once Sernyl was left out of the drug mixture, but we had some saddening experiences before we realised our mistakes.

Stalking black rhino on foot was not easy. They liked dense bush and the smallest twig was enough to deflect a dart. It was different in a vehicle, their habit of charging gave me a chance to shoot them in the rump when they turned. But the first rhino I darted ran when it heard the Land-Rover. Norman Deane drove skilfully over the rough ground and the dart whacked home as the rhino went into a thicket of *Acacia karroo*. Nick and Owen were after it but Nick's stirrup leather slipped as he was galloping through a donga and he fell headlong. The black rhino disappeared into the low country towards the Hluhluwe river. While the guards looked for another, Nick came limping back.

'This is a really dicey game,' he said. 'These black rhino simply melt into the bush and you don't know whether they're waiting for you or not.'

I was worried about the whole capture. Black rhino in my opinion are one of the most dangerous animals in the bush. I had had some unpleasant experiences. One nearly got me on the Makatini flats in 1952, another chased me in Mkuze Game Reserve and I reached a tree just in time. One had pussy-footed after me while I was shooting rations and only the warning shout of a game guard saved me from that curved horn.

In 1955 I was coming back late from a long foot patrol in the Umfolozi Game Reserve, my mind on the billy of tea I was going to drink, and I stumbled on a black rhino cow and calf in the Inyonigazana stream bed. The cow was so close when she charged that her snort deafened me. Fortunately my hat and side haversack fell off, and she hooked them instead. Then on the first wilderness trail conducted in the Umfolozi Game Reserve, the trail party were approaching Mahobosheni camp on the White Umfolozi river when Magqubu yelled a warning '*Ubejane*!' as a black rhino splashed out of a wallow and came straight for us. One man pulled himself up on to a branch with one hand – normally an impossible feat. I crouched behind a tree but not before I felt its coarse skin scrape my arm as it rushed snorting past. If anyone had been injured on that first Trail the whole idea could have failed. The bad publicity would have killed it.

Norman Deane had many brushes with black rhino when he was officer in charge of Hluhluwe Game Reserve and so had Roddy Ward, the ecologist.

Peter Hitchins, who later studied the black rhino full time, had once been chased up a tree and the cow had stood on her hind legs and tried to hook him out.

Ranger Gordon Bailey had seen a favourite horse gored in the stomach, and the intestines spill out onto the veld.

A game guard returning late to the Mahlabashane outpost had been surprised by a notorious black rhino which ripped him from his thigh to his knee. Gatekeeper West had also been caught and had his leg torn open. Another game guard had a lucky escape in Hluhluwe Game Reserve. The black rhino chasing him lunged as he was running and the horn caught his handcuff belt. The guard was flipped into the air and landed on the rhino's back. He bounced off and crawled away.

Black rhino are not animals to be trifled with, but it was understood that no one would ever shoot a rhino in self defence. Our job was to protect them. In spite of their bad reputation they invoked an affection in anyone who had much to do with them. They really were dramatic animals, as Nick said. It was wonderful to watch them running across the veld, or slipping through a dense thicket, or wallowing in a mud hole. I always wanted to put them in a bullfighter's ring and see how long a matador lasted.

After the escape of the first black rhino we discussed other ways of keeping them in sight.

Open country is scarce in Hluhluwe, so rangers and game guards were posted on the highest points and told to watch the rhino's movements once it had been darted.

Bob Murray said that a black rhino bull was lying in an open glade although encroaching acacia scrub might deflect the dart.

I stalked it on foot, mentally measuring the distance from a tall marula I intended climbing if the rhino came for me. I hit it in the right shoulder and ran to the marula tree but the rhino went the other way, much to Norman's disgust; he had hoped it would charge me. The two horsemen cantered off keeping a respectful distance from the rhino and the rangers on the high points shouted out its movements.

22. Gordon Bailey.

23. Ken Rochat – 'never ruffled'

24. On patrol: John Forrest (*left*); the author (*centre*); Nick Steele (*right*).

We ran to a prominent ridge and kept the rhino under observation for twelve minutes, but the drug was having no effect. We watched the rhino walk over the ridge and disappear into the bush. Magqubu tracked it, but lost the spoor in a maze of wildebeest and impala tracks. We scoured the area but found no further sign of it.

The following day Bob Murray went out early to locate black rhino in the Nomagetcha and found four in an unhealthy patch of bush.

I mixed the drug, increased the morphine to 2 grammes, the hyoscine to 200 mgms and diluted it all in 16 c.c. Largactil. To get it to mix properly I had to warm up the plastic bottle, so I left it in the radiator of the Land-Rover with the Capchur gun.

Magqubu and I moved quietly through the bush after one of the four rhino. We got very close but I couldn't shoot. I knew that a piece of grass was enough to deflect a dart, let alone a mass of acacia scrub.

We discussed another method of approach. Nick suggested rushing up to the animals in a Land-Rover and darting them on the run.

We drove straight to the Useme area of the Corridor and at two o'clock Bob Murray pointed out three black rhino browsing on *Acacia caffra* branches. Ox-peckers shrilly gave the alarm call as Norman Deane moved slowly forwards. The rhino were on the alert immediately and their bell-like ears turned towards us. Norman changed down and put the Rover into four-wheel drive low ratio. The vehicle shot forward. The horsemen took up their positions on either side and weaved through the bush, avoiding antbear holes and jumping fallen logs.

I saw Owen's horse rear as a warthog scuttled out of the grass. Norman closed the gap, driving fast and skilfully. A branch swiped me in the face and I fell back, but Magqubu steadied me. Thorns scraped against the doors of the Rover and stumps thumped the chassis. The noise had frightened the three rhino and they ran at a fast trot. Above the screaming engine and the scraping branches I could hear their high-pitched snorting. The ox-peckers that had been flying above the rhino, still calling, veered off. I waited a chance to dart a rhino in the buttocks. There was less chance of the dart falling out and it helped the horsemen follow the right rhino. I fired and the dart went in.

The darted rhino followed a cow and a calf which headed straight for the Hluhluwe Game Reserve. Rangers and guards spread on the hills shouted a commentary. It ran for two miles without any sign of the drug taking effect, then Bob Murray called out that it was near him, and it seemed dazed. We topped a rise and watched the rhino trotting and stopping, keeping up this erratic pattern until it stood under a tree with its back legs splayed. The horses' hooves striking the stones roused it but it soon stumbled to a halt.

The dart had broken off but the needle was still embedded. Two oxpeckers ran up and down the animal's back, looking for ticks. The drug was having some effect but the rhino would not go down, so I shot 100 c.c. Largactil into its shoulder. It ran a hundred yards but Norman cut it off by driving the Rover next to it. The rhino stopped and got its horn under the front mudguard. I gave it more tranquilliser but it kept pushing, and if the Rover had not been there it would have walked away. Fifteen minutes later it was still active and horning the vehicle energetically. Someone jumped on its back to see if the weight would bring it down, but this had no effect. The black rhino, unlike the white, was fighting the drug every inch of the way.

The State Veterinarian took blood samples from the ear veins and Roddy Ward caught various species of biting flies. Bees were attracted by the sweat and *Stomoxys* flies gorged themselves on blood. The rhino had a heavy infestation of ticks, mainly the unpleasant-looking bont tick with the unpronounceable Latin name of *Amblyomma hebraeum*, as well as the rhino tick *A. rhinocerotis*. Sixteen different kinds of ticks were known to exist on the black rhino and six kinds on the white. One of the most remarkable parasites was the *Gyrostigma* which laid its eggs on the base of the horn.

Norman moved the Rover away slowly and we pushed the rhino on to its brisket where it breathed at eleven per minute and sweated heavily on the tail, forehead, chest, and hindquarters. Then without warning, it stood up and greenish liquid poured from its mouth.

'Bile,' Roddy Ward said tersely.

The animal strained forward with fourteen Zulu labourers trying to hold it back. They had an immense struggle to pull it down. I noticed that the mouth was wide open while the animal was under stress.

It rolled over on to its side, looking as though its condition was deteriorating. I decided to give it the antidote but it took us minutes to raise a vein because they were so much smaller than the white rhino and our syringe needles were too thick. I gave it fourteen c.c. intravenously and seventeen c.c. intramuscularly and a minute later it was on its feet. We scattered and it charged Nick who pulled himself into a thin tree just in time.

Twenty minutes later we went close to it in the Land-Rover and I shook a book in its face. It made a short charge. Shortly afterwards, it walked into a tree and stood dazedly looking about, but ten minutes later it had recovered well. We left it and the next day the guards reported that it charged them on sight.

The following day we used the same tactics and rushed in on a group of four rhino lying up on Yidhle hill. They milled around taken by surprise and as I fired I realised I'd darted the wrong animal. It was a big cow and she moved slowly. I realised too late that she was pregnant.

The rhino trotted off towards Ugontshe forest. From a high point, we watched it run into a patch of bush and emerge at the other side minus the dart. The horsemen had it in view and followed it for nearly a mile, trying to prevent it from going into the forest.

'I'll mix another dart,' I told Norman and he and Bob Murray went after the rhino to try to stop it. The darted animal was moving strongly so I decided to give half a gramme of morphine.

Norman fetched me and we approached the cow. She turned and charged. I fired but it was too close. The dart burst and a stream of liquid poured out. Bob Murray drove alongside the animal and managed to stop her. She got her horn under the front mudguard and lifted and dragged the vehicle. One wheel was off the ground. Five minutes later she dropped, then struggled to rise while everyone held on to try to keep her down. I gave more drug with the syringe but already I had a sick feeling. Everything was going wrong with this capture.

I did not know how much drug the rhino had received. It was a very hot day, we were out in the open with no shade and the rhino sweated heavily. I injected penicillin. The tail rose and fell and the rhino shuddered periodically.

The bull appeared on the skyline and trotted to and fro making little mock charges. While the female was being headed off from the forest, the bull had kept nearby and had not charged. It seemed influenced by the passivity of the cow.

Now it was alone and seemed very concerned. A white cattle egret fluttered near and the bull swung on it.

Roddy Ward checked the cow's eyes. They were still pink which was a good sign and I felt a little better and injected more Lethidrone. She reacted and tried to rise, but rolled on to her right side. From this moment, it became impossible to keep her on her brisket. More Lethidrone was injected and she rolled over, struggled a few feet forward on her knees and bashed her head repeatedly on the ground. This behaviour was most distressing and we placed mounds of grass to lessen the shock. At midday, we managed to roll her on to her other side. We tried to get her on to her brisket but she rolled back to her right side and lay with her legs jerking spasmodically. I was now extremely anxious about her condition and worked on the assumption that much of the dose in the second dart had been injected despite the bursting of the syringe. This added to the original dose was proving too much for her.

I injected more Lethidrone and she tried to rise, breathing heavily with mouth open and legs thrashing. She rose partly to her feet but staggered forward. She could not support her own weight. I waited a little then gave more antidote and she began to react favourably. She rolled over on to her brisket by herself and lay, breathing easily. Her recovery was marked. I checked her eye with difficulty as she was conscious of me when I went too close. It was a healthy pink.

Twenty minutes later the temperature dropped sharply and a heavy storm which had been threatening, came sweeping over the hills and broke over us. The change in temperature and the cold rain were too much for her. She raised and lowered her head while her front legs quivered as she tried to rise. At twenty past three she died suddenly.

It was a bad blow. We stood listlessly in the pouring rain looking at her carcass while the unhappy bull watched from the skyline.

In the gathering darkness we cut her open for a post mortem and found a foetus due for birth in about two months. It was a perfect miniature rhino and still pathetically warm. We examined the cow carefully.

There was slight congestion in one lung, fluid in the trachea, and very little blood in the heart. The eyes had turned dark blue, probably due to respiratory failure. The fluid in the small intestine was pale yellow, not the khaki or mustard colour of the black rhino which had been mysteriously dying. The weight of the cow excluding liquid was two thousand and twenty-three pounds. The foetus weighed fifty-four pounds. The only consolation was that we were able to compare her internal condition with those rhino that had been dying.

I wrote to Toni Harthoorn the evening I got back about our failure with the second black rhino. He advised us to wait for Sernyl to add to the morphine mixture. He commented: 'If one cannot get the black rhino onto its feet when it's coming round it will fracture its skull, as the Kenya Game Department experienced with several of their animals. The pregnant animal will, of course, die much more easily from shock or as a result of bumping or any other stress.'

In January 1962 he wrote to say he immobilised a black rhino in Kenya with three grammes Themalon and a quarter gm Sernyl. 'It went like clockwork and it only walked three hundred yards,' Toni said.

Later, with a better drug combination, we successfully immobilised more black rhino and took them to Ndumu Game Reserve.

CHAPTER 20

Mona

We returned to white rhino capture because of the stream of complaints about white rhino in the Mona valley, an area of Tribal Reserve adjoining the Umfolozi Game Reserve.

Owen Letley and I rode across the Black Umfolozi river to meet the local Agricultural Officer and inspect the damage. The country from the main Hlabisa road to the Mona river had been badly overgrazed by cattle and harmed by Africans ploughing up the hillsides. Abandoned mining claims lent an air of depression. Derelict houses, lorries with their engines out, and rusting mining machinery littered the country. But once we crossed the Mona river, just above its junction with the Black Umfolozi, we entered some lovely unoccupied country of tall redgrass, marula trees and small rocky outcrops. Here Cetewayo, the Zulu king, had hidden from the British after the Zulu War of 1879. I was amazed to see that apart from a few trees having been cut for hut poles, there were a good ten thousand acres of virgin land. There were tracks and dung of white rhino about and they had damaged a few mealie fields.

A month later Owen went into the Mona area to establish a paddock for the horses and to get to know the country intimately. He reported back a week later that there had been an influx of people since we had last been there. New fields had been ploughed across tracks we had hoped to use. White rhino had been chased by dogs and by people trying to drive them out of their bushy places. The fruitlessness of these efforts to drive them off was demonstrated by the four bulls who, stayed in a relatively tiny patch of bush almost surrounded by ploughed land. They emerged in the early morning, late afternoons, and at night, or when chased by dogs, but they showed no inclination to change their area.

Other rhino along the Mona river found refuge in a big nthombothi forest, and signs of these animals could be found along the paths where they had made dunghills. Owen estimated that there were between ten to fifteen animals in the upper Mona area.

Owen's Mona valley investigation and report was invaluable. It allowed us to move in on 25 November 1961, ready to begin catching.

We set up camp at Owen's horse paddock, brewed tea, then left to catch the first Mona rhino. Owen was on leave so Nick took a good game guard, and while they saddled the horses and fitted the coronet guards and the chest aprons, which we had recently introduced to protect the horses, John Clark and I cleaned the Capchur gun, mixed the drugs and removed all unnecessary equipment from the Land-Rover. In an hour we were on our way, looking for white rhino.

Nick rode ahead of us to find a route. I was astounded at the number of people who had moved into the area since August. They had established kraals and ploughed up fields where a few months ago there was veld, but there was a population-free belt of about a mile from the Black Umfolozi going north. This belt ran westwards for a good ten miles and it was here that the rhino had been compressed. Magqubu, who was standing on the back of the Land-Rover, spotted a cow and eighteen-month-old calf some four miles from our camp.

I followed the cow, determined to capture our first adult animal. A strong north-east wind blew my scent away but she walked into some thick scrub. I crept forward. I could hear her eating and the calf suckling and making whimpering noises, but even at fifteen yards they were obscured by the thick foliage. Magqubu pointed out her legs but there was no chance of a shot.

We sat watching for about an hour, hoping she would move into a suitable position. Natal robins sang down in the riverine forest and a scarlet sunbird flew about in the blood red flowers of the *Schotia* tree near us. A troop of banded mongoose passed a few feet away but a monkey spotted us and chattered excitedly. The rhino calf became suspicious. It stopped suckling and came towards us. We sat dead still and the calf returned to the cow and continued suckling. I decided to dart the cow first, then the calf.

A quarter of an hour later the drug had coagulated and I had to go back to the Land-Rover for another dose. Nick was waiting at the edge of the thicket sweating heavily in his canvas jacket, for it was a hot day and we were in a valley.

I explained what was going on as I mixed more drug. Magqubu picked up the spoor and we followed the pair into the bush. We had barely found them when the wind swung round and the cow got our scent. She went berserk and hammered a log that was in her way. I had never seen a white rhino behave so viciously. It was obvious that we would have to take care with these Mona rhino; they would not hesitate to kill.

We kept after her for another two hours and just before midday found the two of them lying behind a single bush in an open glade. She had chosen the one place in the whole Mona valley which made stalking impossible. Magqubu went back for the Land-Rover and when it arrived I climbed aboard and pointed out the rhino. The camouflage was so good that neither John Clark nor Nick could see her. We decided to charge up in the Land-Rover and dart her as she ran.

It was the beginning of a long driver-darter partnership between John and me. I pointed out the general direction and John drove forward over the rough veld at thirty-five miles an hour.

The cow heard us coming, got up, turned indecisively once, then ran for the thick bush with the calf just ahead. John caught her up and as I aimed she swerved, John swerved too and I nearly fell off but managed to dart her at thirty miles an hour when we straightened out again, just in time, for ten yards on they disappeared into the bush. Nick and the game guard followed her for three miles as she kept to the fringe of the bush. Then she vanished into almost impenetrable nthombothi forest. Nick lost sight of her. He sent the guard back for us and started cross country in the thick bush to pick up the trail. Leading his horse and following the tracks he found the cow lying in a mealie field.

He came back for us and I saw the calf trying to climb on top of the female. It was a sad sight. We were very short of reinforced needles so I fired a dart with a weaker needle but it bounced off the calf. Normally a calf will not leave the female but this one charged us twice and ran off. I hurriedly prepared another dart. We chased it in the Land-Rover but it escaped us by running into an nthombothi forest.

We returned to the cow at the same time as a bull appeared. It walked out from the bush into a mealie field a hundred yards away. It was clearly aggressive and we took evasive action. These rhino, living among and being so much troubled by human beings, were not only much more alert, their whole behaviour was different. A bond seemed to link them together, as though they had ganged up to fight humanity.

The bull moved off at his leisure and we examined the cow. She had just been served which no doubt accounted for much of the bull's interest in her.

The lorry and crate reached us an hour later and we found the crate was too small. We had made a sled for this exercise which the lorry fetched and we rolled her on to it. But it stuck in the rollers going up and Mona (pronounced Mawna) as she was named by Magqubu, hung upside down for minutes while we tore around trying to get the sled off. We wrenched it free with crowbars, took Mona off and winched her up the rollers straight on to the back of the lorry, trapper style. We put heaps of sacks under her head, made her as comfortable as possible and left for Mpila camp forty miles away.

I decided against antidote as the lorry had to travel over broken country and if Mona struggled, she would do herself a lot of harm. There was no room to load the big rollers on to the lorry so we took the small pair on the back of the Land-Rover.

She only tried to stand up once on the way, and John and the labourers held her down and tightened the ropes. Pressure on the heart and lungs was only noticed on the long upgrades to the Hlabisa hills. Her breathing became laboured and the veins in her ear were rock hard. Africans on the roadside stared incredulously at the huge live beast held down by a few men and some ropes.

It was half past ten as we reached the bomas and a golden moon came up over the horizon. We dragged the rollers off the Land-Rover, got the block and tackle ready and were about to pull Mona off when she stood up. She swayed alarmingly on the back of the lorry, which had no sides. In the dim moonlight we watched, waiting for her to fall. Both her front and back legs were tied and she had only to go a few inches to either side to fall off the truck and kill herself.

'We will have to grab her,' I whispered to John and Nick.

We moved up quietly and led her by her twenty-three-inch horn from the truck. No one knew how far she had recovered from the drugs. The ropes on her legs allowed her to move only a few inches at a time, and she shuffled slowly forward as we gripped her horn and guided her towards the boma.

Her long shadow wavered on the ground as she moved forwards.

A nightjar called, and we spun round in alarm, nerves and muscles taut. The labourers stood well back, only Magqubu came forward to help. We communicated by signals, afraid to speak in case she came to. The ten yards to the boma entrance stretched ahead like eternity and I sweated even though the night air was chilly. Her toes clinked against the stones on the loading ramp and a bush baby screamed down in the valley. I saw Nick and John's strained profiles in the pale moonlight. John held up two fingers: two yards to go.

She stopped a yard from the boma gate and breathed deeply, then sighed with a long exhalation of breath. My mouth went dry. We pulled again and she stumbled the last few feet. As her head went into the boma, sheath knives flashed in the moonlight as we slashed at the ropes binding her feet. I grabbed a syringe and injected twenty c.c. of antidote into her rump. No one spoke until the last gate pole had been wired.

John stayed awake most of the night to make sure she did not wake up, wedge her horn and fight the bomas, but she slept peacefully. The following morning she drank copiously and enlarged her wallow. After watching her wallowing movements we realised she was suffering from swollen udders and was wallowing to try to relieve herself of milk. Two days later she was attacking the pen and the poles creaked and groaned under the strain.

'I'll have to repeat my spider web act,' John said cheerfully. 'But she's using tactics new to me. She lifts herself as high as she can by bracing her nose against the side of the pen, then she starts to batter the poles with her front feet.'

The individual poles held but the whole side would slowly bulge outwards. I went down on the fourth day and John complained of her habit of wallowing in her drinking water. Her pen was turning into one big wallow and the water was mud. John made a shallow concrete water trough in the next pen, then stripped the four feet of dividing wall to make a gate. The sawing, cutting and banging had little effect on her. She kept walking round the boma squelching in the mud.

When the gate was complete she refused to move until late that night when she wandered through the gap, enjoyed her first drink of clear water in nine days and ate a heap of freshly cut *Panicum* grass. The dart wound on her rump turned into an abscess but John lanced it at the right time and she quietened down to a routine life and moved readily from pen to pen.

By the twelfth day, her udders were no longer inflamed or swollen and during the day she became very tame. But at night she walked from boma to boma calling loudly to other rhino below Dengezeni hill. They seemed to be aware of her condition and in the darkness they would come close to her boma. They grew so bold that the labourers had to throw stones at them. They would run off a few yards then come back sniffing and hiccuping as Mona called more loudly. In the early morning John surprised one big bull sniffing at Mona's pen as she stood on her hind legs battering the gate poles, trying to get out.

When two and a half weeks had passed, she was very tame and allowed John to rub her ears and scratch her head, and she would call to him when he came in with a load of grass. They became very attached to each other. We had decided that when a big crate arrived, we would transport her to Ndumu Game Reserve where Boy Hancock, the ranger in charge, was building a boma and a paddock.

John had decided to level out the pen she had turned into a wallow and to build a concrete water trough. Loads of river sand were brought from the White Umfolozi and dumped in readiness. To get the sand into the dirty pen, John had to open the main gate. So Mona was ushered into the adjoining pen, given a feed of green *Panicum* grass, and the main gate was quietly opened and sand moved in with wheelbarrows.

The pen was about three-quarters levelled when I took some visitors down. I did not know what John was doing, and he was so busy he did not see us come. We walked up to the bomas and one man said loudly, 'Good Lord, what a big rhino!'

This brought Mona to her feet. She headed straight for her normal pen in which John had been working. The loose poles were little hindrance and she was in her pen, but the unfamiliar smell of river sand stopped her. John rushed out and tried to replace the gate poles. He had three in place when she saw the movement of the fourth pole. John shouted 'Run' and we all took cover as Mona charged the gate. The poles snapped and Mona was out on the loading ramp.

John described the scene. 'She played football for a minute or two with an empty forty-four gallon drum and knocked it around. Then she looked around to find out what all the excitement was about. Not a human being in sight. Me and my gang were safely imitating crows on the boma walls and the visitors were back in their cars.'

Mona left the drum, turned and sniffed at the broken gate poles, lowered her head and lumbered off into the veld. I saw her grey body moving through the trees then she disappeared. The labourers clambered down from the bomas laughing and chattering about her strength and the way she had broken the poles. John stood with his hands on his hips and philosophically said, 'Well, anyway, I can now finish the pens.'

Chapter 21

Troubles in the Bomas

In December 1961 we went to the Mona valley again. Our plan was first to catch a medium-sized female rhino and keep her in the bomas for two weeks, then to capture a fully mature male and drive non-stop to Ndumu Game Reserve, two hundred miles away.

We searched for miles in the stifling heat along the Black Umfolozi river. It was a cloudless summer day with heat waves shimmering above the grass. The rocks were burning hot to touch and the glare was blinding. Trees wilted, their green leaves twisted into strange dry shapes. The land ached for rain.

I walked along a path next to the river, knowing that on days like this the rhino would lie up near water. The sun beat down on my back and the ubiquitous pepper ticks crawled all over me, prickling in the sweat. The horsemen plodded along, the horses shaking their heads to stop the flies biting at the moisture round their eyes. Owen sat his horse easily and the mounted Game Guard, Khonamangele – Magqubu's son – drooped wearily in the saddle. The rattle of a bridle chain disturbed five rhino in the reeds. They trotted out and made for shade.

I stalked a female but two calves kept trotting towards me, then turning and prancing away. Their eyesight was much better than a mature animal and it took me an hour to stalk a hundred yards. The female was curious too and came towards me. I shot her at fifteen yards but as I fired she turned and the dart entered her ribs. She ran snorting and vanished into the trees. The horsemen followed.

Rib shots seldom worked, but this time I was using a small explosive cartridge, one of a packet given to me by Red Palmer. The cartridge forced the drug in rapidly, unlike the slow movement of the plunger with the acetic acid and carbonate tablet principle.

At two o'clock Khonamangele returned and reported he had found the rhino but it had not gone down. We came upon the animal standing dozily amongst some bushes in the middle of a footpath. The dart needle was bent but she had had just enough drug.

Mbizane (The Caller) was loaded on to a lorry and taken to Mpila and we released her in the boma just before midnight. She was feeding from the hand after a few days and was one of the quietest animals we had.

When we opened the gate from one pen to another, she walked in backwards. She also wallowed far less frequently than the others. The only time she became excited was in the late evening when the wild rhino called from the surrounding bush. As it got darker, Mbizane became frantic and tried to climb her gate. The wild rhino harrumphed, hiccoughed and bellowed in the darkness. Their noises set other animals off and jackal and hyena scavenging on old carcasses began screaming and cackling in the night. But Mbizane settled down after John Clark cured her constipation by adding two pounds of Epsom salts to her drinking water.

Mpandhlana (The Bald One) was a four-thousand-pound, fully mature bull. I had seen him many times when we worked in the area. I badly wanted to catch him and get him to Ndumu Game Reserve. He would be the biggest rhino we moved successfully.

On 8 December the guards spotted him lying up in the shade of a marula. We rushed him in the Land-Rover and I fired as he stood up, but the needle broke and Mpandhlana ran off. I went after him on foot and darted him in the neck. This second needle broke before he had run twenty feet, but the explosive cartridge had injected the contents of the dart. Half an hour later, the horsemen returned to say he was standing back to back with another rhino. The other bull was reluctant to leave his mate and charged us when we were near. We scattered to the trees, shouting at him, then getting down and throwing stones. He pushed home a charge with Owen and nearly hooked him from the horse. Owen was unperturbed and guided his horse in and out of the trees.

Mpandhlana stood listlessly swaying from side to side. The other rhino returned making soft noises in its throat. It defied us for over an hour until Magqubu fired shots which ricocheted along the ground. The sudden loud bangs scared the rhino and we ran forward yelling until it trotted away, swinging its head violently. It turned and came back once more, but we stood our ground, waving our arms and banging on the vehicle doors. It was sad to separate such good friends and I regretted not being able to catch them both.

At six o'clock in the evening we were still trying to get the crate on the lorry. The big winch would not pull the crate the last fifteen feet so we got out the block and tackle. Then local Zulus arrived and kept the crate in position while we rigged up the block and tackle over the cab of the lorry. We greased a pole and pulled the rhino up. The springs sagged as Mpandhlana moved and the planks in the crate creaked under his immense weight. It was dark when we left.

We drove through the night to Ndumu Game Reserve, stopping once among the knob-thorn trees in the Swaziland lowveld to put in sandbags to keep the cold off the rhino. We turned where the Ingwavuma river plunges through the Lebombo mountains, and climbed in low gear up Cecil Mac's pass to the cold plateau. Not a light showed in the tiny Ingwavuma village as our small convoy passed through and down the winding road on the other side of the mountain. We sped along the sandy flats as dawn lit up the sky. Soon the whole Tongaland treeveld sparkled in the early morning sunlight. Spider webs covered in dew glittered amongst grey *Terminalia* trees.

We crossed the rickety bridge over the Ingwavuma river and I smelt the swamps, the heady yellow fever tree flowers, and the crushed figs of the sycamore. Brown water gurgled past on its way to the Pongolo river and the calls of bush francolin, purple-crested louries and fork-tailed drongoes echoed through the forest. Memories of canoeing down the rivers, being chased by hippo and crocodile in the swamps, came flooding back.

I had once been ranger in charge of Ndumu Game Reserve and spent some of the happiest days of my life building it up. The summer was hell except in the coolness of the dense fig forest but the winters were a delight, when birds of every description thronged the pans, when fever trees were yellow, matching the crocodiles lying on pale gold sandbanks.

We drove up the road to where Tonga women in their bright shawls lined up at the store with baskets and basins to buy mealie meal. Others sat under a lone thorn tree selling finger bananas and paw-paws. Young men, lighter skinned than the Zulus, strummed home-made guitars. Their long hair was plastered in white soap and bleached, and they constantly patted it. One small child picked her nose and stared with open mouth at the lorry and the crate on the back. Boy Hancock was troubled by squatters in his reserve too, and he had spread the word about the arrival of a rhino which ate at least one person for breakfast each day.

The big rhino stirred uneasily in the back. It was seven o'clock and he was coming round from the drugs.

We entered the game reserve and I saw Nyamithi pan among the trees and the fig forest at the junction of the Usutu and Pongolo rivers. A single nyala bull with sleek black coat, white ridge and yellow tipped horns leapt across the road and ran, head swept back, into the trees, a lovely sight to greet us after a weary night of driving.

We pulled up at the rough stockade. It had taken fifteen hours to do under a hundred miles.

As we began off-loading, Mpandhlana came to life and viciously put his horn through the top of the heavy crate. There was no chance of giving him an intravenous injection so I rammed the needle into his muscular rump. We intended to keep him in the boma for a week then release him into a ten acre paddock.

Boy Hancock said this rhino reacted differently to Europeans and to Africans. It would tolerate Europeans standing on top of the pen, putting gentian violet on abrasions received during the journey, but as soon as an African climbed up it would charge the gate. This happened several times, and was probably because it had been disturbed and chased by Africans in its former home in the Mona valley.

Mpandhlana was released into the paddock on the 15th and after leaving the pen he ate ravenously. He escaped from the paddock on the same day by breaking barbed wire strands then climbing over the top of a two-foot-six-inch cable. He walked thirty miles inside the game reserve, following the roads, and settled down in the dense Mahemane bush (the name meaning 'I don't know where I am'). It was country not unlike the Mona valley.

We learned much from the translocation of Mpandhlana. It proved that for journeys of a hundred miles it was not necessary to precondition the animal in the boma. By small additions of drugs and tranquillisers we knew it would be possible to transport them even further. The distance was not important; it was the length of time it took to cover the distance that counted.

I phoned Colonel Vincent at our Pietermaritzburg headquarters to say I was confident we could send rhino direct to the Orange Free State under drugs. I told Nick that with the experience we had, I could see that rhino capture would be divided into two categories: rhino to various parks in South Africa, taken there directly from the field under drugs; and rhino tamed in our bomas and sent overseas to zoos or parks too distant for direct translocation. The former had been proved but the latter was problematical and was to cause us much grief before the technique was successful.

The publicity about our success resulted in many requests. George Speidel from Milwaukee cabled asking about the possibilities of getting three rhino. Other zoos from all over the world wrote or cabled, wanting to know the selling price and were not dismayed at paying R6000 a pair.

The Kruger National Park authorities asked for twelve, Rhodesia for eight and the Orange Free State for another four.

We had to increase our staff to cope with the demands. John Tinley, the tall, soft-speaking young brother of my old companion, Ken Tinley, was transferred from Lake St Lucia and took over the Thobothini outpost from Owen Letley. Gordon Bailey, an athletically built young man with a pleasant manner, was recruited and went to Nick Steele at Gome for training. He came to Umfolozi on the day I had darted a crocodile on Lake St Lucia and was bringing it back to put in the Mpafa waterhole at

Umfolozi. He was still wearing city clothes when I told him to help me carry the twelve-foot croc out of the Land-Rover. He showed no alarm. Brian Stevens, another recruit, who was a fluent Zulu linguist and an ex-cane farm manager, moved into new quarters at Mpila. He had the unenviable job of relieving me of mounting clerical work. Before long, these three men were working on rhino capture as well as doing their other work.

John Clark continued at the bomas, improving and altering the pens and looking after Mbizane, who tamed down well and gave us hope for the future. When she was ready we decided to move her to Ndumu too.

So she was darted in the buttock with Largactil and an hour later she was quietly roped and pulled into the crate by ten labourers. At first she was baffled and annoyed by the obstruction, and when the door was slid into position, she began hammering the crate. A side plank was ripped out in one movement and John had to release her from the medium crate into a larger one. She was loaded on to a lorry and started for Ndumu.

By the time John reached Hluhluwe Game Reserve she had made gaping holes in the top of the crate and she was restless to the Umsindusi bridge, then she calmed down and the rest of the journey was peaceful. John arrived at Ndumu Game Reserve in the middle of the night and Mbizane was left dozing until morning. When the crate was off-loaded, she walked out backwards and after a few parting lunges at the crate she began grazing, had a long drink then a luxurious roll in the mud.

We were all pleased at the delivery of the second rhino and John gaily remarked, 'I feel I've won the first major battle and what remains is only a mopping-up process.' He later added, 'in my enthusiasm I had forgotten that no rhino could be shipped overseas on a diet of green grass.'

We all thought the answer was simple: use lucerne. We had overlooked the difficulties John had had getting them to eat indigenous grasses.

While we repaired crates, John Tinley was moved to Thobothi camp to locate more rhino in the Mona valley. Part of his equipment was taken to the Mona-Black Umfolozi junction and carried across by game guards. One guard forded the river when the others were already across. He was about ten yards into the river when a crocodile surfaced close to him. The guard moved back, hitting the water with his sticks, but as he reached the bank the crocodile rushed at him and he only drove it off by beating it on the nose with his knobstick. This was the second drama in a few days.

Khonamangele was stabbed in the leg with an assegai by a poacher at Thobothi camp. We expected trouble and rushed guards to the area, but the show of force soon quietened everything down. Khonamangele was lucky. The blade passed through his leg without damaging any vital part.

Game Guard Jeyi Butulezi was not so fortunate. He was stabbed to death near Mhlanganweni guard camp the following week. One of the Africans caught with the murderer turned State evidence and what he had to say in court was sufficient to have the murderer sentenced to death. We thought this would have a salutary effect, but to our astonishment this same man was caught poaching in the same area a week later.

Poaching was an incessant problem and drained money and manpower. If we relaxed for a week the game reserve would have been overrun and the game wiped out. To the tribal people the game was meat, but it was encouraging to see the interest the urban Africans were taking in wild life.

In late January we crossed the Black Umfolozi into the Mona country and darted a young bull calf. It was badly wounded and in poor condition, but we recognised it as Mona's calf. The Zulus named him 'Msuza' because he was so filled with stomach gases. He was loaded without a crate and taken straight to the bomas and given antibiotics. The next day he drank two gallons of water and a mixture of milk and mealie meal. In a few days he was eating grass from John's hand.

We returned to the Mona area and I darted a rhino, one of a group of nine. Before the drug could work it ran into dense bush and the guards lost the spoor after four hours tracking.

I wrote to Toni Harthoorn about the problem of the drugs not stopping a rhino quickly.

He replied, 'To get a quick knock-down effect with less drug, add hyalondarase to your solution. Best added in powder form from a folded paper.'

It cut down chasing time appreciably.

A large cow, Magqayisa, named after the area we found her in, was captured in early February, and another cow, Masinyana (The One Who Hurries) two days later. Masinyana had just been served and was still on heat. A young bull, named Mtondotondo because of the size of his penis, was caught within a day of Masinyana and John Clark had his hands full. I often used to wake in the early morning to hear his faint shouts and the bellow of bewildered rhino coming round from the drugs, or hear pitiful squealing from the rhino with bad dart wounds.

Each rhino had to be carefully watched while coming round from the drugs; it was too easy for them to wedge their heads in a corner and suffocate. John was intent on taming the rhino, and it was his voice that primarily won them over. He spoke about them as though they were people he knew – visitors could find this disconcerting.

After the cow Masinyana had been at the bomas for three days John approached me wearily one morning and said we would have to move her.

'Last night four rhino arrived at the bomas – all of them bulls. Masinyana is still on heat and she is driving them crazy. It's bad enough having her trying to break out, now the other rhino are helping her, too. She's too large for the pens, all three thousand pounds of her,' he said.

I said we would take her to Ndumu.

She had to be pulled into a crate, and for a quarter of an hour she cunningly knocked the rope away from her head before John lassoed her. She had a tranquilliser to calm her for the journey. It was an easy journey to Ndumu if you overlooked two and a half tons of rhino and crate, and a ton of rollers to assist in off-loading, all on a registered three-ton truck. Fortunately Zululand was still short of traffic inspectors.

Sven Persson was still gathering material for his documentary 'To Catch a Rhino', and he travelled with us.

We waited for daylight to off-load Masinyana. All went smoothly until the moment of opening the crate door. Sven, weighed down by his 35 mm Ariflex, was reluctant to enter the paddock.

'Come in,' I urged him. 'You'll get a good shot of her coming out. It's perfectly safe.'

And to prove it I stood in front of the crate with my own camera. The crate door swung open and she lay quietly inside. I took my photograph then flung a clod of earth to get some action. She was on her feet in a flash and came out snorting. I ran for a Land-Rover. Fortunately she followed me and ignored Sven, for he could never have got out of the way. I dived over the back of the Land Rover just in time to avoid her curved horn. She turned, put her horn under the bumper and jerked the vehicle about. Then she went back to the crate, sniffed all round it and disappeared into the tall grass in the paddock.

Sven had filmed the whole scene then retreated to the cable fence. It was a close shave and he cursed me.

'You nearly had me blady killed,' he snarled. 'And you said it was safe.'

It was a long time before he forgave me.

Masinyana did not stay in the paddock long. Mpandhlana got her scent, smashed the cable fence, and led her out like a happy bride. Boy Hancock later saw the pair grazing peacefully together on the Usutu river flood plain. Two years later she had a calf.

I had just returned to Umfolozi Game Reserve when John Clark radioed me to report that the young Msuza was paralysed in the hindquarters. The dart wound had turned septic. He was unable to even drink water put under his nose.

John mixed glucose, hake liver oil, salt and yeast tablets, which he administered through the anus. Msuza recovered enough to walk round the boma. The next day John gave him more, but Msuza protested feebly. That evening he began whimpering distress calls at a high pitch and seemed to be gaining strength. Twenty minutes later he stiffened, trembled, relaxed, and died.

I looked into his pen and saw him lying there, his eyes wide open and blank, belly beginning to swell. A crow gave its rattling call and an emerald-spotted wood pigeon droned mournfully, 'My mother's dead, my father's dead, all my brothers and sisters are dead, and my heart goes do, do do do.' I walked away sick and demoralised, wondering whether we would ever find a way of stopping infection in dart wounds.

Magqayisa sickened soon afterwards so she was loaded and sent to Ndumu in the hope that freedom would cure her.

The journey was a nightmare. She was weak and fell over and wedged herself in the crate. She had to be dragged out and put back upright, but she attacked the crate and ripped planks off. John injected a tranquilliser and she collapsed on to her side and could not be righted. Her breathing became slow and irregular, a very bad sign. She was dehydrated too. By the time John reached Ndumu she was paralysed in the hind legs. John bathed her eyes and gave her water with a pipe through the anus. This revived her and at midday she drank water unaided and sweated freely. Suddenly she stiffened, cried the plaintive distress calls, shook violently, and died. John had a post mortem and found a bruise extending for six inches on either side of the spine up the sacral hump. This was probably the cause of death.

At the beginning of March 1962 the Madhlozi game guards reported seeing a badly limping mature bull in the country above the Mpafa waterhole.

We darted it, cleaned the wound out, pumped it full of antibiotics, and released it. The guards kept watch for a fortnight and reported that it had fully recovered and was walking normally. An operation such as this, once a dream, had now become a reality, and many rhino were saved. This was some compensation for the deaths of Msuza, Magqayisa and the loss of other rhino down at the bomas.

Later in the month two white rhino, Ondini, a male, and Amatsheni (Amongst the Rocks), a female, were caught in the Corridor and taken to the Willem Pretorius Game Reserve in the Orange Free State. It was an important occasion for us because the Administrator of the Free State, Mr Sand du Plessis, and a member of the Executive Committee, as well as other officials, came to watch the capture. Our Director, Colonel Vincent, was present too.

After a two-hour search for suitable rhino Ondini was darted at eleven o'clock, and crated by one o'clock. Amatsheni was darted after a rough ride across the veld. We were among eight rhino all running at twenty-five miles an hour. Branches were slamming against the capture vehicle and we bumped over warthog and antbear holes. I was screaming at John Clark to turn left, he was trying to avoid crashing into a bull which was swiping at us with its huge head. The Administrator was sitting in front, and being badly thrown about, but he was enjoying every minute of the wild ride. John Clark eventually heard my repeated yells and turned left, so that I could fire the dart into the rhino's fast-moving rump.

We had to wait nearly two hours before a horseman came galloping back to report that Amatsheni had climbed the rocky slope of Ncebe, tumbled and slid down a forty-five degree krantz, and was on the banks of the Black Umfolozi river. When we saw her lying at the bottom of the cliff I thought she was dead, but she only had a few minor scratches.

The problem was how were we going to get her up the hill. There was only one thing to do: walk her up. Mr du Plessis looked at me wonderingly when I explained what we were going to do. Outwardly I tried to spread an air of confidence, but inwardly I wondered if it would turn into a fiasco.

I picked a path amongst the rocky outcrops on the long line of the hill. There was little choice, boulders and trees were everywhere. I mixed a bottle of antidote and injected a small amount into a vein. Amatsheni stood up and everyone unfamiliar with the capture of rhino scattered. We slipped a rope over her head, pulled her tail and she walked forward a few paces. The Zulus chanted and pulled, chanted and pulled, while we pushed from behind. Slowly she moved up the hill, the bass voices of the Zulus echoing downriver. Three or four prancing, singing labourers would leave the main group to push aside boulders and send them crashing down the hillside.

As the hill grew steeper so the singing grew louder and the songs more militant. Magqubu pushed on her flank and made up a song of all our exploits. The others took up the refrain and Zulu and white man pushed and pulled the reluctant Amatsheni. I left a needle in her ear and as soon as there were signs of her slowing down, I injected more Lethidrone from the syringe. Magqubu added this to his song. At the halfway stage I knew, with a surge of pride in these men, that we had won.

There was a roar and a shout when we reached the top and the Zulus collapsed, puffed out.

By six o'clock we had loaded her and the two lorries left for the Free State. The wind had changed to south and storm clouds scudded overhead as the lorries made their way down the eroded road leading from Ncebe to the Tjevu crossing. Lightning forked across the sky and thunder rumbled on the Hlabisa hills. Nick must have read my thoughts, for he said, 'I hope this isn't going to be another Amber episode.'

The following morning I accompanied Colonel Vincent and Peter Potter to the Orange Free State. We had been invited to an official reception honouring the re-introduction of white rhino after an absence of over a hundred years. To our astonishment we met the lorries near the top of Van Reenen's pass, a mere hundred and fifty miles away. It was bitterly cold with a highveld wind howling up the mountain sides. Mist swirled up the valleys and covered the red krantzes.

We stopped the leading truck to look at the rhino. I pulled the canvas sail back and warm air, heavy with the familiar rhino smell, drifted out. Ondini lay on his brisket breathing normally. I administered a penicillin injection against infection and the driver told us of rain and mud beyond Nongoma, lorries skidding in the darkness on the twisting narrow roads, and rain and cold. Amatsheni had knocked her horn off. It looked bad but this was a common hazard. Stockholm tar prevented further bleeding or infection and in time another horn would grow, with a stronger base.

We reached Willem Pretorius Game Reserve early in the morning and the last rhino was off-loaded just before dawn. It was 13 March, two days before my birthday, and I could not have asked for a better present. Ondini had been drugged for a record thirty hours, proof that we could send rhino to the Kruger National Park directly from the field.

Peter Potter and I slept for two hours before the Colonel woke us. He was shaved and dressed and looked as though he had had eight hours' sleep. He was never off balance and at our official reception he spoke brilliantly about conservation. The Administrator in his reply complimented the Natal Parks Board. We then went out to release the rhino into their paddock. Ondini disgraced himself by charging the Administrator who was pulled to safety just in time.

Two more rhino, Rooinek and Boeremeisie, were sent at the end of the month and all four soon settled down in a habitat in which the white rhino had not roamed for a hundred and two years.

Chapter 22

Preparing for Export

By the end of March 1962 I was able to write to Toni Harthoorn and say we had captured eighteen white rhino. I said that as far as morphine was concerned we had probably been overdosing the animals, while the opposite was true of Themalon; but despite all this, the latitude allowed with the drugs enabled us to take all sorts of chances we could never have taken with gallamine triethiodide (Flaxedil).

I explained some of our earlier problems with darts and needles, and how much more efficient we found it to dart from a vehicle instead of on foot. I mentioned too, how we had developed a technique of direct translocation to other reserves. In conclusion I mentioned that 'One of the greatest advantages of the drugs is that you can literally get a rhino out of all sorts of dangerous situations. Had we known what we know now, we would have been able to save even Jonah's life.'

A month later I was able to tell Toni that we had caught another five rhino and had found Sernyl to have a bad effect on white rhino, but a most beneficial one on black rhino. We would also be supplying at least nine zoos with rhino.

With orders for more rhino coming in from Bronx, San Diego and Berlin Zoos, John Clark had to make more bomas. We had trouble with rhino catching their horns in the corners of square bomas and suffocating, so John built round ones.

Gum poles were painted with strong-smelling carbolinium and set in furrows. A tank stand was completed and pipes laid to each boma. Each pen had three gates, one in front and another on either side. An extra holding pen for cleaning purposes was added which proved useful when we attended to injured animals. Land-Rover NPA 733, our darting vehicle, was overhauled and a metal grid with a reinforced bumper added. This gave protection when we had to drive over trees.

We received another order for a pair of rhino from John Seago, the East African game dealer, who asked that the Milwaukee and Chester Zoo rhino be ready for shipment by the end of May. The weather was bad, we were all tired, but I insisted we went out catching again. John Clark kept notes of this particular occasion and when I came to write this book he sent them to me. Here is part of his description.

'Madageni walked into her pen at one in the morning after a terrible fight with the lorry through mud and rain. The two Zulus who had remained at the boma to feed Mtondotondo then informed me that he was getting clever and had given up trying to climb over the boma sides and gates. They were about to explain his new tactics when I got a demonstration. He had found out that if he put his horn in between the two horizontal poles then lifted he could slide it sideways and out. This meant all the gates had to be roped before I could get some sleep.

'Madageni was not much of a fighter. She resorted to more frightening tactics. She refused to eat and got thinner as the days went by. I was on the point of releasing her when I tried one more idea. I gave her the run of three pens with Mtondotondo in the fourth. Twenty-four hours later she started eating, a small amount at first but slowly increasing her intake. During this period nobody was allowed to go near her pens. After a week, I put a little Epsom salts in her water and increased the daily amount of coarse salt. I was afraid that if she became constipated or stopped feeding for any reason, she would never eat again in the pen. Two weeks passed and she was eating extremely well and I began to believe she was on the road to recovery. She confirmed this by trying to climb the gates and battering the walls.'

Madageni was one of the first white rhino ever exported from South Africa. She still graces Chester Zoo in the United Kingdom today.

The following week I darted a rhino the Zulus named Nqabeni (The Refuser) because of his reluctance to succumb to the drugs. We loaded and took him back to the bomas. John Clark complained about what the four-thousand-pound animal was likely to do to the new pens when he came round.

'Those are your worries,' Nick said as he climbed on to his horse.

I travelled with John and Nqabeni to the bomas. Nqabeni staggered out of the crate and charged the gate as the last pole was slipped in. The whole boma shook. John gave me a despairing look as I got into my Land-Rover. A few days later he sent me a report describing his trials with Nqabeni.

'That evening I woke to hear the familiar boma orchestra – creaking of poles, one rhino bellowing and fighting with the other rhino pacing up and down roaring encouragement. This time there was a note of near triumph in the fighting rhino's bellow. I leapt from my stretcher without my trousers but grabbed a khaki shirt which I didn't have time to button and ran to the pens. When I rounded the corner I was just in time to see Nqabeni pop out of his pen like a champagne cork. He saw me and his direction changed. I executed a right about turn at full speed and ran for the nearest rhino crate. Fortunately the door was open and I just made it when he hit the side with such momentum that the two-ton crate moved a full nine inches sideways. I shot up the inspection hatch and got to the top of the crate just in time to wave him a fond farewell as he was swallowed up by the dark bushes. Only then did I realise how close I had come to running full tilt into the horn of an infuriated rhino.'

John showed me the mark where Nqabeni had thumped the crate; even the steel plate was dented.

Rhino No. 21 was a lovely young female I darted after a hair-raising drive through country one would hesitate to take a motorbike through, let alone a Land-Rover. The horsemen took over and roped her after a long and tiring chase.

She fought frenziedly as we dragged her into the crate. As we pulled

25. V.I.P.s visiting rhino bomas; *left to right*: the author with Lord Moran and Dr Werner Schaurte.

26. Feeding time for the babies.

the crate up with the rollers, she rolled over, jammed her horn, and three minutes later was stone dead.

We took her to the bomas, chopped off her small horns and put her in a donga in the open where the other dead rhino had been left. The hyena and jackal soon found her and we heard them howling all night. Not long after dawn the vultures were gliding down and hopping forward to feed. It was part of nature's inexorable law that nothing must be wasted.

This setback depressed us and we rested for a day, but we had orders for far more rhino than we could handle and the bomas had to be filled.

At midday on 18 April I darted another young female in the rump as she ran into the bush below the old nagana airfield in the Corridor. The horsemen took off after her as the dart was brushed off by another rhino. A jet of blood spurted out and ran down her leg. She ran with seven others and as they passed through the bush other rhino lying up in the shade joined them until there were sixteen running together. They all plunged into a ravine in a chaos of squealing calves and clouds of dust. The horsemen were absorbed into a sea of grey animals and occasionally a white helmet and a brown horse appeared in the melée. Eighteen minutes later the horsemen had her roped to a tree.

This had been the most impressive chase I had seen, and how the horsemen had come out of it alive was a mystery. The first thing Nick said was, 'Thank God the horses are fit, a tired horse in among those sixteen rhino – all running with us – could have been disastrous.'

The horses had become extraordinarily fit and when well fed could travel thirty or forty miles a day, but a straight run of seven miles through dongas and up hills did tire them out. The long trek back to camp at night finished them off. It was obvious we needed more horses and trained men who could take over and give Nick and Owen a well-deserved break.

We named the young rhino Malusa (The Herded One) because the horsemen had cut her away from the sixteen rhino and kept going round in smaller and smaller circles until she dropped.

Malusa turned out to be a model rhino. She would lie for hours in her pen uttering a low squeaky call. John swore she was a famous singer reincarnated, until he found she had been stabbed by another rhino in the folds of her hind leg and an abscess had formed. The abscess was difficult to lance but finally it burst. Malusa stopped 'singing' and in three days had doubled her grass consumption.

By the end of May there were nine bomas completed and a trench for a further five dug. Water had been laid on. The perpetual carting of water was a drain on our transport so we ran a plastic pipe from Hugh Dent's house on Mpila down to the boma. This was help to John who could wash out the pens every day and give the rhino a spray on the hot days.

Sometimes a rhino would refuse to move out of its pen at cleaning time and no amount of coaxing helped. John Clark perched on a log above the pen, talking and pleading with the recalcitrant rhino to 'move over'. Then he discovered that the rhino would hesitantly charge a piece of cloth or paper dangled from a stick. A shout from John and the labourers would slip the poles in behind the rhino. Occasionally the rhino panicked and backed, poles snapped resoundingly and cries of pain would rise from all directions as the labourers extricated their bruised fingers. This was our greatest casualty. Someone was always getting his fingers jammed, either by poles, rhino, rollers, or in the loading. My right index finger was permanently disfigured after a rhino moved its foot at the wrong time and crushed my hand against a rock. John was seldom without a soiled bandage on his hand and it was incredible that none of us got tetanus.

There was so much work at the bomas that John Tinley had to be drafted in to help. He was an outstanding ranger, with immense strength. One afternoon while four of us struggled to topple a half-grown rhino bull, John Tinley ran in and bowled the rhino over with his shoulder. He soon had an understanding of the rhino and became an invaluable member of the team.

Work continued steadily at the bomas as more rhino were brought in. Mpugwana (The Fly) was darted in the base of the tail after a thirty-mile-an-hour chase through the bush. She stopped fifty yards from the main road, and a carload of tourists stared at the horsemen trying to tie a rope on to the hind legs of an apparently wild rhino.

Mpugwana was an endearing rhino and John Clark said she soon learned that little tricks, like mock charges at her grass then a short canter with the grass in her mouth, would keep one's attention. If John was not there, or no one paid her any attention for three or four days, she would sulk and go off her food. When John reappeared and scolded her she would perk up and eat double rations.

It was during the capture of Mpugwana that I first got the drug combination in my eyes. In our chases through the bush we had to get so close to the rhino that it was impossible to avoid the spray of the drug as the dart smacked home. The hyoscine opened the pupils and in the bright sunlight the pain was excruciating. Sometimes I was blinded and had to be led to the nearest water – frequently a scum covered wallow – to bathe my eyes. Goggles were no use. They hampered vision and at thirty miles an hour in bush failure to duck at the right moment could mean a broken neck. Eventually we carried a can of clean water on the Land-Rover. Immediately the rhino was darted, John Clark would leap out and pour half a gallon on my upturned face.

When I got the full contents of two darts in my eyes my pupils were twice normal size and I couldn't see very far. I wrote to Toni Harthoorn and asked if he could suggest a remedy. Toni said, 'There is nothing one can do except frequent bathing with water or a solution such as Optrex. The treatment besides washing is dark glasses and rest.' I got the dark glasses but rest was practically impossible.

Mashobeni (The Tail) named because it was a near surgical operation to get the dart out of its tail, tamed very quickly. Mschaurte, a young male, was named after Dr Werner Schaurte, a German who has done much for Umfolozi and the white rhino. Mschaurte suffered a severe dart wound but constant handling tamed him down more quickly than normal. He went to Brookfield Zoo in Chicago.

Meva was a temperamental rhino. John Clark described her as a typical example of the opposite sex. 'She changes from day to day,' he said. 'One morning she will only eat if I hold the grass in my hand and offer it through the gate poles. The next day she will not feed if anyone is within sixty yards of her. It was the same with getting her from pen to pen,' he said. 'One morning she would go into her cleaning pen without hesitation, the following day nothing would move her. I always had to be on my toes as far as she was concerned.

'Once I remember trying to get her to go back to her pen after it had been cleaned, but she wouldn't move. Then in sheer desperation I called her a few choice names. The results were startling, she stormed into the pen and was annoyed for the rest of the day, mock charging every time I went near. I would not like to say whether this was coincidence, or the inflection in my voice,' John said.

Inadvertently some old stocks of lucerne were fed to the rhino. In two days, three rhino started scouring badly. They became listless, lost weight, and lay whining in the corner of their pens. Watery faeces bubbled out of the anus and dribbled in a green stream down the legs. This attracted tormenting flies which settled in a black mass round the eyes and on the mouths of the sick animals. Even the ox-peckers which flocked to the bomas and had become so tame, avoided these rhino. Constant attention and injections of terramycin pulled them through, but later in the year we lost other animals.

Norman Deane phoned me one morning from Hluhluwe; he asked me to bring the rhino capture team to catch another black rhino.

'It's a very old male with a badly damaged hind leg,' said Norman. 'It's probably spent the whole of its life outside the game reserve in tribal reserve number three. For eight years we've been periodically driving the old beast into the Hluhluwe Game Reserve, but the following day it's always back in the Zulu Reserve.'

The recent increase in the human population had reduced the size of its habitat and the black rhino had taken to feeding on pumpkins. The local Zulus were now demanding its removal. When Norman pointed it out to me, I knew there was little chance of it surviving the capture. It was too old.

To get near the rhino, which was in a thicket near an old pumpkin field, Norman had to drive over the veld and along narrow footpaths with steep drops on either side. It heard the Land-Rover and with typical black rhino courage came snorting out to charge the vehicle. It bashed the bumper and knocked the mudguard in, hooked its horn under the springs and rocked us. It was too close to fire so I darted it in the rump as it turned.

Nick and Owen followed it into the Hluhluwe Game Reserve and it collapsed half a mile from the boundary fence. It stumbled about very badly, dragging its leg. The old animal was covered in wounds from fights and from assegais. Both hind legs were scarred by cable snares, and it was blind in one eye. We gave big injections of antibiotics then loaded it up and took it to a specially made boma near the Hluhluwe rest camp. I injected Lethidrone and its condition looked satisfactory.

It tried to rise during the night but could not support itself on its forelegs. Everything was done to keep the animal alive and on the second day after a branch of *Acacia karroo* had been forced into the side of its mouth, it began feeding, eating a variety of plants, mpafa, *Dombeya*, nthombothi, *Rhus natalensis* and *Solanum*. In a few days it had become surprisingly tame, could be hand-fed and enjoyed being scratched around the mouth, ears, and eyes. A harness was made to raise it off its brisket so the front legs could be massaged and exercised to stimulate circulation. Several times it tried to use its legs but could not support itself properly. There was no hope for it and Norman was forced to shoot it.

A post mortem showed severe bruising and a smelly fluid in the joints and tendon sheath. The animal weighed one thousand nine hundred and fifty-three pounds, probably two to three hundred pounds less than it would have weighed in its prime.

Owen Letley had been granted a transfer to the scientific staff just before this black rhino capture and was going to work under Roddy Ward, the finest plant ecologist in Africa. He rode with Nick as a sentimental gesture to the old team. We saw him periodically at Hluhluwe, immersed in his study of grasses.

On 22 May 1962 I was phoned from Durban by a parson who quietly told me that Owen Letley was dead. In a moment of overwhelming, black despair he had taken his own life. The shock stunned me: could so kind and gentle a person be dead? I stared out of the window of my office and one of Owen's horses came down the path. It stopped, looked at me and whinnied. It seemed to know.

It was a long time before we recovered from the impact of Owen's death and we worked harder at rhino capture to try to forget.

Chapter 23

America and Rhodesia

More rhino were caught for the Kruger National Park and were transported directly from the field. They arrived safely after a four hundred and fifty mile journey, the furthest they had so far been transported from the field.

To everyone's surprise Alpheus Ntuli, my personal servant, bored with domestic duties, volunteered to become one of the horsemen. On one of his first chases he and Nick were following a cow and a calf through thick bush in the Mcacaso stream area of the Corridor. They dismounted to follow on foot. The two rhino reached a krantz, could go no further and turned and charged. Alpheus managed to drag his horse out of the way but the rhino cow came for Hom-Hom, the horse Nick was riding, and as Nick climbed a tree the rhino hooked the horse a good six feet into the air. Nick led a limping Hom-Hom out of the bush, his leg wounded but fortunately not broken. Alpheus was too shaken to speak.

Alpheus's horse, Insingisi, which did a splendid job on capture, became blasé after many chases and paid for it with his life. He was gored to death by an irate white rhino that resented his presence at a wallow near the Mpila game guard camp.

Our capture techniques had taken giant steps forward in only a year.

In July 1962 I wrote to Toni Harthoorn: 'We have now caught our fifty-fifth rhino.'

But there was no room for complacency and I was delighted when Ken Rochat rejoined the Natal Parks Board. He had left us two years previously to join the Rhodesian police. A tall, powerfully built but taciturn man, Ken Rochat was one of the most efficient men I had known in the Board's service. Few people knew more about vehicles and mechanical matters and he was also a good horseman. But Ken's greatest virtue was his ability to stay calm under even the most desperate circumstances. He made a very welcome addition to the rhino capture team. John Clark had been offered the chance of taking the Milwaukee rhino to the United States and was due to go at the end of July.

Our equipment had improved out of all recognition. Colonel Vincent had seen that we were supplied with a five-ton Austin lorry with automatic winch, and one morning John Page phoned to say that the Postmaster General had consented to a licence for walkie-talkies. These two things changed rhino capture. The lorry meant we could load animals in formerly impossible positions while the walkie-talkies saved rhino lives; the horsemen could radio their position to us instead of having to gallop back, and we could be with the rhino in minutes.

The first time the walkie talkie was used by Alpheus Ntuli there had been a long silence and Nick and I were worried. Alpheus and another guard had gone after a rhino I had darted, and if the rhino was in trouble we would have to get to it quickly. On this occasion we had no idea in which direction the darted animal and the pursuing horsemen had run and we waited anxiously for an indication of their position so we could race to the spot.

Nick called up over and over again: 'Portable one calling Portable two. Come in Portable two, come in Portable two.'

The radio hissed and crackled but there was no reply. We drove to a higher point and Nick tried again.

'Portable one calling Portable two – come in Portable two, come in Portable two, come in ...'

I looked up into the sky, afraid that vultures would soon be circling and gliding to the mangled bodies of Alpheus and the other game guard.

Twenty minutes passed and still there was no reply. Nick's voice repeated urgently, 'Portable one calling Portable two – come in Portable two.'

At last Alpheus's stuttering voice came faintly over the air. 'Portable one er um I er a-a-a-am receiving you.'

Nick gripped the radio and shouted hoarsely, 'Alpheus, Alpheus, where are you?'

Back came the stuttering reply, 'I-I-I am here.'

'Where is "here" for God's sake,' Nick shouted.

'I-I-I beg your pardon?' Alpheus stuttered.

'Where is "here"?' Nick screamed.

'Here is in the Umfolozi Game Reserve,' Alpheus replied triumphantly.

There was nothing we could do but laugh.

In July John Clark sailed for America with three white rhino for Milwaukee and two for Chicago. With John away everyone had to work overtime at the bomas to tame the rhino. More were due to go overseas and eight were being collected by Rhodesian Parks personnel.

On 18 July we thought we had caught the last rhino for Rhodesia.

'This will give us nearly three weeks to tame them all down,' I said to Nick Steele.

But fate didn't agree.

The Rhodesians arrived at the end of the month, led by Ted Davison, former Warden of Wankie Game Reserve, Rupert Fothergill, hero of Kariba, and John Condy, a veterinary officer. They intended leaving on 9 August but a series of misfortunes delayed them until the end of the month.

It was dry and hot and grass throughout the reserve wilted badly. Vehicles had to range out as much as thirty miles to find green grass to feed the rhino in the pens. By the tenth it was practically impossible to find any. A grey haze covered the land and the temperature climbed steadily to over 105°F.

Gordon Bailey, John Tinley and Ken Rochat were burnt dark brown as they worked at the bomas stripped to the waist in the enervating heat. One thing after another went wrong. We lost two rhino in quick succession before we realised the cause. It was a drought period and the rhino were in a weakened condition. This was worsened while they were recovering from the drugs and refused to eat. Their condition deteriorated so quickly there was little chance of saving them. The bomas had become a depressing place and no one liked being there.

More trouble started when an agent for a zoo refused one of his rhino which had a wound in the shoulder. We had to give him one of the Rhodesian rhino which left us one short, then one died and we were two short; another died and we were three short. All the others recently caught were in poor condition and needed attention day and night. The three men never left the bomas and slept outside the pens of the rhino they were looking after. Fourteen rhino had to be watched over constantly, so there was little rest for any one.

Horns were knocked off, and had to be treated with Stockholm tar; skin abrasions started when the rhino came round and charged the gate, scratching their flanks as they ran past the poles; noses bled from continually hammering the gate poles. But the dart wounds were the worst. Some cavities were so deep the pus had to be cleaned out by the handful.

There was a perpetual stench of iodoform powder, rotting wounds, mixed with the distinct smell of sickly rhino and drying urine. To dress the wounds on a wild rhino took hours of work each day, and when there were as many as nine sick at one time, men worked till they staggered with fatigue. We used long poles, padded at the ends with cloth soaked in medications. The rhino were enticed into a holding pen, we would balance on a crossmember and jab at the wound with the pole and medicated pad. Some of the medicines like acriflavine had to be poured on. Gordon Bailey devised a method of attaching a condensed milk tin to a pole and pouring the liquid gently on. Everything required endless patience because a toss from a rhino's head, or a sudden movement backward would send the tin spinning and hours of work would be wasted. Ken Rochat, Gordon Bailey, and John Tinley never had a meal together, or even a cup of tea. They used to eat and drink as they worked.

Our most trying time was when the rhino would not eat, some for as long as a fortnight. We despaired as their condition worsened. Everything about the rhino changed, even its colour and smell. John Tinley, Gordon, or Ken would spend hours coaxing an animal to take a handful of grass. It would charge the gate in quick bursts, then snort as some one tried to push grass into its mouth. Within three days and in spite of injections of antibiotics, the tell-tale lump of a dart wound would appear. In a week this lump would be a gaping hole which no amount of antibiotics would begin to heal.

In the overall picture of capture the number of deaths in the boma was relatively low, but each sick animal was an individual to us and we watched its progress with ceaseless anxiety. The pitiful cries of an ill rhino wrenched one's stomach. I could never get used to seeing a rhino we had caught in the field with much hard labour, go down in condition and die. But August 1962 was the worst period we would ever experience at the bomas.

Madolo, a fully-grown bull, refused to eat and died, so did Qikiyane and Skebengo, two young females. The dead rhino were dragged out with a winch, loaded on to a lorry, and taken to the 'death donga' nearby. Vultures would circle in the sky, come gliding down to the tall trees and flap, cackling and squawking, to the emaciated carcass. We would hear their harsh shrill cries as they fought over scraps of meat.

Crows would circle, cawing ceaselessly, then the marabous would arrive to dominate the scene.

There were times, when John Tinley radioed to report another rhino dead, that I wanted to give up. I couldn't bear the thought of another carcass being dragged out and given to the vultures.

We tried every possible remedy, and each bit of knowledge helped to overcome the problem. John Tinley suggested green cane tops might tempt the rhino. This was an outstanding success and rhino that had not eaten for weeks fed instantly. Other younger rhino were force fed with a mixture of porridge, salt, and milk.

The moment we lost sight of the individual differences of the rhino, we struck difficulties. Ngazana would only eat his porridge in the half hour following noon; Ngokotshane ate his in the late afternoon from half past four to half past six. Another rhino would only feed if the grass was rattled against a pole. This was probably because the first time it got grass into its mouth someone had rattled a pole.

There was always the problem of noise. Some rhino recovering from the drugs reacted violently to the inevitable racket around the bomas of dung and old grass being scraped out, hammers clanging, or vehicles driving up. Someone thought of playing a wireless in their pens all day. This soon got them used to sound and they settled down fast.

Gordon Bailey discovered other little tricks, such as putting a crate in front of the pen in the early stages, which allowed the rhino to concentrate on one person only as the box obscured most of its view. With one person attending to it all the time it tamed more quickly. Gordon found that once a rhino had been crated it was essential to replace the rear bottom door which was designed so that the dung could be scraped out, otherwise the animal was chafed on its back legs every time it lay down or stood up. The chafing turned into open sores, which attracted flies which in turn infected the wound and within a few days the rhino would be hovering on the verge of death.

When I went down to the bomas, no one needed to come and report to me. I only had to look at their faces to know that another rhino had died or others were going into a crisis. But the three rangers kept a twenty-four-hour watch over their charges. With diligence and innovation the difficulties were slowly overcome.

By 25 August all but three of the rhino for Rhodesia were in their crates. We had to rope some in but the others ran in when something was waved in front of them. By midday all the rhino were crated and plans were made to leave on the morning of the twenty-seventh. But fate had the last word.

The twenty-sixth was a blistering hot day and we had to cool the rhino down with hoses.

'Anyway there's one consolation,' Gordon Bailey said. 'They'll be able to travel over the dirt roads without worrying about getting stuck.'

That evening the wind changed to the south and by ten o'clock it was blowing a gale. I woke early in the morning to hear rain lashing against the windows and water running over the paving stones at the back of the house. I looked down to the bomas and saw lights in the pitch darkness. They were tying canvas sails over the crates to keep the rhino warm.

On the twenty-eighth it was still raining heavily and the weather was

27. A rhino wallow.

28. Building a rhino boma.

bitterly cold. Warthog crept out of their burrows and died of exposure. Game huddled wherever they could find warmth.

The eight rhino did not leave for Rhodesia until the thirtieth. Nick Steele rode over from Gome at noon and we watched the impressive eleven-vehicle convoy churn through the mud of the first leg of the fifteen-hundred-mile journey.

'Well,' Gordon Bailey said impassively, 'I can't say I am sorry to see that lot go.'

Snow was falling in the midlands of Natal when the convoy reached Pietermaritzburg and they spent a bitter night at the showgrounds. The journey ended on 3 September after the rhino had been in their crates for eight days. Some were released at Matopos National Park and others in the Kyle Dam Nature Reserve.

Four years later seventy-four white rhino were transported to Rhodesia in a period of seven months. Over a hundred thousand miles was covered by three trucks taking the rhino straight from the Umfolozi Game Reserve to the Game Reserves of Kyle, Wankie, Victoria Falls, Matopos, and McIlwaine. Some of the journeys lasted forty hours. The only death en route was a cow and a post mortem showed she had been suffering from pneumonia as well as peritonitis.

Thirty-five of the rhino went to Wankie National Park where they were kept in pens and paddocks for a short while. Three wandered into southern Botswana and another was shot dead by a terrorist. By June 1967 over thirty of the thirty-five could still be accounted for in one of the most successful translocations ever undertaken, in spite of the shortage of spare parts and petrol following sanctions against Rhodesia by the United Nations and Great Britain.

On 9 September a four-thousand-pound male rhino, Malaleni, was sent directly from the field to the Kruger National Park. Andrew Brynhard wrote to me that Malaleni was involved in a fight shortly afterwards. He was gashed, and muscles in the right hind leg were severed. He was immobilised and put into a boma for treatment, but his condition deteriorated and he had to be put out. Andrew mentioned building another paddock but I suggested the release of a fully mature bull and cow in a suitable area of the park, and this was agreed to after October 1962.

Between June 1962 and September 1964, ninety-two white rhino were translocated to the Kruger Park. One adult male was attacked by lions and was so badly injured it had to be destroyed. Another won a fight with a lion. Andrew Brynhard told me about a white rhino killed by an elephant at a crater hole near Shingwedzi. A game ranger reconstructed the fight from the surrounding spoor. The rhino had refused to give way, and both animals had fallen down a hundred-foot embankment. The elephant gored the rhino with both tusks on one side and inflicted two deep wounds with single tusk stabs.

Chapter 24

The Fruits of Experience

1962 ended as 1963 began. Badly. Scrawny cattle from the adjacent tribal areas streamed into the western area of the game reserve. All through the day I received reports from game guard and ranger outposts. I was terribly depressed and despondent about everything. Everywhere I went there was something to worry about. I felt I did not have the guts to continue, to fight on.

We had started to build a forty-five mile rhino-proof fence but only a few miles were complete. During one weekend more than a thousand head of cattle were driven into the game reserve and some ranged to within a few miles of the rest camp. Appeals to local officials fell on deaf ears. One senior official in Pretoria even denied that there were any cattle in the game reserve, until Dr Brand, Director of the National Zoological Gardens, published a story in a Transvaal newspaper with photographs of white rhino and cattle together. He re-iterated the danger to the game reserve and asked for the immediate removal of the cattle. There were no more official denials but no preventive measures were taken either, so we decided to take action ourselves and rounded up the cattle to drive them to the Nongoma pound. It was a provocative move. Immediately we were threatened with actions of stock theft. I had wordy battles over the phone with local magistrates and policemen. Mr Douglas Mitchell, the deputy chairman, took up the cudgels and made a strong statement in a national Sunday newspaper.

The lone lion killed a few head of cattle and daily we had rangers and game guards rounding the animals up and driving them over the border. A few months later they were removed but not before depleting the rhino range of much of its lush grass.

We had just recovered from this lengthy and depressing fight when I had news that Colonel Vincent was resigning from the Board's service. It was a dreadful shock to lose this leader. In 1949 Mr Douglas Mitchell offered Jack Vincent the job of Secretary to the Natal Parks Board because he wanted a man who would fight for conservation.

Colonel Vincent was a born naturalist and as a young man had accompanied Rear-Admiral Lynes on ornithological expeditions. He later worked for the British Museum, and had walked from Nyasaland down into Portuguese territory collecting birds, many of which had not previously been recorded. He had been on expeditions into Angola, Ethiopia, and Kenya and had become one of Africa's leading ornithologists. At the outbreak of war he rejoined his old regiment, the Natal Carbineers, became adjutant and fought with them in the campaign against the Italians in Abyssinia and Somaliland, where his knowledge of the country was of great value. His brilliance made him a natural choice for the British Staff College in the Lebanon where he became an instructor. He was the only South African to win the P.S.C. Dagger. As an instructor he excelled in tank tactics and astro navigation and because of his all-round ability was nicknamed 'The Pundit'. At the end of the 1939-45 War he held the highest military degrees in South Africa. He was offered a senior post in the British Army but declined and returned to his farm in the Mooi River district of Natal.

When Colonel Vincent became Secretary the total staff of the Natal Parks Board was eight. By 1963 there were a hundred and sixty staff members. Under Colonel Vincent's expert direction the 1950s and 1960s became an era of expansion as young energetic men were recruited. Norman Deane, Jim Feely, Ken Tinley, John Page, Nick Steele, John Clark, Ken Rochat, Owen Letley, Nick van Niekerk, Boy Hancock, Adriaan Erasmus, Gordon Bailey, John Forrest, John Tinley, Paul Dutton, David

Wearne, and Jan Oelofse were a few of these men. Each one brought skills and enthusiasm to the cause and the Board became recognised as one of the best conservation authorities in the world.

The Colonel – as he was always called by his staff – left in May for Switzerland. He became liaison officer for the International Union for Bird Protection and Secretary of the Survival Service Commission, where he soon made his presence felt. But he left behind a gap which it took many years to fill.

Rhino capture continued and at the end of May I wrote to Toni Harthoorn telling him we had caught our hundredth rhino. He replied jokingly asking whether we intended to retire on reaching our century, but he also had very important news.

'I have been working on a new drug that could be good for the rhino,' he wrote. 'You should catch your rhino with one thousandth part of the morphine dose and so reduce dart trauma.'

This was M99, the drug that changed game capture. It did away with most dart wounds and the rhino began eating far more quickly. It also eliminated the cumbersome twenty c.c. dart.

One of the first people to see M99 in use was a new recruit named John Forrest, sent to Umfolozi Game Reserve for training. A fair haired, blue eyed, fine looking young man, he showed immediate promise of being a good ranger. He understood discipline and got on well with the Zulu game guards and the white officers.

Sir Edward Hallstrom, Director of the Taronga Zoo in Australia, had asked for a pair of white rhino. So we left early one morning for the Umfulumkulu flats and its salty pools, carrying with us the new M99 and small darts. We topped a rise to see fifteen white rhino grazing below Nqoloti. We careered over boulders and old stumps and I was forced to take a snap shot. The dart sailed between the legs of the rhino and the animal ran off in a cloud of dust, the ox-peckers screeching. It was only the third time I had missed since we began shooting from the Land-Rover.

John Clark grabbed the second dart, filled it with acetic acid and we chased another rhino. I fired again as we bumped over a heap of stones and saw the dart hit the rhino in the tail. Ken Rochat and John Forrest disappeared over the brow of the hill, the horses' hooves clattering on the loose stones. Magqubu jumped down from the truck and walked off with his familiar bandy-legged gait to look for the dart.

'He's got no chance of finding it,' John said confidently.

Three minutes later Magqubu returned, holding the dart and smiling.

'Lucky I didn't bet,' John laughed.

I called Ken up on the walkie talkie.

'The rhino has stopped,' he reported.

At that moment two rhino burst out of the bush and ran westwards. I told Ken to leave John Forrest with the rhino, and come back. In the meantime the darted rhino was moving slowly towards the thick bush. I saw John Forrest dismount and carefully tether his horse. The day was still with dazzling bright sunshine and his white helmet reflected light every time he moved his head. The dark grey form of the rhino heavy with sweat kept walking towards thicker bush. I heard John Forrest talking to it soothingly and saw him briefly as he unrolled a hank of nylon rope. Then he vanished and all I could hear was the rhino stumbling amongst trees as it continued forward. Frightened calls of hadeda ibis, guinea fowls taking off and a grey duiker antelope going at great speed marked the progress of man and animal. A helmet glistened for a moment in a dense patch of dark green *Euclea* scrub. I was worried about John. He was still so raw.

'Better prepare another dart,' I told John Clark.

We waited a while, afraid to go forward in case the rhino was not properly drugged and we disturbed it, but at last the strain was too much and we went towards the spot where we had last seen John Forrest.

A rhino burst out of the bush dragging John Forrest at the end of the rope. The rhino ran within a yard of us, obviously doped but still very strong. John Forrest tipped his crash helmet as he passed and said calmly, though a little hurriedly, 'The rhino won't stop, Mr Player.'

We watched speechless as he ran behind the rhino and was drawn into the bush. A minute later we heard a triumphant shout of, 'I've got it, I've got it!'

After all the hard work and excitement John Forrest deserved to see this rhino go to Australia but their Quarantine Department refused permission, so the rhino went to the bomas.

On the morning of 3 July the south wind blew up and by seven o'clock it was gale force, with the trees bending low before it. The wind kept up an unnerving shrieking round the house. It began raining, slowly at first, and gusts splattered against the walls, the windows, and the brown thatch. Then it rained harder and in an hour there were pools of water on all the roads.

I had an appointment in Empangeni and returned that afternoon through Mtubatuba where I met Ranger David Wearne. We drove down to the river where the bridge into the reserve should have been, but there were waves fifteen feet high. The gigantic sycamore figs on the north bank were snapping like twigs and being swept into the swirling water.

We made radio contact with Mpila, and John Clark reported that water had been rushing two feet deep through the pens and that five rhino had died. He was so exhausted and overcome that he could hardly talk, but in a few vivid words he described how he had worked all night trying to get the rhino, some caught only a few days before, into crates – a job normally tackled after the rhino had been six weeks in the boma. With twelve rhino to work with he was attempting the impossible, but he persisted in spite of a strike of his labour. The rhino for Berlin and for Oklahoma were saved, as well as some others, but it was the howling, bitterly cold south wind that quickly sapped the energy of the other rhino and they died one after another.

I crossed into the game reserve by canoe two days later and went to the bomas. It was no wonder rhino had died in that devastation. Water had swirled through the pens more than two feet deep. Red mud lay everywhere. The lucerne and teff grass was soaked through and was already green with mould.

The whole of August 1963 was spent with Ivan Tors of Hollywood, the man who produced the 'Flipper' series. He brought a cast to make the film 'Rhino', including Bob Culp, Harry Guardino, and Shirley Eaton. I acted as technical adviser with the animal shots. Sven Persson, creator of 'To Catch a Rhino', was the cameraman, so our side of the work went relatively smoothly. Rhino capture went ahead as usual which gave the film people many opportunities of unique footage.

M99, the new drug sent by Toni Harthoorn, was used with continued success and I was able to write and tell him we had captured twelve white rhino without loss. Black rhino, blue wildebeest, and zebra were also caught. White rhino were going down in five to ten minutes, instead of twenty minutes to half an hour. This meant we could catch rhino in thicker bush and it saved the horsemen work.

On 12 August I promised Ivan Tors I would catch him a buffalo he needed for a sequence. We left Mpila early on the thirteenth accompanied by Dr Ditman and Dr Wood, two American medical men attached to the film unit. I had had a premonition of disaster two days before so I took extra care.

The guards located a big herd of buffalo near the Tegwan pan and we went straight to the area. We moved through the bush, setting up a herd of zebra. They ran towards the buffalo, which thundered off in alarm. Ken Rochat, who was driving, raced after them and we were amongst the herd in a minute. I aimed and fired at a male, and the dart smacked into the left flank. Ken thought I had missed and he swung the steering wheel. I had just relaxed my grip and had nothing to hold on to. The Land-Rover was going at thirty miles an hour as I flew off. The fear of being run over was uppermost; I remembered letting the gun go then I hit the ground and rolled.

I saw Nick's horse come galloping towards me and as I tried to crawl out of the way it seemed as though I had seen it all before. I yelled to Nick to keep after the buffalo, then groaned and cursed to myself, angry at having fallen off. I felt no real pain until I tried to stand up. My collar bone cracked and I knew it was broken, but what worried me more was the pain in my back when I moved my leg.

The two doctors fixed me up with a bush timber and sweater splint. They gave me a shot of tranquilliser and spoke of using the narcotic. I protested and saw Magqubu grip his rifle – he was not going to let anyone mistake me for a rhino. A little later I felt the shock. I was nauseous and began sweating and shivering, my limbs shaking. It made me appreciate how the rhino go into a state of shock after coming to a standstill when they have been darted. My symptoms were the same.

I was taken to Empangeni hospital and lay there for four days. Nick Steele came down to see me and said that a black rhino was running about Mkuze Game Reserve with a cable snare around its neck. For the hour he was at the hospital I was happy. It took me back to a world I knew, away from the public ward of sick and dying patients, the coughing and spitting, and nurses trundling bottles and bedpans; the smell of ether, methylated spirits, and other disinfectants. It was a relief to get out on the fifth day, even though my back was still painful.

By the time I returned to Umfolozi Game Reserve the snared black rhino had been caught at Mkuze and brought to Umfolozi. It was a female and the Zulus named her Ngozi (Danger). She was given enormous quantities of antibiotics because the cable had buried itself five inches in her neck and had consequently left a deep wound. Fortunately the wire had slipped partially over her forehead, or she would have been strangled. John Clark sat up with her all night and three days later she was feeding from his hands.

There is a marked difference in behaviour between the two species. In the wild the white rhino is very timid, the black rhino generally aggressive. Once the white rhino is caught and taken into the pens it becomes very wild and it takes about six weeks before it is tamed down. With careful handling the black rhino can be tamed in a week.

Ngozi soon learnt about the medicines and she would come forward and lift her head while John Clark poured on the acriflavine or the sulphur dusting powder. She closed her eyes and nuzzled his leg as he scratched her ears and examined the terrible wound. But Ngozi became very restless. She was of course a browser and had been given all the thorns she could eat, but still she was disturbed and walked round the pen, whining softly. John accidentally gave her some grass, which she immediately ate, and we realised what the trouble was; she needed grass. We had always believed that the black rhino was entirely a browser.

When Ngozi had completely recovered we sent her to Ndumu and released her into the wild again. Not very long ago we would have had to shoot animals in her condition, now we could save them.

In September Toni Harthoorn visited us at Umfolozi. He was delighted at the progress we had made, and we drove round the game reserve, reliving the trials and troubles of the early period of rhino capture.

'Do you remember,' Nick Steele said, 'how in the early stages no one ever took food or cigarettes, not even tea. Then tea became a vital part of the capture and the moment a rhino went down water was put on the fire.'

Toni laughed and said, 'Yes, but as soon as the rhino was put in the crate, we forgot about the tea and pushed on.

'Then there were the drugs,' said Nick. 'It was only at the end, when I stopped riding, that I fathomed the drug box.'

Toni recalled the first lesson he had given on drugs and the look of dismay on everyone's face. He described how irritated he felt when every time he started to talk, no matter where he was, the rangers surrounding him immediately pulled out notebooks and pens.

We stopped at a good view point of the grassy plains in the west. White rhino grazed peacefully and the scars of squatters' kraals were healing. We spoke of the excitement and hardships of the very first rhino captured; of Amber and the way she died; of Daisy and the feeling of elation when the new drug combination worked. Our companionship had been forged in the common love of the rhino, worry, and hard work. We all instinctively knew that for the rest of our lives there would be a bond between us.

In a reverie I saw Owen Letley, bare chested and sunburnt, galloping towards us with a smile and a cry of 'It's down!'; of Nick Steele on Zoom with the white mane, fording the ochre-coloured water of the White Umfolozi; of Magqubu striding bandy-legged, his rifle slung across his shoulder as we left the isivivane where the mamba came for me; of tall John Tinley carefully pouring acriflavine on the gaping dart wound in a rhino's buttock. I saw Ken Rochat, quiet and efficient, driving the rhino lorry with incredible skill out of situations where no one else would go. There was John Clark, shoeless and hatless, racing across the veld with a rope in his hands to stop a rhino that had recovered too quickly from the drugs. I could hear the sound of John Kinloch's calm voice on the radio as I passed the message asking for police reinforcements when we were about to be attacked. Umfolozi was the spiritual home of us all.

The first phase of rhino capture was over. The small team of dedicated men it had been my privilege to lead, had achieved miracles. We could look back with justifiable pride over the last three years and say to the world, we have saved the white rhino for you; we have made our contribution to the next generation.

Nick Steele and I were to leave the team but the rhino capture would go on. New men were being trained. John Daniel, Mike Keep, and Graham Root would continue the work we had begun. As long as there was a country or a park that wanted white rhino there would be a Natal Parks Board team to catch the animals.

In 1964 I was promoted to Chief Conservator, Zululand, and was transferred to Hluhluwe Game Reserve. In April I left for a three-month tour of the United States as a guest of MGM and Ivan Tors. I was able to see the beautiful National Parks of the United States and speak to many wild life conservationists. It was a most instructive time and I admired the way the United States led the world in conservation. During my many television and radio appearances I cited our rhino capture as an example of international co-operation: an American invented the gun, an Englishman worked out the drug, and South Africans developed the practical techniques of capture.

In 1966 I returned to America for a short while to read a paper entitled 'The Translocation of the White Rhinoceros : a success in wild life conservation in South Africa'. I was able to report that sixty-three white rhino had been translocated to zoos throughout the world, and two hundred and eighty-two had been sent to other game areas in Southern Africa. Even while I was speaking rhino were on their way to Rhodesia direct from the field, a thousand-mile journey under drugs.

By the end of 1970 a total of eight hundred white rhino had been captured. Of these, four hundred we reintroduced into former white rhino habitats and one hundred and fifty we sold to zoos. The annual aerial count of Umfolozi and Hluhluwe Game Reserves revealed that there were still over a thousand in the two reserves. We needed to continue to reduce this number. I went to Lourenço Marques with David Wearne, who spoke Portuguese, to see Dr de Sousa Diaz and my former colleague Ken Tinley, now biologist in the Gorongosa Game Reserve. The Portuguese authorities agreed to take another fifty-six rhino, thirty for the Maputo Reserve and twenty-six for Gorongosa. We had already put forty in the Maputo Reserve and some had calved. Although the

29. White rhino in Whipsnade Zoo.

30. White rhino inspecting cars at World of Animals, a 550-acre zoo near Dallas, Texas.

reserve was unfenced, very few had strayed beyond the boundaries. The only trouble maker was an old bull that wandered south to the Oro Point lighthouse and charged the building, a rhino Don Quixote.

Of all the areas we reintroduced rhino to, the greatest thrill was seeing a group of white rhino grazing on the undulating grass dunes of Maputo Elephant Reserve. Beyond them was the dark blue of the Indian ocean and I could hear the breakers pounding on the reefs. It was over the long golden beaches that survivors from wrecks walked to Lourenço Marques. I imagined they would have seen the white rhino in similar surroundings. We had brought back life to this paradise that had slept for so long.

Our rhino capture was unique in wild life conservation. Other threatened species had first been taken to zoos, and as they bred they were reintroduced into their original habitats. The white rhino were first reintroduced into their former range in large numbers, then sent to zoological gardens as added precaution. Thanks to the dedication of a few men the gloomy predictions of F. C. Selous in 1898 had been proved wrong. It could be said that the species had been saved for posterity.

Epilogue to the First Edition

They blazed the trails for legions following after,
And bared new treasures to the hungry years.
The Pathfinders – Vance Palmer

The White Rhino Saga tells the story of the years 1960 to 1963 in the Umfolozi Game Reserve. It was the beginning of a great triumph for wild life conservation and for those who dedicated their lives to it.

In the history of wild animals the pendulum of progress has taken many to a point of extinction and beyond. The White Rhino Saga represents one of those unique exceptions where the momentum has carried on to ever and ever safer levels of status. Just how far it can be allowed to ascend is a question of population management and it was this advanced aspect of the situation which prompted the Natal Parks Board decision to send me overseas on a white rhino sales campaign. No one realised at the time that the trip was to take me across a vital new frontier in conservation – the moral boundary separating the ultra non-commercial world of conservation and the cold sphere of big business. We had a hard-won product to sell and it was soon shown to have a definite place in the burgeoning development of Safari Parks all over the world. This demand for white rhino, unlike the requirements of the conventional zoo, called for spectacular group exhibition under semi-natural conditions. This concept promised two potentials, enhanced breeding possibilities and a financially rewarding outlet for our excess rhino.

In December 1969 I left on an extended journey to the United Kingdom,

Europe and America. My objective was to sell groups of twenty white rhino at a time. Allen Payne, an old friend, had made contact with the London Zoological Society and after protracted negotiations with Colin Rawlins, Aubrey Buxton, Lord Zuckerman and Edmund de Rothschild, they were the first to place an order for twenty animals for Whipsnade.

From the United Kingdom I flew to the United States. In San Diego Dr Charles Schroeder, Director of the Zoo, Mr Andy Borthwick and Mr Sheldon Campbell, trustees, agreed to purchase twenty white rhino for the new San Pasqual Wild Animal Park. In Los Angeles Mrs Reese Hale Taylor gave me valuable introductions and Harry Shuster of Lion Country Safari ordered twenty rhino. At Fort Worth, Texas, Harry Tennison, President of Game Conservation International, introduced me to the Hunt brothers of International Animal Exchange, and they bought ten white rhino.

It was a pleasure to be able to report back to the board that leading zoological and commercial institutions of the world were taking the biggest groups yet kept in captivity. I was absolutely confident too that the rhino would breed in the spacious surroundings. Enquiries came from Peking and Moscow. The race to breed the first white rhino out of Africa had begun.

All this required a complete revision of our approach to export, because until now our procedure was geared to shipment of at the most two pairs. David Cook, a close friend and colleague, took over the task of organising shipping, crates, food for the journey and all the other complications. The result was a greater degree of involvement, a change over from the old and convenient ex-Umfolozi Reserve sales basis to F. O. B. Durban and the introduction of a rhinocare service to buyers. This not only reduced the buyers' risk but more important, ensured a high standard of welfare for the travelling animals.

Our debut into this essentially business-like arena was not without its problems but suffice to say that the export operation has become a streamlined routine.

During the first year (1970), 58 white rhino were exported; in 1971 the figure rose to 78; in 1972 our target is an ambitious 180 rhino, half of which had been exported by midyear. Worth almost £250,000, the trade since 1970 shows no sign of faltering and recent negotiations with Safari Park interests dispel fears of a saturated market.

Proven beyond any doubt is the fact that an investment in the conservation of a rare species can reap handsome dividends and is not merely a cultural obligation. As a precedent the White Rhino Saga may well represent an enlightened turning point in conservation ethics and a forerunner of similar projects throughout the world.

That the conservation/economic value of the white rhino should alone be mentioned is to completely overlook the side benefits it has won in international goodwill and other, less apparent, spheres. Natal Parks Board rangers have travelled the world as escorts to consignments, forging new links with their overseas counterparts and adding considerable depth to their personal knowledge and experience. In Natal game reserves the white rhino has helped enrich the fauna through a series of exchange agreements involving the introduction of cheetah and red hartebeest, for decades extinct in Natal. One can go on and on.

Far from being played out this White Rhino Saga continues to bare its treasures and whatever the hungry years may hold this is one conservation exercise which looks to better and better horizons.

Appendix

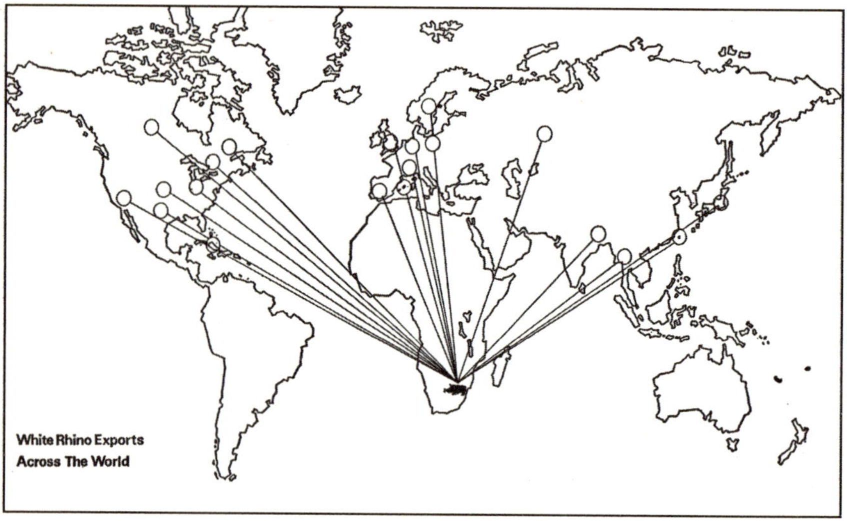

Movement of White Rhino from 1 January 1961 to March 1972:

COUNTRY	PARK OR RESERVE	MALE	FEMALE	TOTAL
Africa				
Angola (10)*	Quiscama National Park	5	5	10
Swaziland (16)	Mlilwane	3	3	6
	Hlane Game Reserve	2	2	4
	Ephvondvo Game Ranch	3	3	6
Botswana (4)	Chobe Game Reserve	2	2	4
Kenya (6)	Meru Game Reserve	3	3	6
Mozambique (85)	Lourenço Marques Zoo	1	1	2
	Maputo Game Reserve	32	39	71
	Gorongoza National Park	4	8	12
Rhodesia (92)	Kyle Dam Game Reserve	13	14	27

* Indicates total number of rhino received

COUNTRY	PARK OR RESERVE	MALE	FEMALE	TOTAL
	Matopos National Park	6	7	13
	McIlwaine National Park	1	2	3
	Victoria Falls National Park	2	2	4
	Wankie Game Reserve	15	20	35
	Henderson Bros. Doddiburn	5	5	10
Zambia (4)	Livingstone Game Park	2	2	4
Transvaal (479)	Hemlock	1	1	2
	Iscor	3	3	6
	Johannesburg Zoo	2	2	4
	Kruger National Park	116	87	203
	Krugersdorp Nature Reserve	2	2	4
	Loskop Nature Reserve	7	9	16
	Mala Mala	25	18	43
	Nelspruit	1	1	2
	Manyaleti Game Reserve	3	3	6
	Pietersburg Nature Reserve	3	2	5
	Pretoria Zoo	2	3	5
	Rondalia Game Reserve	2	2	4
	Rob Ferreira Nature Reserve	1	1	2
	Springs Municipality	1	1	2
	Pontdrift	1	1	2
	Rasinta Farm	1	1	2
	Timbavati Nature Reserve	3	5	8
	Vanderbijl Park Nature Reserve	4	3	7
	Waterpoort	1	1	2
	Komatipoort	2	4	6
	Naboomspruit	2	2	4
	Vaalwater	2	3	5
	Roedtan	1	1	2
Cape (6)	Thomas Baines Nature Reserve	1	0	1
	Grahamstown Nature Reserve	1	2	3
	Tygerberg Zoo Park	1	1	2
O.F.S. (12)	Willem Pretorius Game Reserve	4	4	8
	Bloemfontein Zoo	3	1	4
Natal (85)	Hluhluwe Game Reserve	4	2	6
	Mkuze Game Reserve	6	5	11
	Ndumu Game Reserve	8	10+6 calves	24
	Nyala Game Ranch	1	1	2
	Queen Elizabeth Park	6	4	10
	Ubizane Game Ranch	7	9	16
	Vernon Crookes Game Reserve	3	3	6

COUNTRY	PARK OR RESERVE	MALE	FEMALE	TOTAL
	Midmar	3	3	6
	Subizi Game Ranch	2	2	4
South West Africa (12)	Otjiwarongo	6	6	12
West Germany (7)	Bremen Zoo	1	1	2
	Hanover	1	0	1
	Leipzig	1	1	2
	Gelsenkirchen	1	1	2
East Germany (7)	Berlin	1	1	2
	Dresden	1	1	2
	East Berlin Zoo	0	2	3
Denmark (5)	Copenhagen	2	3	5
Sweden (2)	Kolmarden	1	1	2
Switzerland (4)	Rapperswil	1	1	2
	Zurich	1	1	2
Holland (4)	Rotterdam	1	1	2
	Arnhem Zoo	1	1	2
Japan (4)	Tokyo	1	1	2
	Sindai Zoo	1	1	2
India (3)	Mysore Zoo	1	1	2
	Calcutta Zoo	1	0	1
Cuba (2)	Havana Zoo	1	1	2
Czechoslovakia (10)	Dvur Kralove	3	7	10
Taiwan (4)	Taipei Zoo	2	2	4
Spain (6)	Majorca Zoo	1	1	2
	Barcelona Zoo	1	1	2
	Toledo Zoo	1	1	2
Portugal (2)	Lisbon Zoo	1	1	2
Burma (4)	Rangoon	2	2	4
Canada (6)	Calgary	1	1	2
	Edmonton	1	1	2
	Toronto	1	1	2
United Kingdom (51)	Whipsnade	8	14	22
	Woburn Park	3	3	6
	Longleat	3	3	6
	Regents Park	1	1	2
	Chester	1	1	2
	Windsor Park	3	4	7
	Colchester	2	4	6
United States (138)	Bronx, New York	1	1	2
	Catskill, New York	1	1	2
	Chicago	1	1	2

COUNTRY	PARK OR RESERVE	MALE	FEMALE	TOTAL
	Detroit	1	1	2
	Fort Worth	3	6	9
	San Diego	7	15	22?
	Albuquerque	1	1	2?
	San Antonio	1	1	2
	Los Angeles	1	1	2
	Louisville	1	1	2
	Memphis	2	2	4
	Milwaukee	1	2	3
	New Orleans	1	1	2
	Oklahoma City	1	1	2
	Omaha, Nebraska	1	1	2
	Phoenix, Arizona	1	1	2
	San Francisco	1	1	2
	Tampa, Florida	1	1	2
	World Animal Park, Dallas	4	4	8
	Gladys Porter Zoo, Brownsville	1	1	2
	Lion County Safari	12	28	40
	International Animal Exchange	6	14	20
	Fresno Zoo	1	1	2
Europe (39)	Destination unknown	16	23	39

Grand total as at end of March 1972: 1109

Acknowledgements

I am indebted to my wife Ann for typing the original manuscript and doing the proof reading. My thanks too to Molly Bailey and Nola Steele and Thabite Ntombela for ensuring that we were all fed both night and day.

My grateful thanks are due to the following: the Natal Parks Board for granting permission for this book to be published; Colonel Jack Vincent who as the man behind the scenes was a constant source of inspiration; Nick Steele, Norman Deane, Boy Hancock, Nick van Niekerk, John Clark, Ken Rochat, Gordon Bailey, John Forrest, Bob Murray, Paul Dutton and John Kinloch; John Daniel, David Wearne, Hugh Dent, Brian Stevens, Graham Root and Mark Astrup; Mike Keep, Adriaan Erasmus, Graham Thomson and John Kymdell, all of whom worked long hours without thought of themselves to ensure that the capture of rhino was a success. To Andy Wardell, Herman Bentley, Jimmy Pattenden and their African mechanics who lost many nights' sleep while keeping rhino capture vehicles operating, and to Blythe Pascoe for drawing the maps.

To Nick Steele for his advice about horses' reactions on rhino capture, and John Clark for his notes on rhino behaviour at the bomas. Thanks too to the magnificent horses, Zoom, Tracker, Cherokee and others without whom the initial following of the rhino would not have been possible. To Dr Toni Harthoorn, scientist *par excellence*, who understood the value of field men and never ceased to give them credit; Magqubu Ntombela, philosopher, naturalist, historian, who has been my companion for twelve eventful years; Induna Mzwabantu Masuku and game guards Alphcus Ntuli and Mtembu, and other game guards who loyally supported their European colleagues in every crisis; and to Shadrack Nyawo, radio operator at Mpila.

To the patient Zulu labourers who day after day loaded rhino, pulled crates and carried heavy rollers, yet who always managed to sing; John Page who after his first experience of capture did his best to see we received the necessary equipment.

To Dr Werner Schaurte, Mr Edmund de Rothschild, Mrs Reese Hale Taylor, Mr Aubrey Buxton, Mr Andy Borthwick and Mr Sheldon Campbell, Dr Brand and Dr Schroeder, who befriended the white rhino and always gave help when it was needed.

To the many pressmen who told the world how the white rhino had been saved, but particularly to John Pitts, James Clarke, Roy Rudden, Arthur Bowland, Peter Knowles and John Hughes.

To Pat Waugh and Elizabeth Roy who gave up their spare time to help with the typing of this manuscript.

I must also record my deep appreciation to Mr G. H. Calpin and to Mr Alan Paton who gave me such valuable advice on the setting out of the manuscript.

Finally I am grateful to Jenne Rennie for all her help and expert typing with the new edition. I am thankful too to Frances Perryer for her sage advice and expertise as an editor.

Photographs:
Ray Adler, 30; Gordon Bailey, 24; Fred Campey, 3, 6, 19, 26; Norman Deane, 12; P. M. Hitchins, 8; Mike Keep, 10; *Natal Daily News*, 17, 18; *Natal Mercury*, 11, 15, 27; *Natal Witness*, 1; South African Tourist Corporation, 4; Nick Steele, 25; *The Star*, 16; Zoological Society of London, 29.

Drugs mentioned in the text are:
Flaxedil – gallamine triethiodide;
Scoline – succinylcholine chloride;
Prostigmin – neostigmine methylsulphate;
Largactil – chlorpromazine hydrochloride;
Themalon – diethylthiambutene hydrochloride;
Lethidrone – allylnormorphine;
Morphine – morphine sulphate or morphine hydrochloride;
M99 – 6: 14-endoetheno-7a(2-hydroxy-2-pentyl)-tetrahydro-oripavine hydrochloride.

Index